# ANTITRUST ANALYSIS OF PLATFORM MARKETS:
## Why the Supreme Court Got It Right in *American Express*

David S. Evans
Richard Schmalensee

Competition Policy International, 2019

Copyright © 2019 by Competition Policy International
111 Devonshire Street · Boston, MA 02108, USA
www.competitionpolicyinternational.com
contact@competitionpolicyinternational.com


Printed in the United States of America

First Printing, 2019

Publisher's Cataloging-in-Publication Data
provided by Five Rainbows Cataloging Services

Names: Evans, David S. (David Sparks), 1954- author. | Schmalensee, Richard, author.
Title: Antitrust analysis of platform markets : why the Supreme Court got it right in American Express / David S. Evans, Richard L. Schmalensee.
Description: Boston : Competition Policy International, 2019.
Identifiers: LCCN 2019950801 (print) | ISBN 978-1-950769-41-4 (paperback) | ISBN 978-1-950769-40-7 (hardcover) | ISBN 9978-1-950769-42-1 (ebook)
Subjects: LCSH: American Express Company. | Multi-sided platform businesses. | Competition, Unfair. | Antitrust law. | Commercial law. | Law--Economic aspects. | Law and economics. | BISAC: LAW / Antitrust. | BUSINESS & ECONOMICS / Industries / Financial Services.
Classification: LCC KF1649 .E93 2019 (print) | LCC KF1649 (ebook) | DDC 343.072/1--dc23.


Cover and book design by Inesfera. www.inesfera.com

# Authors' Note

David S. Evans
Richard Schmalensee

This book explores the implications of the U.S. Supreme Court's ruling in *Ohio et al. v. American Express*, and the preceding litigation, for the treatment of multi-sided platforms under U.S. antitrust law. It is based on a series of articles that we wrote (either jointly or individually), leading up to and in the aftermath of the Supreme Court's decision.

We consider that the Supreme Court ruling provides valuable guidance for antitrust analysis in such markets. This book emphasizes the importance for enforcers and the judiciary to take full account of the multisided nature of certain markets, not only in payment services, but throughout the economy (including other types of multisided platforms, which are particularly common in online digital markets).

Although we agree with the Supreme Court's reasoning, this book nonetheless sets out criticisms of the Supreme Court's ruling. We address such criticisms, based on our (and other legal and economic practitioners' and academics') understanding of the modern economic theories on multisided markets. In particular, we underline the need for decisionmakers to take into account any alleged anticompetitive harm and benefits to participants on both sides of a multisided platform, before coming to any conclusion that there has been antitrust injury as a result of any given conduct.

Of particular importance, and emphasized throughout this book, is the need to undertake a full rule of reason analysis of conduct in multisided markets, consistent with both long-standing antitrust precedent and modern economic theory. A proper assessment must take into account the multisided nature of certain markets in all steps of antitrust analysis, whether the issue at hand relates to alleged monopolization, co-ordinated behavior, or a merger. Given the prevalence of multisided platforms, similar allegations of antitrust harm are sure to arise time and again in the years to come, and there are many unanswered questions. We hope this book makes a timely contribution to the ongoing debate.

For convenience, as Appendices, we also include the text of the U.S. Supreme Court's ruling, an *amicus* brief filed jointly by 28 antitrust professors, an *amicus* brief filed jointly by 8 economists, and the brief filed by the U.S. on behalf of the petitioners.

# Contents

Authors' Note..................................................................................................5

**CHAPTER 1**
Introduction ................................................................................................. 9

**CHAPTER 2**
Where's the Harm? ..................................................................................... 23

**CHAPTER 3**
The Rule of Reason ...................................................................................... 39

**CHAPTER 4**
Under and Over Enforcement ..................................................................... 51

**CHAPTER 5**
Two-Sided Red Herrings .............................................................................. 57

**CHAPTER 6**
All That Jazz .................................................................................................. 67

**APPENDIX 1**
Supreme Court Decision...............................................................................81

**APPENDIX 2**
Brief for the United States as Respondent Supporting Petitioners ...................................115

**APPENDIX 3**
Brief of 28 Professors of Antitrust Law as *Amici Curiae* Supporting Petitioners ................... 153

**APPENDIX 4**
Brief for *Amici Curiae* John M. Connor, Martin Gaynor, Daniel Mcfadden, Roger Noll, Jefferey M. Perloff, Joseph A. Stiglitz, Lawrence J. White, and Ralph A. Winter in Support of Petititioners....................................................................................183

Authors' Bios ...............................................................................................205

# CHAPTER 1

# Introduction

Around the year 2000, economists recognized that platforms, like payment card networks, differ in important ways from traditional businesses, like automobile manufacturers.[1] In the ensuing decades, digital platforms have become more prominent players in the economy, domestically and globally. Antitrust courts, enforcers, and practitioners have been sorting out whether traditional methods of analysis need to be modified for platforms and, if so, how. An important issue concerns how to define markets for platforms that serve two, or more, intertwined groups of customers and how to assess the competitive effects of proposed mergers and suspected monopolistic practices that involve platforms.

The U.S. Supreme Court made an important contribution to this debate in its June 2018 decision in *State of Ohio et al., v. American Express (AmEx).*[2] Whether you agree with it or not, it is a seminal decision that sets the rules for addressing antitrust claims for platforms in the United States. The authors are not disinterested parties. The decision cites our work extensively and we submitted an *amicus* brief to the court. This book is based on a series of articles that we wrote leading up to and in the aftermath of the Court's decision.

This chapter sets the stage by summarizing the economics of multisided platforms and providing an overview of the Court's decision. It then summarizes the remaining chapters.

## A. Economics of Multisided Platforms

A multisided platform is a physical or virtual place at which participants can enter into beneficial exchanges, which the platform facilitates by helping participants find good matches and consummating an interaction. OpenTable, for example, is a restaurant reservation service. Using a website, app, and other software, it enables diners and restaurants to find each other and for diners to make, and restaurants to

---

1  Evans and Schmalensee (2016).

2  *Ohio v. American Express Co.*, 138 S.Ct. 2274 (2018). The U.S. Department of Justice was the lead plaintiff in the cases below. It decided not to join the States in seeking certiorari, so the States are the plaintiffs in the Supreme Court case. After cert was granted, the Justice Department ended up filing a brief for plaintiffs and participating in oral arguments.

take, reservations. The diners and restaurants are the two sides of this platform. Some platforms have more than two sides. Google's search platform, for example, connects websites, users, and advertisers. To simplify the exposition, we focus on the two-sided case.

Of course, two members of distinct groups could just meet and agree to interact with each other. A two-sided platform, however, reduces the transaction costs, or frictions, between the two parties thereby making it easier for parties to find each other and complete an exchange of value. When OpenTable started out, restaurants often had to have someone to answer the phone to take reservations, which were then written down in a book; diners often had to call several restaurants to find a table on a particularly busy night. Many tables went empty because it was inefficient for diners and restaurants to make suitable matches. OpenTable reduced the friction in making reservations for diners and restaurants. The diners saved time and had more choices while the restaurants earned more profit from filling unused capacity.

Two-sided platforms can coexist with bilateral exchange. Some users may not face significant transaction costs for dealing directly with each other or may not be able to afford the platform's services. Many restaurant reservations are still made directly between a diner and a restaurant.

## 1.   Indirect Network Effects and Positive Feedback Loops

Economists who have contributed to the literature on two-sided platforms use the term "indirect network effects" to refer to the situation in which participants on one side of the platform value having more participants on the other side with whom they can have a mutually beneficial interaction. Two-sided platforms have indirect network effects for at least one type of participant. OpenTable has indirect network effects for diners, who value access to more restaurants, and restaurants, which value access to more diners.

Indirect network effects arise for two related reasons. First, with more potential partners on the other side, there is a higher probability of finding a partner with whom a value-increasing exchange is possible. If more diners use a restaurant-reservation platform, the restaurant has a greater chance of filling empty tables. Diners have a greater chance of finding a table when and where they would like to dine if there are more restaurants. Second, with more potential partners on the other side, it is possible to find a better match—that is, one that generates more value. A passenger on a ride-sharing platform, for example, will get a ride more quickly if there are more drivers available, and a driver will spend less time reaching a rider if more are looking. Drivers and riders therefore waste less time when there is a greater density of passengers and drivers on the platform in a local area.

Indirect network effects refer to increasing the pool of *relevant* partners for each type of user, not the sheer number of participants in the platform. What matters for having a valuable interaction is finding a partner with whom a user can enter into a valuable exchange. In the case of OpenTable, for example, an available restaurant in Boston, MA isn't relevant to someone who wants to go to dinner in Charleston, SC; and a diner who wants sushi at 7 pm on Friday night isn't relevant to an Italian restaurant that has a table available at that time. By increasing the *density* of relevant partners for each user, platforms become more attractive to users by increasing the probability and quality of a match.

Indirect network effects result in a positive feedback loop between the two sides. When more members of one group join the platform, such as passengers, the platform becomes more valuable to the other group, such as drivers, which leads more members of that group to join. Then the platform becomes even more valuable to the first group, the passengers, leading even more of them to join.

These positive feedback loops, which are sometimes referred to as the virtuous circle, drive the growth of platforms. Figure 1 shows an example based on Uber that has been presented by industry commentators. Positive feedback effects help a platform grow as a result of increasing the participation by both sides. But feedback effects also work in reverse resulting in contraction. If a platform experiences a loss of users on one side that will make the platform less valuable to the other side, leading to a loss of those users, resulting in further losses on both sides.

**Figure 1: Positive Feedback Effects Associated with Uber's Platform**[3]

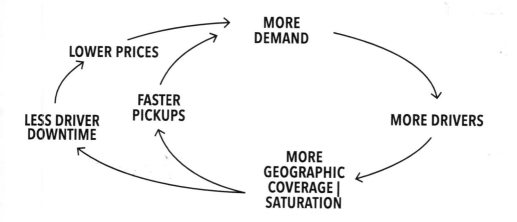

---

3  Gurley (2014).

Studies of two-sided platforms typically find that managing these indirect network effects, and the resulting positive feedback loop, is a central part of starting and running these businesses. When a platform starts out, for example, it cannot provide a valuable service to members of either group unless it has members of both groups on board. This results in the well-known "chicken-and-egg problem" for platform startups. A platform needs to figure out how to get enough of both types of participants to join. As they mature, platforms must balance the interests of both groups, because business decisions that affect the value to one group from using the platform affects the value to the other group.[4]

## 2. Interrelated Prices, Price Levels, and Price Structures

The prices that different types of users pay for platform services are interrelated. Platforms have to select prices that balance the participation of each group against the profits from that group. A higher price for one group reduces the demand from that group, which makes the platform less valuable to the other group. The platform therefore has to juggle prices to find ones that maximize its profits, taking price and demand on both sides of the platform into account.

The economic theory of two-sided platforms shows that the best price to charge to either group does not necessarily track the costs of serving that group. A platform may charge a low price to one group, even below cost, to attract that group and then a high price to the other group to interact with the first group. OpenTable, for example, doesn't charge people to make reservations—in fact, it gives them rewards points and meal discounts for doing so—and makes its profits entirely from the restaurants. The fact that prices do not track costs for each group of participants separately sets two-sided platforms apart from single-sided businesses.

An important consequence of this interrelationship is that the prices charged to either group are not informative, by themselves, about the degree of competition for the platform. A platform could be highly profitable even though it charges a price to one group that barely covers costs, and it could be just making a competitive return even though it charges a price to one group that greatly exceeds costs. For the same reason, it is not possible to make sound inferences about changes in profits from the change in prices or costs on any one side. The impact of any change on overall platform profit depends on the feedbacks between the two groups as well as the extent to which the platform changes prices or other terms of service to the other group.

---

4 In theory, the presence of indirect network effects could lead to natural monopoly for platforms. Since the value of the service provided is greater when there are more users for both groups, it is most efficient for one firm to serve the market, all else equal. In practice, platforms can try to differentiate themselves by appealing to particular types of users (horizontal differentiation) or through trading off price and quality (vertical differentiation). Nevertheless, the existence of indirect network effects, like scale economies, necessarily limits the number of firms that compete for providing a platform service, and that is what typically appears in platform markets.

This interrelationship of prices leads to another important difference with competition among single-sided, traditional firms. In a traditional market, the main effect of one firm attracting a customer from a rival is that the firm's revenue increases, and the rival's revenue decreases. In competition between two-sided platforms, there is another effect. By attracting a customer from one group served by a rival, a firm increases the value of its service to the other group while the value of the rival's service falls if that customer no longer uses the rival's service. For example, when Lyft persuades passengers to use its ride-sharing platform instead of Uber, it not only gets additional revenue, it also makes its platform more attractive to drivers. As a result, to understand competition, and the sources of competitive constraints, economic analysis must consider the platform overall and not just competition for one group.

Making apples-to-apples comparison of prices for platform services also requires accounting for indirect network effects. At given prices, a platform that gives members of one group access to more members of the other group is providing a more valuable service. That is obvious in the case of ride-sharing platforms. For a given cost per ride, a ride-sharing platform provides a more valuable service to drivers if it provides access to more passengers. With more passengers, there is less risk that no passenger will be available when the driver needs one, and the driver won't have to wait as long for a passenger. Thus, drivers would be willing to pay more for access to a platform that provides access to more passengers.

## 3. Transaction Platforms

Many two-sided platforms ultimately offer services to two different types of users at the same time. These "transaction platforms" always have different types of users at either end of an interaction with the platform intermediating between them. A restaurant reservation takes place on a platform such as OpenTable, for example, only when a diner agrees to make, and a restaurant agrees to take, a reservation for a particular time.

There is a strong presumption that transaction platforms have significant indirect network effects between both groups, and powerful feedback loops, as both types of users are seeking more valuable interactions. It is the nature of exchange that the likelihood of finding a beneficial match, and the expected value of that match, generally increases with the number of relevant choices.

Businesses that want to compete for serving the parties to these transactions must necessarily compete for both groups. A restaurant-reservation platform could not provide reservation services to diners if it lacked restaurants; and it could not provide reservation services to restaurants if it lacked diners. And, in competing for both groups of users, transactions platforms have to account for the strong indirect network effects between the two sides, the resulting positive feedback effects, and interrelated pricing.

The fact that there is a simultaneous exchange between participants on a transaction platform does not necessarily mean that the parties *join* the platform at the same time. For example, it is unlikely that a restaurant and a diner would both sign up for OpenTable at the same time. Given that transaction platforms help facilitate these transactions they often provide other services prior to actual transactions taking place. OpenTable, for example provides diners with a website for search and they provide reservation-management software to restaurants. They may provide other ancillary services that raise the platform's value to one or both groups of users because they help persuade some to join and use the platform, which increases indirect network effects. Lyft, for example, rents cars to its drivers.[5] The two parties that enter into a transaction do not necessarily incur charges for using the platform at the same time. The platform may decide to impose fees before, after, or contemporaneously with the transaction.

## 4. Attention Platforms

Ad-supported media businesses, such as newspapers, are platforms that use content to attract viewers and sell ads to businesses that want to market to those viewers.[6] The way these businesses internalize externalities, and the feedback loops between the two sides, are different than in the case of transaction platforms, such as restaurant-reservation businesses, that facilitate a direct exchange between a buyer and seller.

Advertisers would like to present messages to consumers in the hope of persuading them to buy their products. If consumers could be confident that the message was valuable to them, perhaps because it provided information on a sale price for a product they want to buy, they should be happy to receive that message. But, even if it was possible to target messages so precisely, advertisers want the opportunity to persuade people who are not initially receptive to buy their products, people who wouldn't willingly hear the message. Advertising can also be annoying since marketers seek ways, including hyperbole, to get people's attention. Thus, while consumers might like to receive some advertising, they don't normally want to receive as many messages as advertisers would like to deliver.

Nevertheless, so long as advertisers value delivering a message more than a consumer values avoiding the message, there's an opportunity for an exchange that makes them both better off. Ad-supported media emerged in the 17th century to solve this problem. Newspapers produced content that got people to spend time looking through the paper. They then sold advertisements that appeared in their pages. The advertisers hoped that people would see their ads, some of those people would be interested, and they would make a sale as a result. The content compensated the newspaper reader, and the advertising revenue compensated the newspaper for producing and distributing the content.

---

5  Lyft (n.d.).
6  Evans (2019).

Unlike a transaction platform, an attention platform may be helping to sell something that the buyer doesn't value and therefore needs to be paid to take. Media businesses, unlike transaction platforms, also do not have to provide a service to two types of participants simultaneously or at all. While a business that wants to sell advertising usually needs to have content, a business could decide to just sell content and not have advertising.

## B. *American Express* Decision

In *American Express*, the U.S. Supreme Court examined how to apply the rule of reason analysis in a situation in which the challenged conduct involved a company that was a two-sided transaction platform. The District Court had decided that the analysis should begin by examining a relevant market comprising the merchant side of the credit card networks since that is the side on which the conduct occurred. The Appeals Court decided that the right market was the market in which the two-sided credit card networks competed. The Justice Department, the state plaintiffs, American Express, and various parties that submitted *amicus* briefs advocated a variety of approaches for dealing with platforms under the rule of reason. What follows is a brief summary of the Court's majority decision. Chapter 2 provides a detailed analysis and the full decision appears at the end of this volume.

### 1. Definition of Two-Sided Platforms

The Court began by noting that, according to economists, a "[t]wo-sided platform offers different products or services to two different groups who both depend on the platform to intermediate between them."[7] It cited a more fulsome description, based on our work, that "'[t]wo-sided platforms' serve distinct groups of customers who need each other in some way, and the core business of the two-sided platform is to provide a common (real or virtual) meeting place and to facilitate interactions between members of the two distinct customer groups."[8]

Following the economic literature, the Court highlighted that indirect network effects are a key feature of two-sided platforms: "Two-sided platforms differ from traditional markets in important ways. Most relevant here, two-sided platforms often exhibit what economists call 'indirect network effects'"[9] Indirect network effects refer to the situation in which the value realized by members of one group of customers is higher when they can interact with more members of the other group of customers.

---

7  *Ohio v. Am. Express Co.*, 138 S. Ct. 2274, 2280 (2018).

8  Evans and Schmalensee (2008).

9  *Ohio v. Am. Express Co.*, 138 S. Ct. 2274, 2280 (2018).

This description of two-sided platforms is broadly consistent with the economic literature on two-sided platforms, which considers a well-defined class of businesses that have these characteristics.[10]

## 2. Economic Implications of Indirect Network Effects for Two-Sided Platforms

The Court then noted the well-documented theoretical and empirical implications of indirect network effects for two-sided platforms. "Due to indirect network effects, two-sided platforms cannot raise prices on one side without risking a feedback loop of declining demand."[11] The point established in the literature is that, by increasing price on one side, the platform reduces the number of participants on that side, which makes the platform less valuable to the other side. The platform accounts for these feedback effects in setting profit-maximizing prices to each side.

The Court observed that pricing features of two-sided platforms discussed above had important implications for considering prices in antitrust analysis. "[T]he fact that two-sided platforms charge one side a price that is below or above cost reflects differences in the two sides' demand elasticity, not market power or anticompetitive pricing."[12] Furthermore, "[p]rice increases on one side of the platform likewise do not suggest anticompetitive effects without some evidence that they have increased the overall cost of the platform's services."[13]

These interrelated pricing issues, which flow from significant indirect network effects for two-sided platforms, are important to the Court's conclusion that it is necessary to consider a single platform market comprising both sides.

## 3. The Strength of Indirect Network Effects

The key issue is whether the indirect network effects are substantial enough to make pricing to the two sides interdependent even if the business is a two-sided platform. The Court says that "[a] market should be treated as one sided when the impacts of indirect network effects and relative pricing in that market are minor."[14] To put this another way, the Court said that a market should be treated as one-sided when the core concerns for error based on examining the price on one side noted above do not apply. In this context, relative pricing refers to the ability of the platform to adjust prices to either side to recover costs and make a profit.

The Court then goes on to give newspapers as an example of a platform in which indirect network effects are minor. It says that indirect network effects work only in one direction for newspapers: advertisers would like more readers, but "read-

---

10 Evans and Schmalensee (2018c).

11 *Ohio v. Am. Express Co.*, 138 S. Ct. 2274, 2285 (2018).

12 *Id.* at 2285-6.

13 *Id.* at 2286.

14 *Id.* at 2286.

ers are largely indifferent to the amount of advertising that a newspaper contains." It goes on to say that "[b]ecause of these weak indirect network effects, the market for newspaper advertising behaves much like a one-sided market and should be analyzed as such."[15]

## 4. Transaction Platforms and the Degree of Indirect Networks

The Court draws two important implications from the dependence between the two sides for transaction platforms.

*[handwritten: ⋆⋆ Really imp't]*

The first is that transaction platforms are likely to have pronounced indirect network effects and interconnected pricing. "Because they cannot make a sale unless both sides of the platform simultaneously agree to use their services, two-sided transaction platforms exhibit more pronounced indirect network effects and interconnected pricing and demand."[16]

The second is that transaction platforms necessarily compete on both sides. "Evaluating both sides of a two-sided transaction platform is also necessary to assess competition. Only other two-sided platforms can compete with a two-sided platform for transactions."[17] To put this another way, two-sided analysis is unavoidable for transaction platforms because they necessarily raise the core concern of wrongly inferring market power and anticompetitive effects from prices on one side.

## 5. Rule of Reason Analysis for Two-Sided Platforms

In applying this analytical framework to credit card networks, the Court concludes that there is a single platform market in which rivals compete for transactions. "For all these reasons, '[i]n two-sided transaction markets, only one market should be defined.'… Accordingly, we will analyze the two-sided market for credit card transactions as a whole to determine whether the plaintiffs have shown that AmEx's anti-steering provisions have anticompetitive effects."[18] Market power has to be assessed at the platform level given the interdependence of prices. To assess whether there was an anticompetitive exercise of market power it is necessary to consider whether the overall price of transactions was raised above the level that would have occurred but-for the challenged conduct or the output of transactions was reduced below the level that would have occurred but-for the challenged conduct.[19]

---

15  *Id.* at 2286. The Court cites *Times-Picayune.*

16  *Ohio v. Am. Express Co.*, 138 S. Ct. 2274, 2286 (2018).

17  *Id.* at 2287.

18  *Id.* at 2287.

19  The Supreme Court decision refers to this as relative to the competitive level but this seems just unartfully phrased as the case law is clear that it is but-for the challenged conduct.

As the Court noted, "AmEx uses its higher merchant fees to offer its cardholders a more robust rewards program, which is necessary to maintain cardholder loyalty and encourage the level of spending that makes AmEx valuable to merchants."[20] That is, AmEx's business strategy was to charge relatively higher prices to merchants and relatively lower prices to cardholders, but this did not mean that AmEx charged a higher overall price. The Court's conclusion was "That AmEx allocates prices between merchants and cardholders differently from Visa and Mastercard is simply not evidence that it wields market power to achieve anticompetitive ends."[21]

## C. Overview of the Remaining Chapters

Chapter 2 describes the evolution of the *American Express* case through the courts, the areas of agreement, and where the higher courts departed from the lower court. The District Court had found that American Express was a two-sided transaction platform that provided joint services simultaneously to cardholders and merchants. But it then chose, by adopting a single-sided merchant services market, to analyze the effect of the anti-steering provisions at issue solely on one side of these simultaneous transactions. The District Court also decided that case law prevented it from considering the effect of the conduct on the other half of the transactions even at the second stage of the rule of reason. The Supreme Court, and the Appeals Court, disagreed, and insisted on looking at competitive effects in a single market. They found that the plaintiffs had failed to prove antitrust injury to platform competition for transactions in the relevant market in which the platforms competed.

Chapter 3 then presents the reasoning behind our *amicus* brief to the Supreme Court which considered some of the alternative proposals before the court. We observe that, in recent years, the federal courts' analysis of the competitive effects of conduct challenged under the Sherman Act's rule of reason, which generally includes market definition as a critical step, has been properly guided by sensitivity to business reality and sound economic analysis of the conduct at issue. When it comes to two-sided platforms, we argue that courts should adhere to that same flexible but principled approach and avoid rigid alternatives that would apply regardless of the platform, conduct, or fact-pattern.

In briefs before the court, the U.S. Department of Justice as well as some law professors and economists proposed analytical frameworks that would have, first, required courts to restrict the relevant antitrust market to the side of the platform that is the subject of the challenged conduct and, second, would have then excluded the impact of the conduct on the other side of the platform for the purposes of establishing anticompetitive effects under the first stage of the rule of reason inquiry. We explain why such a rigid approach could lead courts, and possibly require them, to ignore business reality, sound economics, and fact patterns in analyzing alleged anti-

---

20  *Ohio v. Am. Express Co.*, 138 S. Ct. 2274, 2288 (2018).

21  *Id.* at 2288.

competitive conduct by platform enterprises and defining relevant antitrust markets. Following this approach would result in tribunals wrongly exonerating behavior that is anticompetitive or wrongly condemning behavior that is not. We explain why this approach should be rejected in favor of accounting for the business realities of two-sided platforms just as the courts have generally done for enterprises.

One might argue, as some have done, that having courts focus on an overall platform market might close the door to plaintiffs and thereby encourage platforms to escape antitrust scrutiny. In Chapter 4 we show that the two-sided analysis of platform businesses isn't pro-defendant or pro-plaintiff. By accounting for business reality and modern economics, it helps courts and enforcement agencies reach the right decision and thereby reduce the likelihood of false negatives as well as false positives. Sometimes two-sided analysis is essential for uncovering how conduct harms competition and consumers. Other times it helps establish that conduct is innocuous or beneficial. Fears, and hopes, that two-sided analysis will discourage enforcement efforts are misplaced.

A surprising amount of debate leading up to the Supreme Court's decision in *American Express*, and the commentary following this landmark ruling, seem to trivialize and marginalize the modern economic learning on multisided platforms. Despite these efforts, the Supreme Court ultimately embraced the economic literature on these business models, as had both courts below. Chapter 5 debunks five red herrings that have been floated in the debate: (1) the two sides are just complements, nothing new there; (2) everything is two-sided, or who's to know what's two-sided; (3) as industries mature two-sidedness goes away; (4) markets must be one sided since the services to the two sides aren't interchangeable; and (5) two-sided analysis "devastates" antitrust law. The Supreme Court's decision has raised a host of interesting issues, including how to deal with two-sided platform businesses that look different from American Express's credit card platform and what sort of evidence is necessary or sufficient in markets with platform businesses to establish competitive effects. Like any Supreme Court decision, not every word was chosen as carefully as it might have been, and clarifications will be needed going forward. The large and evolving literature on two-sided platforms will prove helpful to sort that out, and we anticipate that the courts will embrace this constructive approach.

As we noted above, the Court focused on transaction platforms, thereby leaving the proper antitrust analysis of attention platforms, which include large online advertising platforms including Facebook and Google, uncertain. We take this up in Chapter 6. The *American Express* dissent argued that the Court had already decided how to apply the rule of reason analysis to two-sided platforms in *Times-Picayune,* and got it right then, but got it wrong in *AmEx*. *Times-Picayune* is a shaky foundation for that proposition. In that case, the Government had alleged *per se* tying involving advertising and monopolization of the dissemination of news and advertising. By the time the case reached the Supreme Court it was mainly about *per se* tying and didn't pose the particular two-sided issues that concerned the Court in *American Express*. After dismissing the *per se* tying claim, the Court provided a short rule of reason analysis which is consistent with considering the newspaper platform overall and not just one side. In particular, the lower court had analyzed the Government's predation claims for the newspaper by considering the platform in its entirety, and the Court relied on its conclusion. While this is clearly a subject to which the Supreme Court will have to return, we believe that the underlying principles of *American Express* apply more broadly to many attention platforms, although the details of the analysis may differ.

The Supreme Court decision, including the dissent, appears at the end, with hyperlinks to the relevant academic literature cited for readers of the digital version of this book. We have also included the briefs by the U.S. Department of Justice and a group of law professors and economists which lay out alternative approaches to the one we advocated.

# CHAPTER 2
# Where's the Harm?

Many criticisms of the Supreme Court decision seem to be based on the rejection or misunderstanding of the economics literature on multi-sided platforms on which the District Court, the Appeals Court, and the Supreme Court all relied. There was no serious debate that American Express was a two-sided transaction platform. Nor about the key findings of the economic literature on these businesses. The key issue concerned how to evaluate harm when a company serves two interrelated set of customers which turns greatly on market definition.

## A. The District Court's Background Findings on the Case

The U.S. Department of Justice, together with the State of Ohio and other states, brought the case against American Express in 2010. Before addressing the merits of the plaintiffs' lawsuit, the District Court provided some background on the payment card business and the use of anti-steering provisions as well as other issues.

When a purchase is made with a general-purpose credit or charge (GPCC) card, the merchant pays, to a third party, a fraction of what it charges the buyer. Most of that payment, the merchant fee, goes to the firm that issued the card: American Express in the case of American Express cards, and a bank in the case of Visa or Mastercard cards. Historically, AmEx has had a "spend-centric" business model: it has focused on attracting consumers who are likely to spend heavily, in part by offering more generous rewards for using its cards than Visa or Mastercard issuers had typically done. It has financed its reward programs by charging higher merchant fees than Visa or Mastercard. Visa and Mastercard issuers, in contrast, had "lend-centric" business models: they did not focus on attracting heavy spenders and made much of their money by lending to cardholders.

Despite the higher AmEx merchant fees, and even though most AmEx cardholders also carried one or more Mastercard and Visa cards, the AmEx card was accepted at around 6.4 million U.S. merchant locations. But it was *not* accepted at around 3 million U.S. merchant locations that had chosen to accept Visa and Mastercard.[22]

---

22 *U.S. v. American Exp. Co.,* 88 F.Supp. 143, 204 (2015).

Since the 1950s, AmEx's contracts with merchants that had chosen to accept its card generally prohibited merchants from using both price and non-price forms of what has come to be called "steering."[23] Steering via price would involve the merchant imposing special surcharges on purchases made with AmEx cards rather than other GPCC cards.[24] Non-price steering would involve the merchant trying in other ways—by pleading hardship, disparaging AmEx, or posting "We Prefer Visa" signs—to persuade customers who carried and perhaps had presented their AmEx cards instead to use a means of payment that was less expensive for the merchant. If they did so, customers would generally give up some standing in the AmEx rewards program and possibly use a less preferred card from their standpoint. There were similar anti-steering provisions in Visa and Mastercard merchant contracts.

Beginning in the late 1980s, Mastercard and Visa mounted campaigns aimed at persuading consumers that their cards were more useful than AmEx cards and persuading merchants to steer consumers toward their cards using non-price methods. These two campaigns together were effective: between 1990 and 1995, AmEx's share of GPCC volume declined from 25 percent to 20 percent. AmEx responded by strengthening and enforcing the anti-steering provisions in its merchant contracts.

In 2010, the U.S. Department of Justice (DOJ) and several states charged that the restrictions on *non-price* steering in the merchant contracts of AmEx, Visa, and Mastercard were unreasonable restraints of trade and thus violations of Section 1 of the Sherman Act. Independent class-action cases brought by groups of merchants challenged the restrictions on surcharging.[25] The plaintiffs' case thus had nothing to do with direct restrictions on price competition at the merchant level, and certainly

---

23 *U.S. v. American Exp. Co., 88* F.Supp. 143, 161 (2015). American Express was launched in 1958. At the time Diners Club was the dominant GPCC system in the US. See, Evans and Schmalensee (2005) at pp. 57-59.

24 There have never been restrictions on giving discounts from list price for the use of cash or other means of payment. The AmEx contracts' restrictions on steering via price did not bar surcharging relative to cash, checks, or debit cards, only relative to other GPCC cards.

25 The merchants' suit against Mastercard and Visa was brought in 2005 and was finally settled in January 2019. Both networks now permit surcharging with disclosure requirements and limits on the charges: See, Visa (2019); Mastercard (2019). In 2008, another group of merchants challenged all of AmEx's anti-steering provisions. Individual merchant cases and a putative merchant class action challenging AmEx's provisions were consolidated in 2011. In January 2019, the trial court ordered both parties to proceed to trial using the two-sided market definition in the Supreme Court *AmEx* decision: Memorandum and Order, *In Re: American Express Anti-Steering Rules Antitrust Litigation*, 11-MD-2221 (NGG) (RER) (January 14, 2019). On April 12, 2019, the individual merchant cases were dismissed with prejudice pursuant to a joint stipulation between the parties that settled the litigation on undisclosed terms. There is a pending motion to dismiss and compel arbitration of the class action. It seems that all of AmEx's anti-steering restrictions are still in force. See, American Express (2019). Complicating this picture, ten states and Puerto Rico had anti-surcharge laws in effect in 2016. Several of these have been voided as impermissible restrictions on commercial speech, and the validity of others is being litigated. See, National Conference of State Legislatures (2016).

nothing to do with discounts for cash or debit cards, despite some commentators' claims to the contrary.[26]

An important theory of harm, in the case that was brought initially, was that the restrictions on non-price steering by the three leading systems unreasonably limited the ability of smaller GPCC systems, like Discover, to compete by charging low merchant fees. Visa and Mastercard, which accounted for 68.3 percent of GPCC volume in 2013,[27] agreed to drop their restrictions on non-price steering, thus greatly weakening the plausibility of that theory as applied to AmEx alone.[28] The plaintiffs nonetheless persisted, as did AmEx, and a seven-week trial ensued during the summer of 2014.

## B. The District Court's Rule of Reason Analysis

The District Court issued a 97-page decision in February 2015.

### 1. District Court Findings on AmEx as a Platform

At trial, experts for both sides described AmEx as a two-sided platform. The court agreed, citing a number of works from the relevant economics literature. The judge noted the existence of indirect network effects between merchants and consumers on the two sides of that platform. This ready acceptance of the economic literature on multi-sided platforms is in marked contrast to the strenuous attacks on that literature that has appeared in later commentary on this case,[29] some of which we discuss below.

The judge went on to describe AmEx as a two-sided *transactions* platform:[30]

> ...the two sides of the platform are brought together to consummate a single, simultaneous transaction, and the products provided by the platform are consumed in fixed proportions by the consumer and the merchant.

That finding became a key predicate of the Supreme Court's decision.

---

26  See, for instance, Hovenkamp (2019).

27  *U.S. v. American Exp. Co.*, 88 F.Supp. 143, 188 (2015).

28  Nevertheless, the District Court found that AmEx's restrictions on non-price steering, the only restrictions at issue in the case, by themselves "...render it nearly impossible for a firm to enter the relevant market by offering merchants a low-cost alternative to the existing networks." The testimony from Discover on which this finding apparently rested, however, referred to a period in which Mastercard and Visa also had restrictions barring both price and non-price steering. *U.S. v. American Exp. Co.*, 88 F.Supp. 143, 213-214 (2015).

29  Evans and Schmalensee (2018c).

30  *U.S. v. American Exp. Co.*, 88 F.Supp. 143, 155 (2015).

Having found that AmEx was a two-sided platform, the judge faced a critical choice that has been discussed at some length in the academic literature: whether to define a single market linking both sides of the platform, or to carry out the analysis working with two closely coupled markets.[31] He chose to describe the GPCC business as consisting of two markets, one involving AmEx and merchants and the other involving AmEx and consumers. He then decided to limit consideration to the merchant side of the business in the first step of the rule of reason analysis and thus to consider initially whether AmEx's policies in that market had unreasonably restrained competition.[32] As we will discuss below, he also decided that he could not consider any pro-competitive benefits from the consumer market in the second step of the rule of reason analysis.

This single-sided market approach basically precluded the court from considering the implications of its own finding that AmEx was a two-sided transaction platform. It had to view the facts of the case through a lens that distorted the business reality the court itself had emphasized.

## 2. The Choice of Market Definition and the Rule of Reason

In principle, the conclusions of an *economic* analysis of the effects of a challenged practice by a two-sided transactions platform should be the same whether based on consideration of a single platform market or two closely coupled markets corresponding to each side. Unfortunately, the conclusions of a *legal* analysis under the three-step structure of rule of reason analysis in U.S. courts can depend critically on this choice of market definition. In particular, the single platform market definition allows consideration of all the relevant evidence and accounts for the business realities surrounding platform competition, while the side-specific platform market definitions suppress this evidence and distort business reality.

Under the rule of reason, plaintiffs have the initial burden of showing that challenged conduct harmed competition. If they do so, the defense has an opportunity to demonstrate pro-competitive benefits. In principle, if both sides meet their burdens, the finder of fact must balance pro- and anti-competitive effects. As a

---

31  A useful overview of that discussion is provided by Wright and Yun (2019). See also Affeldt et al. (2014) and, for a different view, Katz and Sallet (2018).

32  After excluding debit cards and other forms of payment from the relevant market, the trial judge found AmEx had a 26.4 percent share of GPCC transactions volume. Despite this relatively small share he found that AmEx had sufficient market power to affect competition and proceeded to analyze the effects of the challenged conduct. *U.S. v. American Exp. Co.*, 88 F. Supp. 143, 207 (2015). We take market power as given for the analysis below even though one could quarrel with the court's finding. For example, the court found that AmEx's cardholders' loyalty was "…critical to the court's finding of market power…" even though that loyalty was, at least in large part, purchased by AmEx through its generous rewards program. The Court of Appeals disagreed, holding that there is no reason to intervene because of market power that depends on rewards and prestige: *U.S. v. American Exp. Co.* 838 F.3d. 179, 204 (2016).

practical matter, however, if plaintiffs succeed at the first step, defendants have a very difficult task.

The *American Express* case illustrates why. First, it isn't clear that the court could consider the other side-specific market in the second stage of the rule of reason inquiry. The trial court judge noted that pro-competitive benefits on the consumer side, in "a separate, though intertwined antitrust market," could not be used to offset anti-competitive effects on the merchant side.[33] Second, after finding that a practice is anti-competitive in the first stage, courts seldom give much weight to pro-competitive benefits in the second stage. In this case, the judge essentially ignored the tight linkage between the two markets he had defined: AmEx's pro-competitive justifications for its conduct are not discussed until the last 14 pages of the 97-page District Court opinion.[34]

When a challenged practice clearly has effects on both sides of a two-sided transactions platform, as in this case, to exclude either side of the platform in the first step of the analysis is to bias the result. After all, the output (transactions consummated by both sides), the price of that output (paid by both sides), and the profits earned (contributed by both sides) necessarily depends on both sides. Once a court has found that a business is a two-sided transaction platform, it makes no economic sense to ignore the consequences of the challenged conduct for half of the parties to the joint transaction. And in the case of transactions platforms, the most natural way to take into account the impact of the challenged conduct on both sides of the same transaction is to define a single market for the service of connecting the two sides. Doing otherwise means, as a practical matter, the court ignoring pro-competitive benefits for the other interlinked side or putting little weight on this evidence.

## 3. What the District Court Missed by Looking Just at One Side

In this case, it is instructive to suppose that the trial court had decided to take a serious look at the consumer side of the platform in the first step of the analysis and that AmEx had fully availed itself of this opportunity. AmEx could have made a good argument for the facial reasonability of its anti-steering provisions in light of general

---

33 *U.S. v. American Exp. Co.*, 88 F.Supp. 143, 229 (2015). It seems unsettled whether under U.S. case law it is possible to consider the benefits from a related market. Several eminent law professors who filed an *amicus* brief in support of the plaintiffs before the Supreme Court said it was not appropriate to do so. The U.S. Department of Justice seemed sufficiently uncertain about this that they advocated that the Court find that those benefits could be considered. See "Brief of 28 Professors of Antitrust Law as Amici Curiae Supporting Petitioners" *State of Ohio, et al. v. American Express Company, et al.* (2017) No. 16-1454 (SCOTUS); "Brief for the United States as Respondent Supporting Petitioners," *State of Ohio, et al. v. American Express Company, et al.* (2017) No. 16-1454 (SCOTUS).

34 Justice Breyer, in dissent, would have allowed the benefits from the interlinked market to be considered in the second step of the rule of reason. He then noted the likely futility of that defense: "A Sherman Act §1 defendant can rarely, if ever, show that a pro-competitive benefit in the market for one product offsets an anticompetitive harm in the market for another." *Ohio v. American Express Co.*, 138 S.Ct. 2274, 2302 (2018) (Breyer, J., dissenting).

business practice. As one commentator asked, rhetorically, when the DOJ complaint was initially filed,[35]

> [T]he larger question is whether … American Express, or any firm, could possibly violate the Sherman Act by telling agents that are distributing its services as well as the services of its competitors that once the customer has expressed a clear preference to use its service rather than a competing offering, the agent must accept the consumer's preference.

*[handwritten: Not sure about this. Is it free-riding?]*

In addition, if the District Court had been able to look at the platform as whole, AmEx might have been able to make its free-riding argument more persuasive. After all, why would a merchant decide to accept the AmEx card and then to try to persuade customers not to use it rather than simply not accepting the card unless accepting that the AmEx card generated incremental business? That incremental business must have resulted from investments by AmEx, on which some merchants who wanted to engage in non-price steering wished to ride free.[36]

AmEx could have gone on to note that it is common for two-sided platforms to restrict the behavior of participants on one side in order to benefit those on the other side. For instance, OpenTable terminates the accounts of diners who are no-shows four times in a 12-month period.[37] This rule is an inconvenience to diners but clearly benefits restaurants. Similarly, AmEx's restrictions on non-price steering by merchants clearly benefitted its cardholders: it freed them from being hassled to give up rewards in order to lower merchants' costs. Or from just being hassled when they'd like to pay and get out of the store. These restrictions enabled AmEx to offer a more attractive product by ensuring what it called "welcome acceptance."[38]

Experience abroad provides additional support for the direct consumer benefit from rules that restrict merchant steering. Australia and the United Kingdom both prohibited card networks, including American Express, from forbidding merchants from imposing surcharges which is the leading price-based steering method.[39] Both found that, of the merchants who surcharged, some did so opportunistically.[40] The surcharges sometimes greatly exceeded the fees merchants paid. Most troubling, some online merchants imposed these fees at the end of the check-out process as an extra fee—a practice known as "drip pricing." Having persuaded the consumer to go through the purchase process and enter their payment details, the merchant

---

35  Brown (2010).

36  On this point, see the discussion by the Court of Appeals, *U.S. v. American Exp. Co.*, 838 F.3d. 179, 204 (2016).

37  OpenTable (n.d.).

38  *U.S. v. American Exp. Co.*, 88 F.Supp. 143, 156 (2015). This point was accepted by the Supreme Court: *Ohio v. American Express Co.*, 138 S.Ct. 2274, 2289-90 (2018).

39  Reserve Bank of Australia (2010).

40  Reserve Bank of Australia (2016); Office of Fair Trading (2012).

anticipates that the surcharge at the end won't dissuade them for completing the purchase.[41]

Australia revised its regulations to limit the surcharges so they could not exceed merchant fees.[42] The United Kingdom has prohibited merchant surcharging altogether.[43] Puerto Rico and ten U.S. states have passed legislation that prohibit merchants from imposing surcharges.[44] Under the single-sided market approach, a court could not consider the possibility that American Express was prohibiting surcharges to protect its cardholders from opportunistic behavior, nor could it consider any consumer benefits that this protection provides.

To address the charge that its restrictions on non-price steering nonetheless constituted an unreasonable restraint of trade that reduced consumer welfare, AmEx would stress that payment systems compete for *transactions*, which requires them to cater to both merchants and consumers. It would point to the many merchants that had elected not to accept the AmEx card because of its high merchant fees as evidence that price competition is alive and well in the GPCC card business. It would remind the court that it did not restrict merchants' ability to offer discounts for cash, checks, or debit cards and that their ability to charge more when more expensive payment systems were used—to surcharge—was not an issue in this case. The only competition that was suppressed by the AmEx restrictions at issue was merchant jawboning aimed at the customers of a firm with a 26.4 percent share of GPCC transactions' volume.

All of these arguments go to the heart of the question that should have been before the court at the first stage of the rule of reason—did the practice restrict competition among two-sided transaction platforms?—but couldn't be considered under the single-sided definition adopted by the District Court in this or similar cases.

## 4.  The District Court's Single-Sided Evidence on Antitrust Injury

Plaintiffs stressed evidence that AmEx had market power and that the anti-steering provisions restricted one form of non-price competition which some merchants testified that they would have employed but for those restrictions. And, as noted above, the District Court was somehow persuaded that the AmEx restrictions on non-price steering had, by themselves, made it "nearly impossible" for Discover or other systems to compete on the basis of low merchant discounts.[45]

*NB — If X surcharges → makes AX less attractive at Y, Z etc. (w/ a rewards card)*

*Not apply to D.*

---

41  Fletcher (2012).

42  Reserve Bank of Australia (2016).

43  HM Treasury (2018).

44  National Conference of State Legislatures (2016).

45  *U.S. v. American Exp. Co.*, 88 F.Supp. 143, 213-24 (2015).

The rest of plaintiffs' evidence relied on by the District Court seems to add little economic substance to this.[46] Plaintiffs stressed that AmEx had increased its merchant discounts substantially over the 2005-2010 period with only a slight decline in merchant acceptance, though these increases were in response to earlier increases by Mastercard and Visa. AmEx was selling a differentiated product in a concentrated market, and generally offering higher consumer rewards, so price differences and price changes are hardly symptoms of competitive breakdown. Plaintiffs were unable to persuade the trial judge that AmEx charged supra-competitive prices, or that it earned supra-competitive profits, or that its merchant fees were above those of Visa and Mastercard. So, in the end, plaintiffs did not provide any quantitative evidence showing a *causal* link between AmEx's more stringent enforcement of its ban on non-price steering and any change in market competition.

Perhaps a trial court that considered both sides of the platform in this fashion in the first step of the rule of reason analysis would nevertheless have found that AmEx's restrictions on non-price steering constituted an unreasonable restraint of trade and that consumer welfare was on balance reduced by it. But we think that looking at the interlinked consumers and merchants together, in a single platform market, would more likely have revealed just how weak the DOJ's case was and would have led to a decision for AmEx by the District Court. In the actual world, the District Court found that AmEx had violated Section 1.[47]

## C.  Market Definition and Antitrust Injury on Appeal

In 2016 a three-judge panel of the Court of Appeals for the Second Circuit unanimously reversed the District Court, largely on the grounds that the correct product market definition was GPCC transactions:

---

46  On what follows in this paragraph, see *Ohio v. American Express Co.*, 138 S.Ct. 2274, 2288 (2018). The District Court also noted that in the absence of surcharging or discounting, the cost of AmEx's merchant fees is paid by all consumers at merchants that accept AmEx cards, even those consumers that don't use AmEx cards. It argued that this could result in a regressive subsidy from poor consumers who use cash to rich consumers who use AmEx cards: *U.S. v. American Exp. Co.*, 88 F.Supp. 143, 216-7 (2015). The claim that GPCC cards result in cash users subsidizing card users (and poor people subsidizing rich people) is often made by commentators on *American Express* as well as by the plaintiffs. The point isn't as obvious as it may seem at first blush. Merchants incur significant costs from handling cash, after all, and cash-intensive and card-intensive users seem likely to tend to patronize different merchants. The unpublished paper by Schuh, Stavins, and Oz, which is often cited in support of the cash/poor subsidy point demonstrates the fragility of the evidence on this point. Schuh et al. (2011) at Slide 18. They find no cross-subsidy if the merchant pass-through rate is 50 percent or less, which is within the range of pass-through rates found in the literature, and report results based on 100 percent pass-through. For an overview of evidence on pass-through rates see Chang et al. (2015).

47  *U.S. v. American Exp. Co.*, 88 F.Supp. 143, 238-9 (2015).

The District Court's definition of the relevant market in this case is fatal to its conclusion that AmEx violated §1.[48]

It held that by looking only at services to merchants, plaintiffs had not established antitrust injury in the relevant antitrust market, the market for transactions. The Second Circuit then declined to have the full court reconsider the panel's decision.

The State plaintiffs appealed, and the Supreme Court granted certiorari in 2017. It issued its decision in June 2018.[49] In that decision, the majority began, almost exactly as the District Court and the Court of Appeals had done, by defining two-sided platforms and indirect network effects, citing much of the relevant economic literature, and concluding that AmEx is a two-sided platform:

> As the name implies, a two-sided platform offers different products or services to two different groups who both depend on the platform to intermediate between them.[50]

This description of two-sided platforms has been criticized as being over-inclusive, notably by Justice Breyer in dissent,[51] and some have argued that it would enable almost any business to claim special treatment because it is two-sided.[52] Like the District Court and the Court of Appeals, however, the Supreme Court majority cited relevant studies in the economics literature with more systematic, and less-inclusive, definitions. The literature cited by the Supreme Court includes a 2008 paper of ours, for instance, that offers a less-inclusive definition that is widely accepted in the economics literature:[53]

*Isn't if "argue not PM. TJPM."*

> Two-sided platforms serve two distinct groups of customers who need each other in some way, and ... provide a common (real or virtual) meeting place ... *to facilitate interactions between members of the two distinct customer groups.*"

This context and the lower court decisions demonstrate that the majority was not departing from the now-voluminous economics literature on this point. That literature is entirely consistent with the proposition that, even though multi-sided platforms are increasingly important, many businesses, large and small, are not multi-sided.

---

48  *U.S. v. American Exp. Co.*, 838 F.3d. 179, 196 (2016).

49  *Ohio v. American Express Co.*, 138 S.Ct. 2274 (2018).

50  *Id.* at 2280.

51  *Id. at* 2298-2300 (Breyer, J., dissenting).

52  Sagers (2018).

53  Evans and Schmalensee (2008); Evans and Schmalensee (2018c); Wright and Yun (2019); Affeldt et al. (2014); and Katz and Sallet (2018).

Like the District Court and the Court of Appeals below, the majority went on to find that AmEx operates a transaction platform, with indirect network effects running in both directions, providing a joint product simultaneously to two parties engaged in a transaction.[54] And like the Court of Appeals, it found that given this finding it was appropriate to define a single relevant market for GPCC transactions, rather than two different markets for merchant services and consumer services.[55] As with the Court of Appeals, it also found that the plaintiffs' evidence on antitrust injury was completing wanting.

Given that market definition, the Supreme Court found that evidence on merchant fees, on which "plaintiffs stake their entire case," was "unpersuasive" absent more.[56] The majority noted the lack of evidence of supra-competitive pricing of transactions and cited the District Court's finding that there was no reliable evidence on AmEx's transactions' prices or profit margins, nor conclusive evidence about whether AmEx charged more than its competitors.[57] The Court also took note of evidence that AmEx's price had increased from 2005 to 2010, but it found, properly, that an increase in price by a single firm, not found to have engaged in supra-competitive pricing, during a period of output growth did not establish an anti-competitive effect. It went on to point to evidence of vigorous competition among networks. It affirmed the judgement of the Court of Appeals.

It is worth repeating that this outcome was largely dictated by the findings of the District Court. There wasn't any dispute among the parties that AmEx was a two-sided platform, the District Court found that it was a transaction platform, and the District Court didn't cite credible evidence that would establish that the anti-steering provisions had caused antitrust injury. The Supreme Court decision was not like Athena, full born from the head of Zeus. It was the logical outcome of the District Court's findings but for the trial judge's decision to ignore the consumer side of the two-sided transaction platform.

## D.  Justice Breyer's Dissent and Other Criticisms

The Supreme Court's conclusion that the facts in *American Express* should be viewed through the lens of a single market for transactions, which we have endorsed above, seems to have attracted the most hostile commentary. In dissent, Justice Breyer argued at length that it is simply wrong because it aggregates complements—services to merchants and services to consumers—rather than substitutes.[58] The majority's market definition has been described by prominent commentators as "incoherent"

---

54  *Ohio v. American Express Co.*, 138 S.Ct. 2274, 2280 (2018).

55  *Id.* at 2287.

56  *Id.*

57  *Id.* at 2288.

58  *Id.* at 2297-2301 (Breyer, J., dissenting).

and "economic nonsense."[59] In contrast, the economics literature generally indicates that a single-market lens may be more appropriate for use in some cases involving two-sided platforms, depending on fact patterns and analytical convenience.[60]

The *American Express* majority has *not* erred in treating complements as if they were substitutes for purposes of market definition. Rather, it has defined a market for the product, GPCC transactions, that is produced by the card systems by combining merchant-side and consumer-side complements in *production*. Antitrust markets of this sort are hardly novel. Left shoes and right shoes are plainly not substitutes in consumption. Rather, they are complements in *production*. They are combined to produce the product of interest to both suppliers and demanders: pairs of shoes. Similarly, engines and brakes are complements in production that are combined, along with other complementary inputs, to produce automobiles, potentially a relevant antitrust product market.

Justice Breyer said in the oral argument that the two sides were just like "nuts and bolts" and in his dissent like "tires and gasoline."[61] Professor Carlton, who has made the same point in earlier writing, has another analogy:[62]

> Steel and rubber are used to make a golf club, but it would make no sense to claim that steel and rubber are in one market.

But there is nothing obviously wrong with defining a market for golf clubs, which, as Professor Carlton notes, are produced by combining the two complementary inputs he mentions along with other inputs. These comparisons, and the complement point, seem to willfully ignore a voluminous literature on two-sided platforms that, since the early 2000s, has recognized that the two-sides aren't just ordinary complements.

The definition of "transaction market" adopted by the District Court and quoted above emphasizes fixity of proportions as well as simultaneity.[63] Fixity of proportions is central to the examples in the preceding paragraph and other similar examples, as well as to the production of GPCC transactions. It is hardly irrelevant, as the Supreme Court majority said, that "...credit cards determine their market share

---

59 These descriptions are from Wu (2019) and Hovenkamp (2019).

60 Wright and Yun (2019); Affeldt et al. (2014); and Katz and Sallet (2018). Justice Breyer cites us (Evans and Schmalensee (2008) and Evans and Schmalensee (2018c)) for the proposition that in some cases it is appropriate to ignore linkages between the two sides of a platform (*Ohio v. American Express Co.*, 138 S.Ct. 2274, 2300 (2018) (Breyer, J., dissenting)). We still agree with that proposition, but *American Express* is not one of those cases.

61 Transcript of Oral Arguments at 22, *Ohio v. American Express Co.*, 138 S.Ct. 2274 (No. 16-1454); *Ohio v. American Express Co.*, 138 S.Ct. 2274, 2298 (2018) (Breyer, J., dissenting).

62 Carlton (2019).

63 *U.S. v. American Exp. Co.*, 88 F.Supp. 143, 155 (2015).

by measuring the volume of transactions they have sold."[64] The plaintiffs used those same shares which of course are exactly the same from both sides of the two-sided transaction platform.

The Supreme Court found that the plaintiffs "have not carried their burden to prove anticompetitive effects in the relevant market."[65] Justice Breyer in dissent argued that as a legal matter, market definition was unnecessary if "proof of actual detrimental effects" on competition were at hand.[66] We have argued above that the evidence for "actual detrimental effects" presented to the District Court was weak when considered on one-side of the platform and incomplete by refusing to consider the other side of the platform.

Apart from the facts in this case, we believe that as an economic matter, it is essential to consider market definition and, more fundamentally, market power in Sherman Act rule of reason cases, even if market boundaries are often blurry and market power often eludes quantification. The use of "direct evidence" to prove anti-competitive effects in *American Express* illustrates why.

In discussing proof of actual detrimental effects, for instance, Justice Breyer noted that American Express raised its merchant fees 20 times in five years without losing appreciable market share.[67] Since Visa and Mastercard were also raising their merchant fees over the same period, it seems at least plausible that the JCB card, which issued cards in several U.S. states until 2018 but had a trivial share of GPCC card volume,[68] also raised its merchant fees. Is that fact, taken alone, à la Justice Breyer without the market context, proof that the JCB card's conduct had actual detrimental effects on competition?

Justice Breyer also pointed to testimony from numerous merchants that they would have engaged in steering but for AmEx's anti-steering restrictions.[69] Suppose the JCB card's merchant agreements also had anti-steering provisions to which some merchants objected. Would that constitute evidence that those agreements had had anti-competitive effects sufficient for a Sherman Act Section 1 violation? If the JCB card had market power, perhaps. But without more than the quantum of market power that comes from selling a differentiated product, a firm's unilateral conduct simply cannot have any appreciable impact on competition in a relevant antitrust market. JCB's hypothetical anti-steering provisions may be a restraint of trade in the

---

64  *Ohio v. American Express Co.*, 138 S.Ct. 2274, 2286 (2018). The District Court found that transactions' volume was the best indicator of market share: *U.S. v. American Exp. Co.*, 88 F.Supp. 143, 189 (2015).

65  *Ohio v. American Express Co.*, 138 S.Ct. 2274, 2287 (2018).

66  *Id.* at 2296 (Breyer, J., dissenting), citing *Indiana Federation of Dentists*, 476 U.S., at 460-61, 106 S.Ct. 2009.

67  *Id.* at 2293 (Breyer, J., dissenting).

68  Wikipedia (n.d.).

69  *Ohio v. American Express Co.*, 138 S.Ct. 2274, 2296 (2018) (Breyer, J., dissenting).

literal sense, but without market power they simply could not be an unreasonable restraint of trade, the requirement for an antitrust offense. Thus, if *Ohio v. American Express* imposes a new requirement to consider market-level effects when attempting to prove anti-competitive effects from direct evidence, as some commentators have argued,[70] we do not think this is a bad development.

If nothing else, *Ohio v. American Express* stands for the proposition that the now well-established economics of multi-sided platforms cannot be ignored in anti-trust litigation. The Supreme Court and the Court of Appeals followed the District Court and found that AmEx was a two-sided transactions platform, and all three decisions cited some of the voluminous relevant economics literature in support of those findings. Aside from how to treat market definition it doesn't appear that the basic economics was controversial at all.

Nonetheless, Justice Breyer complains that "The phrase 'two-sided transactions market' is not one of antitrust art …"[71] This seems to be correct but, in light of the history of antitrust law and policy, irrelevant. At the time the Sherman Act was enacted, and for quite some time after, modern microeconomics and industrial organization theory, including game theory, hadn't even been developed. "Barriers to entry" was not a term of antitrust art from 1890 until sometime after the concept emerged in the economics literature in the 1950s, and the hypothetical monopolist (or SSNIP) approach to market definition was unheard of in antitrust litigation from 1890 until the publication of the 1982 merger guidelines. Over the decades, antitrust lawyers and courts have proven able to incorporate new developments in economics in pursuit of more economically rational antitrust outcomes.

Despite the volume of economics literature on multi-sided platforms that has been produced over nearly two decades, Professor Hovenkamp argues that multi-sided platform theory may be something of a fad, the implication being that courts should curb their enthusiasm for it.[72] The analytical value of multi-sided platform theory is not seriously disputed among economists, however, and economic research on multi-sided platforms shows no sign of slowing after nearly two decades.

Finally, some have argued that taking the multi-sided platform literature seriously will dramatically weaken antitrust enforcement.[73] Taking the correct economics into account may complicate at least some cases. But the argument for weakened,

---

70  Kully and Vardner (2018).

71  *Ohio v. American Express Co.*, 138 S.Ct. 2274, 2298 (2018) (Breyer, J., dissenting).

72  Hovenkamp (2019) argues that the economic theory of multi-sided platforms may follow the trajectory of contestability theory and recede into relative obscurity. We think this very unlikely: contestability theory rested on very strong assumptions and was controversial from its inception, while the economic theory of multi-sided markets is much more robust and has been almost universally accepted among economists.

73  Compare Wu (2019) and Evans and Schmalensee (2018b). Professor Wu's argument is distinct from that advanced by Kully and Vardner (2018), which has nothing to do with two-sidedness.

rather than more accurate enforcement, is an argument that courts will be persistently confused by defendants, despite plaintiffs' best efforts at adducing relevant economic evidence of harm to competition. In the end, the case against American Express failed because the plaintiffs didn't have any credible evidence of harm to competition. Vertical restraints can harm platform competition, and when they do, plaintiffs should be able to demonstrate that with quantitative and qualitative evidence.

## E.  Conclusion

In light of the substantial and growing economic importance of multi-sided platforms, it is hard to see a responsible alternative to taking seriously the economic literature that helps understand their unique characteristics. Professor Jean Tirole, Nobel Prize-winning economist and co-author of pioneering work on two-sided platforms (which he calls two-sided markets) has described essential elements of the necessary, if difficult, path forward:[74]

> Regulators, then, will need to refrain from mechanically applying traditional principles of competition policy.  When it comes to multi-sided platforms, these principles simply are not applicable in many cases.  New guidelines for adapting competition policy to two-sided markets would require that both sides of the market be considered together, rather than analyzed independently, as competition authorities still sometimes do.  This will require care and a new analytical approach.  But this is better than misapplying traditional principles or simply treating these sectors as legal no-go zones for competition authorities.

Sound antitrust policy has always focused on market-specific competitive realities rather than just applying abstract theory.  In markets with multi-sided platforms, new learning has made it clear that competitive realities often differ fundamentally from those in ordinary single-sided markets.  New tools may well be necessary to apply traditional principles appropriately in markets with multi-sided platforms, but there is no reason to abandon those principles.

---

74  Tirole (2019).  Professor Tirole's pioneering work on multi-sided platforms was cited in all three *American Express* decisions.

# CHAPTER 3
# The Rule of Reason

*American Express* raised fundamental issues regarding the proper application of the Sherman Act's rule of reason to platform enterprises that, like American Express, connect different types of customers with interdependent demands – merchants and consumers in the case of *AmEx*.

## A. Competing Approaches to the Rule of Reason

In submissions to the Supreme Court in *AmEx*, the U.S. Department of Justice and some law professors[75] and economists,[76] as *amici curiae* in support of Petitioners, proposed to require courts in such cases to restrict the relevant antitrust market to the side of the platform that is the subject of the challenged conduct,[77] and then to exclude the impact of the conduct on the other side of the platform for the purposes of establishing anticompetitive effects under the first stage of the rule of reason inquiry.[78]

This approach would apparently apply to all platform enterprises, for all possible challenged conduct, and for all possible fact patterns. It would be a substantial departure from the courts' long-standing emphasis on understanding business reality and employing sound economic analysis. Since platform enterprises are a large and

---

75 The "Petitioner *Amici* Law Professors" refers to the brief filed by the 28 Professors of Antitrust Law as *Amici Curiae* Supporting Petitioners (Dec. 14, 2017).

76 The "Petitioner *Amici* Economists" refers to the brief filed by *Amici Curiae* John M. Connor, Martin Gaynor, Daniel McFadden, Roger Noll, Jeffrey M. Perloff, Joseph A. Stiglitz, Lawrence J. White, and Ralph A. Winter in Support of Petitioners (Dec. 14, 2017).

77 Brief for the United States as Respondent Supporting Petitioners at 35–40; Petitioner *Amici* Law Professors at 17–20; and Petitioner *Amici* Economists at 30–31.

78 Brief for the United States as Respondent Supporting Petitioners at 20-27; Petitioner *Amici* Law Professors; Petitioner *Amici* Economists at 30–31. The *amici* law professors and economists would further exclude consideration of procompetitive benefits on the other side of the platform in the second stage of the rule of reason inquiry. *See* Petitioner *Amici* Law Professors at 32–34; ; Petitioner *Amici* Economists at 23. We note that the Justice Department does not go to this extreme. It argues that the courts should consider procompetitive benefits on the other side of the platform in the second stage of the rule of reason analysis. Brief for the United States as Respondent Supporting Petitioners at 52.

growing portion of the economy, adopting this rigid framework would fundamentally transform the rule of reason. And, as we show below, it would lead to condemnation of procompetitive conduct in some cases and exonerating anticompetitive conduct in other cases.

The risk of error from ignoring customers on one side of a platform during the first stage of the rule of reason analysis is heightened for platforms that provide services that, by their very nature, are jointly and unseverably consumed by two different types of customers.[79]

In these cases, the platform can charge either or both types of customers for the service that both consume jointly in order to recover the platform's costs and make a profit. A restaurant reservation service, for example, provides a valuable service only when it enables a person wishing to dine at a restaurant to make a reservation and a restaurant to take that reservation from that prospective diner. The reservation service can charge the diner, the restaurant, or both for this service.

To determine whether a restraint is anticompetitive, where, as in the restaurant reservation example, the platform's matching services are joint and unseverable, the presumption at the first stage of the rule of reason should be to consider the impact on both sets of customers, on how much they jointly pay, and, ultimately, on the overall output of the jointly consumed service.[80] Conduct that increases the overall output of a service should be commended, not condemned, as that is a central virtue of competition.[81]

This is not a matter of burden-shifting. There is simply no way to know, especially in the case of a platform that provides a service that customers on each side consume jointly, whether a practice is anticompetitive without at least considering both types of customers and the overall competition among platforms. That analysis must, therefore, happen at the first stage of the rule of reason to assess whether the conduct is anticompetitive or not.

The assertion by the *AmEx* Petitioners and some of the *amici* in support that the relevant antitrust market for a two-sided platform *always includes* the side of the

---

79 Examples include online marketplaces, stock exchanges, dating businesses, messaging platforms, and payment networks.

80 As is always the case with the rule of reason, the inquiry ultimately concerns the impact of the conduct on the market price and output. *See, e.g., NCAA v. Board of Regents of Univ. of Okla.*, 468 U.S. 85, 113 (1984) (calling higher prices and lower output "hallmarks of anticompetitive behavior").

81 Some *amici* economists even want to discourage the courts from looking at the standard signals of competitive harm—price and output—because, despite received antitrust doctrine, they contend that lower prices and higher output may be undesirable. That would eliminate the main navigational tool that the courts have used with great success in rule of reason inquiries. Those *amici* economists would have the courts wade into the sea of two-sided platforms without a compass for the rule of reason. Petitioner *Amici* at 20, 34–35.

platform on which the conduct has occurred and *always excludes* the other side of the platform conflicts with sound economics. This assertion is clearly wrong for platforms that provide services that are jointly consumed, and unseverable, by the customers on each side. In such cases, there is a single service that is subject to competition, and it is that service that is interchangeable among the customers that use it. For example, while the benefits that diners and restaurants each obtain from an online reservation service are not reasonably interchangeable, the service they jointly consume *is* reasonably interchangeable with services provided by other online restaurant reservation services.

In submissions to the Supreme Court in *AmEx*, some law professors, economists, and the U.S. Department of Justice, all as *amici*, write as if they are asking the Court to conduct rule of reason business as usual. In fact, they are insisting that the courts *always* view *all* platform enterprises through a uniquely narrow and distorted lens. The Court should reject this request and, instead, take business reality and the facts on the ground into account in applying the rule of reason to two-sided platforms, as courts do in cases involving all other enterprises. There will be matters—especially involving platforms that provide joint and unseverable matching services—in which, to minimize errors, the courts will need to consider both sides of a platform. There will also be some cases in which it may be possible to address certain issues by considering only one side of a platform. NB

## B. One-Sided Analysis of Two-Sided Markets

The Court's decision in *Times-Picayune*, relied on by *AmEx* Petitioners, illustrates how different modes of analysis can make economic sense in practice, depending on the violation alleged, the specific issue considered, and the facts on the ground.[82]

The issue presented to the Court was whether a newspaper publisher, with a two-sided platform for readers and advertisers, engaged in a Sherman Act Section 1 tying violation by requiring advertisers to place ads in one publication as a condition of placing ads in another publication. The Court disposed of the issue based on its finding that advertisers had sufficient choices of where to place ads so that the business leverage necessary for an anticompetitive tie was absent.[83] There was no apparent reason to examine the impact of the tie on readers to assess whether there was an antitrust violation involving tying, given the Court's treatment of tying at that time.[84] Moreover, for the purposes of assessing whether the newspaper publisher had the bargaining leverage to impose an anticompetitive tie, it was sufficient to consider only competition for advertising.

---

82  *See Times-Picayune Publishing Co. v. United States*, 345 U.S. 594 (1953).

83  *Id.* at 611–13.

84  One could imagine other sets of facts that would make it necessary to consider both sides for a full understanding of anticompetitive and procompetitive effects in tying cases.

In contrast, in analyzing whether the newspaper publisher engaged in preda-tion in violation of Sherman Act Section 2, the District Court examined whether the platform as a whole—taking both readers and advertisers into account—was operat-ing at a loss.[85] The District Court compared revenue from both sides and the costs on both sides.[86] This two-sided arithmetic helped support the District Court's conclusion that there was no Section 2 violation, which the Supreme Court accepted without criticism.[87] Since newspapers typically lose money on the reader side while making money on the advertising side, it would ignore business reality and make no economic sense to look at either side in isolation for predation analysis purposes.

Predatory pricing makes particularly clear how the failure to account for the interdependent demand between the two sides can result in a tribunal concluding that conduct is anticompetitive when it plainly is not (a false positive), and finding that conduct is not anticompetitive when it plainly is (a false negative).

A tribunal could reach a false positive conclusion if it found predatory pric-ing based on the platform charging a below-cost price on one side.[88] That is com-mon profit-maximizing behavior for two-sided platforms even when they operate in competitive industries. A French commercial court made that mistake in finding that Google Maps engaged in predatory pricing by providing websites with free mapping software.[89] A Paris Appeals Tribunal reversed,[90] relying on an opinion by the French Competition Authority. This opinion, along the same lines as the "District Court's" in *Times-Picayune*, states that revenue and cost on both sides of the platform should be considered.[91]

A court could also make a false negative finding. Suppose, contrary to the ac-tual facts, that Times-Picayune Publishing had reduced advertising prices for its evening

---

85   *United States v. Times-Picayune Publishing Co.*, 105 F. Supp. 670, 677 (E.D. La. 1952) (evaluating arguments about allocating "revenues and expenses" from both "advertising and circulation" in determining whether one of the defendant's two papers "was operated at a loss").

86   *Id.* As a matter of economics this approach is equivalent to comparing the overall price charged by the platform, based on a weighted average across readers and advertisers, and the overall operating costs incurred by the platform, based on a weighted average across readers and advertisers. This approach is consistent with the two-sided price-cost comparison we rec-ommend in our Oxford Handbook paper. *See,* Evans and Schmalensee (2014) at 423–25.

87   *Times-Picayune Publishing Co. v. United States*, 345 U.S. 594, 626–27 (1953).

88   For a survey of issues in analyzing predatory pricing cases for two-sided platforms see Amelio et al. (2017).

89   Tribunal De Commerce [TC] [ordinary court of original jurisdiction] Paris, Jan. 31, 2012, Case No. 2009061231.

90   Cour d'appel [CA] [regional court of appeal] Paris, civ., Nov. 25, 2015, Case No. 12/02931.

91   Autorité de la Concurrence [French Competition Authority], *Rendu à la Cour D'appel de Paris Concernant un Litige Opposant la société Bottin Cartographes SAS aux sociétés Google Inc. et Google France* [Report to the Paris Court of Appeals Concerning the Litigation between Bottin Cartographes SAS and Google Inc. and Google France] ¶ 50 (Dec. 16, 2014).

paper without raising prices to readers and that, although the advertising prices were greater than the cost of providing advertising, doing so resulted in operating the evening paper at an overall loss because of losses on the reader side. Assume further that this pricing structure had forced its rival out of business, since the rival could not match the lower advertising prices without sustaining large losses, and that Times-Picayune Publishing then recouped through higher reader and advertiser prices.

If, in this hypothetical, the District Court had defined an advertising-only market and evaluated the predatory pricing claim based only on whether price was greater than cost in that market, then the court would have concluded that Times-Picayune Publishing had not engaged in predatory pricing when in fact it did. The two-sided approach actually adopted by the District Court in 1952 would have saved it from making that false negative determination.

False negatives and false positives can arise from any rule of reason analysis in which the finder of fact ignores one side of a platform. There may be situations in which the interdependence between the two sides of a platform is unimportant or can be neglected because of the particular issue at hand. As in any rule of reason inquiry, however, the courts should analyze the challenged conduct in light of business realities and the overall fact pattern before deciding what evidence to consider.

## C. The Heightened Risk for Transaction Platforms

For platforms that provide two groups of customers with a service that they must consume jointly, and where the challenged conduct necessarily affects both types of customers, there is a strong presumption that, as a matter of economics, the rule of reason analysis, at the first stage, should consider the impact of the challenged conduct on both groups of customers.

Joint consumption is not an essential aspect of the services provided by many platforms. For instance, people can watch ad-supported television, enjoy the content, and ignore the ads. Although advertisers hope that enough consumers will pay attention to their ads to justify the cost, content and ads are not necessarily consumed jointly. Providing content and providing ads are severable. It is possible to provide content without ads, and some consumers are willing to pay for programming without ads. As a result, two-sided ad-supported television faces competition from single-sided premium cable channels and streaming video providers.

Some platforms, however, provide a service that, by its very nature, must be jointly consumed by two customers and cannot be separately provided to one or the other. Consider an equity exchange such as Nasdaq. The service involves helping buyers and sellers find each other and engage in trades. The service is jointly consumed: the buyer and seller agree to terms and then consummate a transaction. The exchange service is also unseverable since it is not possible to provide it just to buyers or just to sellers. Any enterprise that wants to be in this business must provide the service to both groups.

When a service is jointly provided, a party and a counterparty stand at opposite ends of the service. In some cases, the same platform participants could be on either end of the service depending on their circumstances. People can, at different times, be both senders and receivers of messages on a messaging platform (e.g. WhatsApp) and both senders and receivers of funds on a person-to-person money-transfer platform (e.g. Venmo). In other cases, the parties and counterparties are necessarily distinct. Heterosexual dating platforms (e.g., Match.com) connect members of opposite sexes, and payment card networks (e.g., American Express) connect cardholders and merchants.

In all these cases, the platform must decide how to split the cost of the service between the parties that consume it jointly and unseverably. OpenTable, for example, charges restaurants $1.00 and diners $0.00 for reservations made through the platform.[92] The price it charges for a reservation would still be $1.00 if it charged restaurants $0.75 and diners $0.25 for each reservation or any other set of numbers that added up to $1.00.

It would not make economic sense to analyze the conduct of a platform that provides a service that is jointly consumed by looking only at what customers on one side pay for the service and receive from it. Businesses of this sort never provide a transaction to only one side of the service, and every interaction has a party and a counterparty that both benefit from the service.

The economic surplus generated by each interaction equals the total difference between the values both parties place on the interaction minus the total costs they incur. The platform determines the division of this surplus between the two sides through the prices it charges each. Competition between platforms that provide joint and unseverable services, like competition between ordinary single-sided businesses, leads to greater economic surplus by encouraging lower prices, better quality, and higher output.

A platform with market power that provides a service that is jointly and unseverably consumed could, like any other firm with market power, engage in conduct that would harm competition. Evidence on whether the challenged conduct has made buyers worse off, or would be likely to do so – through some mix of higher prices, lower output, and lower quality – would typically be important, or certainly useful, for that assessment. Conduct that, at the market level and taking both sides into account,

---

92 We have simplified this pricing structure to aid exposition. In fact, OpenTable also charges restaurants a monthly access fee and provides reward points to diners based on how many reservations they make so diners pay a negative transaction fee. *See* Evans and Schmalensee (2016).

does not reduce the quality of the service or raise the total cost of the service would ordinarily not reduce total market output or buyers' surplus.[93]

There is a strong presumption that conduct that affects one party to a jointly consumed service has an impact on the other party consuming that service and sharing its cost. In determining prices to maximize its profits, the platform must take the interdependent demands of both parties into account. Conduct that affects one side of the jointly consumed service necessarily affects the other side. Therefore, it would be necessary to consider both sides of the platform that provides the jointly consumed service at the first stage of the rule of reason inquiry to determine whether challenged conduct has harmed consumers and the competitive process.

Considering the impact of challenged conduct on both sides of the interaction is very different than the usual evaluation of procompetitive benefits in the second stage of a rule of reason inquiry in at least two different ways.

First, it is possible that the conduct harms parties on which a restraint has not been imposed, and failure to consider both sides of the platform involved at the first stage of the rule of reason inquiry could lead to a false negative. A job matching platform with market power, for example, might require employers to list jobs exclusively with it in exchange for lower prices. If this prevented the entry of other job sites, however, the firm imposing the constraint could charge higher prices to jobseekers. To properly assess whether challenged conduct harms competition, then, the first stage of the rule of reason inquiry should consider the impact of the conduct on both parties, most naturally by considering the impact on total market prices and market output.

Second, it is possible that the conduct benefits parties on one side of the platform. That benefit is part of the economic surplus generated by the interaction between the parties and should be accounted for in determining whether the practice reduces consumer welfare. Consider a money transfer platform that lowered prices to senders so they received a subsidy, and increased prices to receivers by a smaller amount, thereby resulting in a lower total price, higher demand, and greater output. Its pricing could look predatory on the sending side even though this change in pricing structure reduced the total price for money transfers and increased the output of money transfers. In this example, it is not that there are procompetitive benefits that offset anticompetitive effects; rather, there are no possible anticompetitive effects to begin with. *See Note on 206*

---

93 The *AmEx* Petitioners, and some of the *amici* in support, claim that the total cost of the service to both types of customers is not relevant because competition should determine the relative prices to the two sides. Brief for the United States as Respondent Supporting Petitioners at 18, 42–46; Petitioner *Amici* Law Professors at 20, 23–24; Petitioner *Amici* Economists at 15. It is not possible, however, to reliably determine if conduct has harmed competition and consumers through a distortion in relative market prices without considering both sides of a two-sided platform at the start of the analysis, since competition takes place on both sides.

And therein lies the fundamental error in the arguments about impermissible balancing put forward by the *AmEx* Petitioners and *amici* in support. The first stage of the rule of reason analysis involves determining whether the conduct is anticompetitive. The economic literature on two-sided platforms shows that there is no basis for presuming one could, as a general matter, know the answer to that question without considering both sides of the platform.

## D.  Market Definition and Two-Sided Competitive Constraints

Market definition is normally an important step in the analysis of competitive effects. The basic principles for determining the relevant antitrust market are no different for platform enterprises than they are for other enterprises. The relevant antitrust market should consist of the suppliers that compete with the firm or firms of primary interest and impose significant competitive constraints on that firm or those firms. That principle has been at the core of the economic analysis of market definition since the early 1980s.[94] It is essential that market definition faithfully reflect business realities to identify and assess competitive constraints from suppliers that compete with the firm or firms of primary interest.

A firm that operates a two-sided platform faces competitive pressures on both sides of the platform that restrain its ability to raise prices or restrict output on either side on both sides of the platform.[95] Consider, for example, competing shopping malls. If one mall decided to reduce its subsidy to shoppers—by charging for parking or reducing amenities, for example—some of those shoppers would shift their demand to other malls. Because of that fall in traffic, the demand by retailers for locating at that mall would decline, therefore reducing the rents the mall could charge. Competitive pressures on the retailer side therefore constrain the mall's ability to profitably lower the subsidy to shoppers.

The magnitude of these competitive constraints, however, and the relationship to challenged conduct, will vary across matters before the courts. Sometimes these cross-side competitive constraints could be economically significant, making it a mistake to exclude competition for customers on one side from the set of competitive constraints on competition for the other side. In other cases, these cross-side competitive constraints could be small enough to ignore. In some cases, even though these cross-side competitive constraints are significant, it may be convenient to proceed at the first stage by assembling the competitive constraints separately for each side into

---

94  The modern approach to market definition, with its emphasis on competitive constraints rather than mere interchangeability, is generally understood to have begun with the U.S. Department of Justice's 1982 Merger Guidelines. The basic approach in the guidelines is generally used by economists. Werden (2003); Carlton (2007); Shapiro (2010). Also see *Comcast Corp. v. Behrend*, 569 U.S. 27, 44 (2013) (citing the most recent iteration of the Merger Guidelines).

95  For surveys of the economic literature on market definition for two sided platforms, see Affeldt et al. (2014); Wismer and Rasek (2017).

two markets and then consider the linkages between them.[96] In all cases, it is important at the first stage of the rule of reason analysis to respect the reality that two-sided platforms are in the business of linking their two sides.

In their filings in *AmEx*, some *amici curiae* supporting the Petitioners are asking the Court to *require*, as a matter of law, that the relevant market for assessing challenged conduct by *all* platform enterprises *never* include competition for the customers on the other side of the platform. This rigid approach would exclude relevant competitive constraints on the conduct at issue and is therefore inconsistent with modern approaches to market definition and basic rules of evidence. It would also prevent the courts from accounting for the business reality of platform enterprises when it is important to do so.

The fundamental error in imposing this novel limitation on the court is most clearly seen for platforms that provide services that are jointly and unseverably consumed. In these cases, participants are consuming the same service, just standing at different ends. Any enterprise that provides the service would have to compete for both types of customers. The value of the service to one type of customer depends on their ability to interact with the other type of customer. A platform that is more successful at attracting one type of customer necessarily makes it harder for its rivals to attract the other type of customer. Defining a market that included just one type of customer would be inconsistent with business reality, as there is no rational competition for one side without the other, and it would ignore the competitive constraints coming from competition for both groups.

The *AmEx* Petitioners, and the *amici* in support, base their proposal for confining market definition for platform enterprises on two false premises.

The first false premise is that the purpose of market definition is to mechanically identify products that are interchangeable. Examining the extent to which consumers can substitute the products of different suppliers is often an important element in identifying those suppliers that should be included in the market because they impose significant competitive constraints. However, the analysis of the interchangeability of

---

96 For a discussion of considering linked markets versus a single market see Wismer and Rasek (2017) at 4-7.

products is not an end in itself.[97] It is just a means for helping the court identify relevant competitive constraints.[98]

The second false premise is that the interchangeability between the services received by opposing sides of a platform is somehow relevant for assessing competitive constraints. To see the error in their analysis, consider competition among person-to-person money transfer services. It is true that the service provided to a person who sends money is literally different from, and not interchangeable with, the service provided to a person who receives money. Defining separate markets for sending money and receiving money, however, would ignore the core business reality that suppliers compete for transactions between senders and receivers. The transactions between senders and receivers are substitutable across platforms. An increase in the price of the transaction by one platform—almost no matter how that price is divided between the sender and receiver sides—would tend to result in an increase in demand for other platforms.

In the cases of platforms that provide a service that is jointly and unseverably consumed, the observation that the customers are at different ends of the service is irrelevant and should not be used to remove important competitive constraints from the relevant market. Platforms that provide similar jointly consumed services are substitutes for each other, and their products are interchangeable as a matter of business reality. Market definition for platforms that provide services that are jointly consumed and unseverable should therefore focus on identifying suppliers that provide services that are interchangeable in this sense, which typically accords with business reality.

## E.  Conclusion

The history of the application of the rule of reason shows the importance of allowing the courts to consider all economic evidence that is potentially relevant for determining whether conduct is anticompetitive or not, including new economic

---

97  Wismer and Rasek (2017) at 253; Easterbrook (1984) at 22 ("Market definition is just a tool in the investigation of market power…").

98  It is not uncommon for courts and antitrust authorities to define relevant product markets that include products or services that most customers would not consider to be reasonable substitutes. For example, the market for hospital services may include heart transplants, brain tumor surgery, and appendectomies, which patients and doctors would not consider to be interchangeable. *See, e.g., FTC v. Penn State Hershey Medical Center*, 838 F.3d 327, 338–45 (3d Cir. 2016) (including local hospitals that constrain the defendants' pricing of general acute care services and incorporating new economic learning for determining relevant geographic markets); *FTC v. Advocate Health Care Network*, 841 F.3d 460, 468, 471–73 (7th Cir. 2016) (including "abdominal surgeries, childbirth, treatment of serious infections, and some emergency care" in the relevant product market and adopting new economic learning for relevant market definition).

learning.[99] There is certainly no basis in economics for putting special blinders on the courts when it comes to considering platform enterprises, as requested by the Petitioners and some of their *amici* in *AmEx*. Doing so would be a radical departure from the flexible but principled approach that the Court has taken, with great success, in applying the rule of reason to a wide variety of businesses, conduct, and fact patterns.

Nat'l vs local = Inp't.

---

99  *See, e.g., Leegin Creative Leather Products, Inc. v. PSKS, Inc.*, 551 U.S. 877, 889–91, 897–99 (2007) (citing new economic learning as a justification for ending the *per se* illegality of vertical resale price maintenance agreements, which had been the law for a century, and instructing courts to take economic considerations into account when applying the rule of reason).

# CHAPTER 4

# Under and Over Enforcement

The two-sided analysis of platform businesses isn't pro-defendant or pro-plaintiff. By accounting for business reality and modern economics, it helps courts and enforcement agencies reach the right decision and thereby reduce the likelihood of false negatives as well as false positives. Sometimes two-sided analysis is essential for uncovering how conduct harms competition and consumers. Other times it helps establish that conduct is innocuous or beneficial. Fears, and hopes, that two-sided analysis will discourage enforcement efforts are misplaced.

## A. Two-Sided Mistakes

Managing a two-sided business requires getting these participants on board, in the right proportions, getting them to interact with each other, and helping them secure gains from trade. This is seen from considering one key business strategy, setting prices, but it extends to many other aspects of running these firms. Just as both sides matter to platform executives, both sides matter to antitrust analysts. Any practice that affects the demand by one set of customers has an impact on the demand by the other set of customers. Positive feedback effects between the two sides tend to magnify these impacts. A shopping mall that imposes an exclusivity requirement on an anchor store will tend to get greater foot traffic from shoppers who have to come to patronize that store. That might inconvenience those shoppers but might enable the mall operator to attract smaller stores, which benefits those shoppers.

These two-sided effects are also important for conduct that affect competitors. A practice by a rival that affects one side, such as by reducing demand, has an impact on the other side, and feedbacks between the two sides magnify these effects. A shopping mall that imposes an exclusivity requirement on an anchor store could make it more difficult for a competing mall to get traffic and recruit other stores.

Whether these cross-side impacts are material is an empirical question, but one could not know the answer without considering both sides. When they are important, antitrust analysis, like economic analysis more generally, needs to account for the implications of interdependent demand.

Accounting for business reality, and using the appropriate economic models, should tend to minimize errors. Consider conduct that directly affects customers on one side of a platform. Analyzing conduct on just that side could reach a false negative by ignoring harms on the other side and a false positive by ignoring benefits on the other side. There doesn't appear to be any *a priori* reason to believe that doing the correct two-sided analysis should increase errors in making decisions concerning antitrust matters or that it should disproportionately reduce false positives relative to false negatives.

Comcast's proposed acquisition of Time Warner Cable illustrates the potential for false negatives. These companies operated local cable systems but never in the same zip code. Given this lack of overlap the parties, as well as many analysts and commentators, argued that there was no possible anticompetitive harm. Viewed from a single-sided perspective that position is obviously correct since the merger wouldn't change the choices available to consumers.

These cable systems, however, operated two-sided platforms. As Internet Service Providers (ISPs) they connected households and Internet content providers and as Multichannel Video Distribution Providers (MVPDs) they connected households and video programming providers. Focusing just on the households that participated on one side ignored the possible impact of the merger on the Internet content providers and video programmers as well as the possible feedbacks between those participants and households.

The U.S. Department of Justice found that the merger would increase bargaining leverage over Internet content providers and video programmers and thereby impose harm on those customers.[100] Moreover, the merger would increase the risk that the parties would use their control over broadband access to soften competition between the MVPD businesses and the emerging streaming video business, thereby harming consumers. These conclusions are predicated on the lack of competition on the household side. Consumers have few good alternatives for broadband service, and the costs of switching are high. The merger wouldn't change this competitive situation on the household side but it would on the other Internet content and video programming sides through the agglomeration of these households into larger bottlenecks.[101]

Predatory pricing illustrates the possibility of both false positives and false negatives. Profit-maximizing platforms often set prices above marginal cost on one side and below marginal cost on the other side. These skewed pricing structures persist in the face of competition. There is therefore no basis for inferring that a firm is engaging in price predation from the fact that price is below cost on one side. The traditional price-cost test applied to one side leads to a false positive decision.

---

100  Hill et al. (2015). Also see, Baer (2015).

101  Evans presented economic studies to the FCC and Justice Department, on behalf of Netflix, concerning the competitive effects of the transaction, and Schmalensee also did to the FCC, on behalf of trade association. Evans (2014).

A French predatory pricing case against Google Maps shows this danger. Bottin Cartographe sold mapping software that buyers could embed in their websites for the purpose of showing people directions. Google provided mapping software to websites for free but in return secured the right to deliver ads when people clicked on the directions shown; it also had a paid premium service. Bottin Cartographe sued Google for predatory pricing in the French commercial court.

The lower court agreed, on the grounds that Google charged websites nothing for a service that had positive marginal cost.[102] The Paris Appeals Court reversed that false positive finding.[103] It relied on an analysis by the French competition authority, which showed that Google Map's revenue exceeded its costs after accounting for the advertising revenue that resulted from people viewing the free ad-supported maps.[104]

Of course, two-sided platforms can engage in price predation by lowering their overall prices below the profit-maximizing levels to drive out rivals and then recouping profits after they have secured monopoly power. A single-sided analysis, however, wouldn't necessarily detect this behavior and could reach a false negative finding.

Consider a city with two daily newspapers and suppose, as is usually the case, that the profit-maximization results in a pricing structure in which readers pay less than marginal cost and advertisers pay more than marginal cost. The dominant newspaper reduces advertising prices so that they are below the profit-maximizing level but above marginal cost and leaves reader prices unchanged. As a result, it loses money overall since the profits on the advertiser side do not cover the losses on the reader side. The smaller newspaper can't survive at the lower advertising prices and exits.

A single-sided analysis would focus on the conduct on the advertiser side since that is where prices are being lowered. It would find that prices are greater than marginal cost and therefore conclude that there was no basis for a price predation claim. That is a false negative. A two-sided analysis accounting for prices and costs on both sides would prevent this error.

Single-sided analyses can reach false negatives or false positives for any conduct involving two-sided platforms for the same reasons they can arise in predatory pricing. Examining one side provides an incomplete picture of the benefits and costs of the conduct to customers as well as to the platform and a distorted view of what's happening to competition among platforms. Filling in the picture by considering

---

102  Tribunal De Commerce [TC] [ordinary court of original jurisdiction] Paris, Jan. 31, 2012, Case No. 2009061231.

103  Cour d'appel [CA] [regional court of appeal] Paris, civ., Nov. 25, 2015, Case No. 12/02931.

104  Autorité de la Concurrence [French Competition Authority], *Rendu à la Cour D'appel de Paris Concernant un Litige Opposant la société Bottin Cartographes SAS aux sociétés Google Inc. et Google France* [Report to the Paris Court of Appeals Concerning the Litigation between Bottin Cartographes SAS and Google Inc. and Google France] ¶ 50 (Dec. 16, 2014).

both sides and accounting for the linkages between them provides a complete view. That could expose anticompetitive behavior, or reveal the procompetitive reasons for conduct that looks dubious viewed from one side.

## B.  Both Sides Now, Friend or Foe

Some of the advocacy presented to the Supreme Court and in its aftermath fails to appreciate that single-sided analysis of two-sided platforms can result in false negatives as well as false positives. The U.S. Department of Justice and several of *the Amici* in support of the state plaintiffs essentially argued that the courts should confine rule of reason analyses to the side of the platform on which the conduct has taken place for the first stage of the rule of reason analysis.[105] That approach would help secure a verdict against American Express and could help plaintiffs in other similar cases. But it would also make it more difficult to secure verdicts against platforms in which conduct on one side inflicts harm through its impact on the other side.

More generally, applied across all platform enterprises, there is no apparent reason to expect that the single-sided approach would tend to reduce false negatives more than false positives. From the standpoint of antitrust enforcement, the Justice Department has therefore taken a shortsighted approach towards analyzing conduct by platform businesses.

Some commentators seem to think that two-sided analysis will give tech companies a free pass to engage in anticompetitive conduct.[106] To begin with, two-sided analysis accounts for business reality and gets the economics right.  If that analysis doesn't find that conduct harmed competition and consumers, then chances are that the conduct isn't anticompetitive.

It is hard to predict the net effect of single-sided analysis versus two-sided analysis on tech companies, but there's no apparent reason why tech foes should be rooting for single-sided analysis and tech friends should be cheering for two-sided analysis.  A good default position would be to advocate two-sided analysis when there is significant interdependent demand on the theory that getting the right answer is probably best, on average, for everyone—at least for consumers.

---

105   The Justice Department argues that benefits to the other side could be considered in the second stage of the rule of reason analysis. See, Brief for the United States as Respondent Supporting Petitioners at 43-47, 52. Remarkably, Petitioner *Amici* Law Professors and Petitioner *Amici* Economists argue that the courts should not consider pro-competitive justifications involving the second side even in the second stage of the rule of reason analysis. See Petitioner *Amici* Law Professors at 32-34; Petitioner *Amici* Economists at 23.

106   Bernstein (2018) ("Even the most extreme scenarios could be immune to antitrust complaints if the tech platforms could argue that benefits accrue to someone else, said Tim Wu, a professor at Columbia Law School. 'Don't you realize you're insulating a whole class of business from the reach of the law?'")  See also, Petitioner *Amicus* Open Markets Institute.

# CHAPTER 5
# Two-Sided Red Herrings

The Supreme Court's recent *American Express* decision has raised a host of interesting issues, including how to deal with two-sided platform businesses that look different from AmEx's credit card platform and what sort of evidence is necessary or sufficient in markets with platform businesses to establish competitive effects.[107] The large and growing economics and business strategy literature on two-sided platforms, now almost two decades old,[108] will be helpful in sorting out these and other issues, as the extensive citations to that literature by the District Court, Appeals Court, and Supreme Court indicate.[109]

Unfortunately, a considerable amount of the recent debate in the U.S. on how to conduct antitrust analysis of two-sided businesses has involved attempts to trivialize or marginalize the findings of the relevant economics literature. This is surprising because there have been no critical comments on the main papers in this literature, which have appeared in leading economics journals beginning in 2003. A co-author of the seminal paper on two-sided platforms was awarded the 2014 Nobel Prize in Economic Science for a body of work that included this subject.[110] In the *AmEx* litigation, the District Court and Appeals Court both cited this literature without any criticism.

---

107 *Ohio v. American Express Co.*, 138 S.Ct. 2274 (2018). Some platforms have more than two sides, and all that we say here also applies to such multisided platforms.

108 That literature began around 2000 with circulation of working paper versions of Rochet and Tirole (2003). Other key contributions include Rochet and Tirole (2006); Armstrong (2006); and Weyl (2010). There are no articles in serious economics journals, including the ones that published these papers, that argue that the theories described in these foundational pieces are wrong. For nontechnical surveys, see generally Rysman (2009) and Evans and Schmalensee (2014). The online appendix to the latter paper lists over 350 significant economics articles published through December 2012, https://papers.ssrn.com/sol3/papers.cfm?abstract_id=2185373. The Harvard Business Review has been publishing articles for managers on two-sided platforms since 2006. See, Eisenmann et al. (2006).

109 *Ohio v. American Express Co.*, 138 S.Ct. 2274 (2018); *U.S. v. American Exp. Co.*, 88 F.Supp.3d 143, 165 (2015); and *U.S. v. American Exp. Co.*, 838 F.3d 179 (2016).

110 The Nobel Prize (2014) "Press Release: The Sveriges Riksbank Prize in Economic Sciences in Memory of Alfred Nobel 2014," (October 13, 2014), https://www.nobelprize.org/prizes/economics/2014/press-release/.

In what follows we discuss five red herrings — assertions that have been used to marginalize the role of the extensive economics learning on two-sided platforms in antitrust analysis.

## A. It's Just About Complements, Like Gasoline and Tires

The first red herring says that there is really nothing novel about two-sided platforms because the services on the two sides are just complements, and the courts know what to do (and not to do) with complements.[111]

In order to process transactions between merchants and cardholders, American Express must provide services to merchants and different services to cardholders, and the prices to either group will affect that group's participation on the platform and thus the attractiveness of the platform to the other group. In oral argument, Justice Breyer contended that this interdependence in demand is simply what characterizes complements, like nuts and bolts.[112] In his dissenting opinion, he compared the different services to gasoline and tires.[113] In an *amicus* brief, eight economists compared them to tennis balls and tennis racquets.[114]

This argument has no merit. It does not appear anywhere in the serious economics literature on two-sided platforms. None of the economics journals that have published the key theoretical articles have published critical responses that say that the theory of two-sided platforms is retreading well-known concepts about complements. The claim is simply wrong.

Two complements are usually both sold to the same customers; that's the reason why the price charged for one of the products affects the demand for the other. In contrast, American Express provides merchant and consumer services to members of distinct customer groups. The price charged to one side of the AmEx platform affects demand on the other side because of indirect network effects: merchants care about how many consumers use the card, and consumers care about how many merchants accept it.

Two complements can be and often are sold by different firms. Many convenience stores sell tennis balls without selling tennis racquets, and companies often specialize in selling gasoline or tires but not both. By contrast, AmEx must serve both merchants and consumers to stay in business and must do so essentially simultaneously.

Finally, two-sided businesses like AmEx always facilitate interactions between customers on both sides of the platform. But you can buy gasoline without having any interaction with anyone who bought a tire.

---

111  For a related discussion see Filistrucchi (2018).

112  *Ohio v. American Express Co.*, (No.16-1454) (Oral argument February 26, 2018) at 22-24.

113  *Ohio v. American Express Co.*, 585 U.S. 11-12 (2018) (Breyer J., dissenting).

114  Petitioner *Amici* Economists at 4.

## B. If Any Business Is Two-Sided, So Are Almost All Businesses

The expansive variant of this red herring says that all businesses deal with members of more than one group — retailers, for instance, deal with both suppliers and customers — and therefore antitrust defendants will claim their business is two-sided. According to Professor Sagers, one of the signers of the *amicus* brief by lawyers in support of the Petitioner,

> ... we can expect every antitrust defendant and their sister to start claiming their business is two-sided, and lower courts will find reason within the theory to give their claims the time of day. After all, even a brick-and-motor retail store is "two-sided" in the sense that it must balance the demands of suppliers and customers.[115]

Katz and Sallet provide a lighter version of this red herring. They claim there is a "lack of consensus regarding the definition of a platform [and] it is much harder to distinguish single-sided businesses from multisided ones than one might initially expect[.]"[116] They conclude that,

> [g]iven the lack of definitional consensus regarding multisided platforms, coupled with the prospective applicability of existing definitions to a vast range of firms, it would be a mistake for antitrust enforcement to dramatically differ based on the threshold, and easily manipulable, question of whether a defendant is classified as a multisided platform.[117]

This suggests that there is an ongoing debate about the definition of two-sidedness. But there is no such debate. We believe that most, if not all, economists who have worked in this area would consider businesses to be two-sided platforms when there are (a) indirect network effects between members of at least one of the two customer groups and members of the other group; (b) these indirect network effects are strong enough to affect business conduct; and (c) the platform facilitates interactions

---

115  Sagers (2018).

116  Katz and Sallet (2018) at 2148.

117  *Id.* at 2152.

between members of the two groups.[118,119] Moreover, the serious economics literature often identifies the same narrow set of businesses, defined by these characteristics, as two-sided. There are other nuances involving two-sided platforms. People who write articles in this area, including us, often include an abbreviated definition that doesn't go into all of these characteristics, which of course doesn't mean that they aren't recognized.

The definition commonly used by economists is narrow enough to exclude most ordinary, one-sided businesses. Supermarkets deal with both customers and suppliers, for instance. And supermarket customers may care about the variety and quality of goods on offer, but suppliers to supermarkets generally care only about their sales, not the number or characteristics of shoppers. More critically, supermarket customers and supermarket suppliers do not interact. Anchor Steam does not know that one of us has just bought a six-pack of their beer, just that a six-pack has been sold. There may be businesses for which this definition does not yield a clear conclusion, but they seem to be rare, and detailed inquiry into the facts of real businesses will usually resolve the issue.

The vast sea of doubt and uncertainty portrayed by some commentators on the definition of two-sidedness doesn't correspond to the now vast economics literature on this topic. The courts should not get sucked into a "what about" argument that makes a spurious claim that some business is two-sided — for example, "brick-and-mortar stores" — using a definition that isn't employed in the economics literature to avoid serious analysis of businesses that are likely to be two-sided based on a widely accepted definition and analytical methods.[120]

---

118 After suggesting that there is an ongoing debate, Katz & Sallet assert that a good approach for antitrust purposes "is to define a firm as a multisided platform when *cross-platform network effects* occur in at least one direction and the firm facilitates interactions between two or more groups of users, can set distinct prices to different user groups, and has market power with respect to these groups." *Id.* at 2150. With the exception of the market power requirement, this definition is, in our experience, consistent with how economists working in this area define two-sided platforms in practice. And Katz and Sallet (2018), note 26, observe "Our inclusion of market power is meant to capture the likely circumstances in which antitrust issues arise, not to suggest that all firms with multisided business models have market power."

119 In his dissent, Justice Breyer notes that Rochet and Tirole (2006) also specify that if a business is a two-sided platform, the volume of transactions it manages "depends on the structure and not only the overall level of fees charged." Like Katz & Sallet, we tend not to stress this condition, as it is an implication of indirect network effects in the absence of arbitrage between the two sides that would make it impossible for the platform actually to determine the effective price structure. As Rochet and Tirole (2006) put it, the structure of charges "is relevant only if the two sides do not negotiate away the corresponding usage and membership externalities." We are not aware of evidence that platform businesses cannot use the price structure to balance demand because of arbitrage which would in any event be difficult given that platforms can often charge membership as well as transaction fees. [ Need to consider ]

120 Sagers (2018).

Justice Breyer says under the *AmEx* majority's definition, two-sided platforms are "commonplace."[121] While the majority's definition is arguably less narrow than the one advanced above, the economics literature has found that many businesses are in fact two-sided, and it is widely recognized that this model has become more important as a result of the Internet and other related technologies.[122] That is why two-sided platforms have attracted increasing attention among competition authorities around the world.[123]

We agree that some definitions of two-sidedness that have been advanced outside the economics literature are so broad as to imply that almost any business can be described as a two-sided platform. There is some merit to Justice Breyer's criticism that the definition employed by the *AmEx* majority was incomplete.[124] But that's an argument for tightening up definitions in antitrust analysis, not throwing out an uncontroversial body of economics learning, and ignoring substantial cross-side effects when the facts show they are important.

## C. Two-Sidedness Is Irrelevant in Mature Markets

This two-part red herring applies to mature markets with two-sided platforms, one in which all or almost all potential customers are engaged with one or more platforms. It is first argued that as a market matures, indirect network effects at the market level weaken and ultimately vanish when the market is fully mature. It is then argued that this change implies that indirect network effects at the firm level also weaken with market maturity and vanish in fully mature markets. Thus, even if firms were two-sided platforms before their market matured, once it has matured, it is argued, the links between the demands on their two sides have vanished.

To our knowledge this two-part argument was first made in expert testimony in the *Sabre* case and was accepted by the trial court.[125] It was repeated in an *amicus* brief to the Supreme Court in the *AmEx* case.[126] In the economics literature it has only

---

121 *Ohio v. American Express Co.*, 138 S.Ct. 2274, 2299 (2018) (Breyer J., dissenting).

122 Evans and Schmalensee (2016); Parker et al. (2016).

123 OECD (2018); Federal Trade Commission (2018).

124 *Ohio v. American Express Co.*, 585 U.S. 15-18 (2018) (Breyer J., dissenting). Justice Breyer points out that the majority decision did not reference the point, made by Rochet & Tirole, that for a business to be two-sided the price structure must affect the overall volume of output. Rochet and Tirole (2006) at 664-665. Rochet & Tirole, being aware of their own definition, refer to credit cards as two-sided platforms in this paper as well as in their seminal 2003 publication. Also, we noted above, this role of the price structure is an implication of indirect network effects in the absence of arbitrage and is therefore a consequence of a business being two-sided rather than a defining characteristic.

125 *U.S. Airways, Inc. v. Sabre Holdings Corp. et al.* 105 F. Supp. 3d 265 (2015).

126 Petitioner *Amici* Economists.

appeared as an assertion, without theoretical or empirical support, in a three-sentence paragraph in a single article.[127]

The argument that indirect network effects at the industry level generally weaken as a market matures is somewhat plausible, though we know of neither theoretical arguments nor empirical evidence that supports it. But even if it is true, it is not at all plausible that indirect network effects at the *firm level* are absent in mature markets. To see this, suppose there is a fixed number of possible participants on each side of a set of competing platforms and that all will join one or more platforms regardless of price or small changes in the number of participants on the other side of the platform. In this case, membership demand at the *market* level by each group is independent of the other group's demand at the margin, regardless of price, and indirect network effects at the margin are effectively absent at the market level.

Suppose further, to track the *Sabre* case, that one group of customers multihomes by participating on all platforms (the airlines) and the other group of customers single-homes by participating on only one platform (the travel agents). The price charged by any individual platform to the single-homing group determines the extent to which travel agents join that platform versus competing platforms. That in turn determines how much the multi-homing group would pay for access to that platform. But even with perfectly fixed demand at the market level, if an *individual platform* charged travel agents too much (or subsidized them too little) it could lose all of those customers, and the airlines would have no reason to use that platform. That result is consistent with the effective absence of indirect network effects at the market level because, by assumption, all airlines and all travel agents would still join one of the remaining (competing) platforms. But, in this extreme hypothetical case, there would be one less platform competing in the market.

Thus, even if indirect network effects are weak or absent at the market level because the market has matured, there is no reason to think that they are weak or absent at the level of the individual firm. Making that assumption would be very likely to lead to an erroneous evaluation of individual firm conduct.

## D. Lack of Interchangeability on Two Sides Implies Two Separate Markets

In an *amicus* brief to the Supreme Court in the *AmEx* case, a group of antitrust law professors presented an absurd market definition for two-sided platforms, proceeded to demolish it, and argued that their demolition proved that single-sided analysis was always appropriate.[128] They began by noting that the two groups served by two-sided platforms consume different services that are often not interchangeable. The services AmEx provides to merchants are clearly not good substitutes for the ser-

---

127  Shy (2011).

128  Petitioner *Amici* Law Professors at 17-20. Justice Breyer seems to accept this argument: *Ohio v. American Express Co.*, 585 U.S. 15-17 (2018) (Breyer J., dissenting).

vices it provides to consumers. They went on to argue that it would, accordingly, make no economic sense to include both sets of services in the same market, so that services to each group must be analyzed separately.

This is a very bright red herring. Consider competition among person-to-person money transfer services. It is true that the service provided to a person who sends money is literally different from, and not interchangeable with, the service provided to a person who receives money. Defining separate markets for sending money and receiving money, however, would ignore the core business reality that suppliers compete for transactions between senders and receivers. Transactions between senders and receivers *are* substitutable across competing money transfer platforms. An increase in the price of the transaction by one platform—almost no matter how that price is divided between the sender and receiver sides—would tend to result in an increase in demand for other platforms. Platforms that provide similar jointly consumed services compete with each other, and their products are interchangeable as a matter of business reality.

Market definition should therefore focus on identifying suppliers that provide services that are interchangeable in this sense, which typically accords with business reality and sound economics.[129] The objective of market definition is to identify competitive constraints. Since the early 1980s, the modern approach to market definition accordingly focuses on the ability of a firm or firms of interest to raise price above competitive levels.[130] It is not possible to make that assessment by looking at one side of a service that is consumed jointly by the two sides. The claim that one should exclude the other side of the transaction from the market because it isn't "interchangeable" is a red herring because it focuses on a service that the platform cannot provide separately and ignores the service that the platform provides jointly.

Let's be clear on why this red herring is very dangerous. Through the rhetorical sleight of hand that different sides of the transaction aren't interchangeable we are led to exclude the other side of the jointly consumed transaction, and the business realities of jointly competing for both sides, from the analysis.[131] Luckily, American courts are skeptical of market definitions that do not accord with business realities, as the plaintiffs found in *AmEx*.

---

129  Thus in the *AmEx* case, we have supported defining the market as consisting of payment services provided by AmEx and competing platforms Evans and Schmalensee (2018a). Economists supporting Petitioners seem at times to agree with us on this point: they assert that "… the relevant competition occurs at the platform level (i.e. competition among the credit card companies)." Petitioner *Amici* Economists, p. 15.

130  *See generally* Werden (2003); Carlton (2007); Shapiro (2010).

131  Another approach, which may be superior in some settings not involving the provision of services that are jointly and inseverably consumed, is to define separate markets for the services to each group the platform of interest serves but to take due account of the linkages between them in analysis. The more appropriate approach depends on both the facts of the case and the question at issue. A general rule that would require defining separate markets and ignoring linkages between them, which the antitrust law professors seem to advocate, makes no economic sense.

## E. Considering Two-Sidedness Explicitly Will Devastate Antitrust

The colorful language is from Professor Wu.[132] This is as much a red herring, a distraction from substance, as the other assertions we have examined here. There is simply no reason why accounting for the business realities of two-sided platforms and relying on uncontroversial economics learning is going to do anything other than help courts and competition authorities make better decisions. If it does, modern antitrust analysis has a bigger problem than dealing with two-sided platforms. One-sided analyses of two-sided platforms can result in false negative decisions in addition to false positive ones.

## F. Conclusion

The *American Express* decision necessarily left many issues unresolved, but it has made it clear that future cases will need to take the economics of two-sided platforms seriously. This will improve the quality of antitrust decisions. Around the world there is constructive discussion on how to do that, driven by the growing importance of platform businesses and recognition that they are in fact different from traditional ones in important respects, and that modern economic learning can help competition authorities and courts properly enforce the antitrust laws for them.

---

132  Wu (2019).

# CHAPTER 6
# All That Jazz

New Orleans is famous for Mardi Gras, Creole cuisine, Dixieland Jazz, and, of course, *Times-Picayune*.[133] That is a 1953 Supreme Court decision involving the only morning newspaper in the city at the time. It has gained recent fame in the debate over the proper antitrust analysis of two-sided platforms leading up to the *American Express* decision. *Times-Picayune* was featured in the dissent and the majority opinion distinguished it briefly.[134]

The dissent said the Court had already decided the central market definition issue before it—the other way. *Times-Picayune* concluded, it argued, that antitrust analysis of two-sided platforms, like newspapers, should focus narrowly on the service provided by the side of the platform subject to the challenged conduct.[135] The relevant antitrust market pertained to that side, and not the platform overall. There was no need to consider the other side. The majority decision distinguished *Times-Picayune* on the grounds that it was appropriate to analyze newspaper advertising as single-sided because the indirect network effects that connect the groups served by platforms were minor, given that readers did not care about advertising.

This chapter takes a closer look at the journey of *Times-Picayune* from a complaint filed by the U.S. Department of Justice, to the District Court, and then to the Supreme Court. The majority decision in *Times-Picayune*, and the lower court decision the Court relied on in part, don't provide much support for the notion that an antitrust analysis under the rule of reason should consider just one side of a two-sided platform. Even in the case of newspapers.

*Times-Picayune* is a useful case study of platform competition. The Government's complaint described a plausible strategy for destroying a platform competi-

---

133  *Times-Picayune Publishing Co. v. United States*, 345 U.S. 594 (1953).

134  *Ohio v. Am. Express Co.*, 138 S. Ct. 2274, 2286, 2295 (2018).

135  *Id.* at 2295 (Breyer dissenting opinion). The Justice Department and various *amici* in support upholding the District Court decision, based on a merchant-specific market, also cited *Times-Picayune* prominently as having already decided the issue. See Brief for the United States as Respondent Supporting Petitioners at 36, 39; Petitioner *Amici* Law Professors at 22; Petitioner *Amici* Economists at 3.

tor which could be relevant to other cases involving ad-supported platforms. The case provides insights for determining conditions when that strategy could work, and when it is implausible. This old newspaper case remains relevant for the antitrust analysis of other ad-supported media including digital platforms.

## A. The Government's Case

The U.S. Department of Justice filed a complaint against the Times-Picayune Publishing Company ("Company") on June 14, 1950.[136] At that time, the Company published the Times-Picayune, the only morning newspaper in New Orleans, the New Orleans States ("States"), an evening newspaper which the Company had purchased in 1933, and a Sunday newspaper ("Times-Picayune & States"). The other significant newspaper in New Orleans, the Item, had evening and Sunday editions. These newspapers earned money from paid circulation and advertising. There were three categories of advertising: local display, general national, and classified.

The Government claimed that the Company engaged in an unlawful tie by offering advertising only as a unit at combined rates in both morning and evening newspapers. The "unit rule," as it was called, applied to classified and general advertising but not to local display advertising.

The Government also alleged that the Company "[u]sed the dominant advantage … of the Times-Picayune to injure and destroy competition" for its evening and Sunday newspapers by (a) engaging in the tie; (b) using profits from the morning paper to subsidize arbitrarily low rates for advertising in the evening paper; and (c) "increasing the number of pages in the evening paper without a corresponding increase in revenue for the purpose of inducing and forcing circulation and advertising from the Item to the States."[137] (There were also a few other claims that are peripheral to the main story and were rejected by the District Court.)

These practices, according to the Justice Department, restrained competition in the "dissemination of news and advertising" and were an attempt "[t]o monopolize … the dissemination of news and advertising."[138] Indeed, the Justice Department had described a strategy for ruining competing ad-supported media platforms that could be plausible with the right set of facts.

---

136  *United States of America v. The Times-Picayune Publishing Company, et al.* Complaint, No. 2797 (Eastern District of Louisiana, June 14, 1950).

137  *United States of America v. The Times-Picayune Publishing Company, et al.* Complaint, No. 2797 (Eastern District of Louisiana, June 14, 1950) at pp. 8-9.

138  *United States of America v. The Times-Picayune Publishing Company, et al.* Complaint, No. 2797 (Eastern District of Louisiana, June 14, 1950) at p. 6.

## B. Ad-Supported Media

Economists have considered ad-supported media businesses two-sided since the start of the economic literature on platform businesses.[139] An ad-supported media business serves both advertisers and readers. There's a twist compared to other platforms, though. Advertisers appreciate having access to more readers, but readers may not appreciate being exposed to more advertising. In this case, there are positive indirect network effects on one side but not on the other. It turns out, though, that having positive indirect network effects on one side is enough for the economic theories of two-sided platforms to apply, even if the other side has negative indirect network effects.

Indirect network effects aren't the whole story, though.[140] Even if consumers don't like ads, they do like content. And they can't get content, or as much of it, if the media business can't sell advertising, which funds production of that content and is the *raison d'etre* for this content. Unfortunately, while they might like to get the content at subsidized prices, without the advertising, they are unlikely to find a willing media business for this proposition. These ad-supported media businesses are also known as attention platforms since they are in the business of trading consumer mindshare.

The basic business model for attention platforms has some similarities to the credit card networks considered in *American Express*. Ad-supported media provide readers with content to get them to come to the platform. They generally charge readers prices that don't nearly cover the cost of producing and distributing content. The content is the reward for coming to the platform and being exposed to advertising. The "content reward" plays a much more important role than "reward points" for payment cards, but they both result in a payment to one side to use the platform. Ad-supported media then sell advertisers access to those readers through ads that are interspersed throughout the content. The details of this vary by medium, but the principles are common.

For ad-supported media and for credit card networks there are separate prices to two distinct groups of customers; those prices are interdependent and effectively negative to one side, and the businesses must compete for both types of customers. Of course, there are differences as well, most notably that readers may not like being connected to advertisers, unlike cardholders who do value being connected to merchants.

So long as there are sufficient entry barriers the Justice Department described a clever and coherent strategy for destroying a competitor and monopolizing a market in its *Times-Picayune* complaint. The morning-evening advertising tie could have deprived the Item from earning enough advertising revenue to fund its content, and with less content it would attract less circulation, which in turn would make it even

---

139  Rochet and Tirole (2003) at 990; Anderson and Gabszewicz (2006).
140  Evans (2019).

less attractive to advertisers. Meanwhile, the low advertising prices and an unprofitable expansion of content on the part of the States could have forced the Item to lose advertisers and readers and incur unsustainable loses. The combination of these strategies could have pushed the Item below critical mass and send it into a death spiral.[141]

The Company would have demolished its evening and Sunday competitor. Then it could have exercised anticompetitive market power by raising advertising prices, cutting content, or raising circulation prices. It could also have killed off a potential competitor for its morning newspaper. Since the reader and advertiser sides of the platform are intimately intertwined, its strategies would have harmed both customer groups. Of course, the facts would have to support these claims.

## C. The District Court Decision on Predation and Tying

The U.S. District Court for the Eastern District of Louisiana issued a decision on May 27, 1952.

### 1. Market Definition, Dominance, and Separate Products

The District Court concluded that the three newspapers at issue "are the only significant media of news, advertising and other information disseminated regularly for residents of New Orleans through publication and circulation of newspapers." The Company claimed that its morning, evening, and Sunday newspapers were editions of a single newspaper. The judge rejected this on the ground that the papers had different appearances and content. As we will see, that finding was key.

The trial judge found that the Times-Picayune, the morning paper, was the dominant newspaper. "For at least twenty years," according to the court, "the Times-Picayune has been the largest newspaper in New Orleans in circulation, advertising lineage, and number of pages published." The Company's manager of general advertising had claimed, the judge noted, that the Times-Picayune is "the back-bone of any advertising effort" in New Orleans. "Enjoying as it does a monopoly position in the morning field, and an enormous advantage in circulation, advertising lineage, and number of printed pages," the judge continued, "newspaper advertisers who desire to cover the New Orleans market must, of necessity, use the Times-Picayune as a medium for the advertising." In effect, the trial court found that there was a separate market for morning newspapers since neither readers nor advertisers had substitutes.

The District Court's description of the business is silent on whether readers have any interest in seeing advertising.

---

141  See Whinston (1990) for the classic discussion of using tying to foreclose competition by preventing traditional scale economies. The two-sided strategy is similar but exploits demand-side scale economies resulting from indirect network effects. In both cases, since the tie imposes a cost on buyers, the strategy is profitable only if it eliminates the competitor. It is not possible to address that issue for a two-sided platform without considering both sides and the interdependencies.

## 2. The Unit Rule and Tying

The District Court examined the advertising contracts for classified and national advertising that had the unit rule. Put in terms of the modern language for analyzing tying, the judge found that the tying product was in a dominant position, that the defendant forced customers to take the tied product, and that the unit applied to a substantial portion of the market. He concluded that,

> "The Times-Picayune, because of its monopoly position, has been able to force buyers of advertising space to purchase what they do not want, space in the States, in order to purchase what they require, space in the Times-Picayune. The very fact that the defendant corporation was able successfully to impose the unit rate on general and classified advertising tends to prove the monopoly position which the Times-Picayune enjoys...."[142]

In addition to finding an unlawful tie, the trial judge found that the purpose of the unit rule, which was found to violate Section 1 of the Sherman Act, was to harm the Company's only evening rival.

> "[It] is apparent from the record that it was also the intention of the [Company] to restrain general and classified advertisers from making untrammeled choice between the afternoon newspapers in purchasing advertising space, and also to substantially diminish the competitive vigor of the Item, the States' only competitor in the afternoon field."[143]

The same findings showed that the unit rule also violated Section 2 of the Act. The District Court found that the Company used the unit rule to attempt to monopolize "that segment of the afternoon newspaper general and classified advertising field which was represented by those advertisers who also required morning newspaper space."

The District Court was silent as to the impact of the unit rule on the dissemination of news and did not conclude that it had prevented the Item from operating a viable newspaper.

## 3. Tying, Predatory Pricing, and Content Expansion Under Section 2

As the District Court judge put it, "Considerable evidence was offered by the Government to establish that the defendants maintained a rate structure which, considered as a whole, resulted in the operation of the evening States at a loss." The Company's books showed that the States was operating at a profit, but the Government claimed that was the result of questionable allocations.

---

142 *United States v. the Times-Picayune Pub. Co.*, 105 F. Supp. 670, 678 (E.D. La. 1952)
143 *United States v. the Times-Picayune Pub. Co.*, 105 F. Supp. 670, 678 (E.D. La. 1952)

The judge found, however, "nothing in the evidence which would indicate, much less establish, that the States at any time was operated at a loss." He was persuaded by testimony from the Company's auditor that more careful allocations would not reveal that the States was operating at a loss.

The Justice Department and the District Court agreed on one thing though.

The relevant question was whether the States, which derived income from circulation and advertising, was operating at a loss. They both considered the platform as a whole. The Justice Department did not argue that the advertising rates were below cost for serving an advertising market. Rather, it argued that the combination of expenditures on content, which attracts readers, and advertising and circulation prices resulted in the States operating at loss. And the Item couldn't compete with that. Only a platform level analysis, that considered prices and costs overall, could address that monopolization claim.

Thus, the Government ended up victorious only on the claim that the unit rule was an unlawful tie that restricted competition for afternoon advertising. It was defeated on the claim that the States was operated at a loss to destroy competition.

## D. The Supreme Court Decision on the Unit Rule

The Times-Picayune Publishing Company appealed the decision that the advertising contracts with the unit rule violated Sections 1 and 2 of the Sherman Act. The Court, in a 5-4 decision issued on May 25, 1953, found they did not.

### 1. The Newspaper Business

The Court situated the case in the newspaper business in the mid-20th century. "The daily newspaper, though essential to the effective functioning of our political system, has in recent years suffered drastic economic decline." It noted that the number of daily newspapers in 1951 was the lowest it had been since the turn of the 20th century. In fact, daily newspaper competition "has grown nearly extinct."[144]

The Court recognized that "[a]dvertising is the economic mainstay of the newspaper business." After reporting that "more than two-thirds of a newspaper's total revenues flow from the sale of advertising space" it noted that, [o]bviously, newspapers must sell advertising to survive." Competition from other mass media—radio, television, and magazines—had reduced newspapers' share of total national advertising expenditures from 79 percent in 1929 to 35 percent in 1951.

---

144 *Times-Picayune Publishing Co. v. United States*, 345 U.S. 594, 602-603 (1953).

## 2. The Tying Claim

Tying is a *per se* violation of Section 1 of the Sherman Act, according to the Court, when the seller has a monopoly position in the market for the tying product and when it forecloses competitors from "any substantial market."[145] In evaluating the *per se* claim the Court concluded that the key issue was whether the Times-Picayune occupied a dominant market position because it was the sole morning daily in New Orleans.

The Court described the two-sided features of the newspaper business. It noted that "every newspaper is a dual trader in separate though interdependent markets; it sells the paper's news and advertising content to its readers; in effect that readership is in turn sold to the buyers of advertising space."[146] It said that the case only concerned the advertising market which was the subject of the tie and that "dominance in the advertising market" was decisive in determining the legality of the unit rule.[147]

The Court stated it didn't think that the Times-Picayune was dominant in the advertising market. It noted that the morning paper's share of "both general and classified linage over the years hovered around 40%".[148] That conclusion assumed, however, that the relevant market consisted of general and classified advertising in all three papers.

Critical for that assumption, the Court rejected the trial judge's finding that these newspapers were separate products from the standpoint of the advertiser.[149] According to the Court, just because readers may distinguish between the papers, doesn't necessarily mean that advertisers do.[150]

> "But that readers consciously distinguished between two publications does not necessarily imply that advertisers bought separate and distinct products when insertions were placed in the Times-Picayune and States. So to conclude here would involve speculation that ad-

---

145   *International Salt Co., Inc. v. United States*, 332 U.S. 392, 396 (1947). Of course, the antitrust law on tying has evolved considerably since then including the seminal decision in another case situated in New Orleans. See *Jefferson Parish Hosp. Dist. v. Hyde*, 466 U.S. 2 (1984).

146   *Times-Picayune Publishing Co. v. United States*, 345 U.S. 594, 610 (1953).

147   *Times-Picayune Publishing Co. v. United States*, 345 U.S. 594, 610 (1953).

148   *Times-Picayune Publishing Co. v. United States*, 345 U.S. 594, 612 (1953).

149   The Court noted that newspaper advertising might compete with other forms of advertising but lacked evidence on this. *Times-Picayune Publishing Co. v. United States*, 345 U.S. 594, 611-612 (1953).

150   There doesn't appear to have been any evidence on the extent to which morning and evening readers were substitutes for classified and general advertisers. The morning and evening papers could have tried to differentiate themselves to attract readers with different characteristics that were relevant to advertisers. For example, the morning paper could have skewed towards women and the evening paper towards men.

vertisers bought space motivated by considerations other than customer coverage; that their media selections, in effect, rested on generic qualities differentiating morning and evening readers in New Orleans."

That finding didn't just support the finding of lack of dominance. It defeated the tying claim since, from the standpoint of the advertiser, there was a single product and not two.

> "Here, however, two newspapers under single ownership at the same place, time, and terms sell indistinguishable products to advertisers; no dominant 'tying' product exists (in fact, since space in neither the Times-Picayune nor the States can be bought alone, one may be viewed as 'tying' as the other); no leverage in one market excludes sellers in the second, because for present purposes the products are identical and the markets the same.... In short, neither the rationale nor the doctrines evolved by the 'tying' cases can dispose of the Publishing Company's arrangements challenged here."[151]

There was no *per se* violation of Section 1, based on unlawful tying, because there was no separate tied product and there was no dominance once the two alleged tying and tied products were considered together.

## 3. The Unreasonable Restraint of Trade Claim

The Court then turned to whether the unit rule was an unreasonable restraint of trade under Section 1. It articulated the rule of reason analysis as requiring it to determine the amount of business controlled, the strength of the remaining competition, and "whether the action springs from business requirements or purpose to monopolize". It then eviscerated the District Court's finding that the unit rules were unreasonable restraints of trade.

Earlier the majority decision had reported that local display advertising accounted for 44 percent of total revenue (including circulation), classified 13 percent, and general display 14 percent. The District Court had rejected bundling claims related to local display, leaving only 27 percent for the Court to deal with.

The Court noted that the unit rule for classified ads was adopted in 1935 to compete with the Item. At that time the Item operated a morning and evening newspaper which together carried more classified ads than the Company's. The Item suspended its morning newspaper in 1940. It was also common practice among newspapers with morning and evening editions.

Over the next decade the Item's share of classified advertising linage declined

---

151 *Times-Picayune Publishing Co. v. United States*, 345 U.S. 594, 614 (1953).

by three percentage points overall (from 23 percent to 20 percent) and by five percentage points considering only the evening papers (from 37 percent to 32 percent). The unit rule was instituted for general advertising in 1950, by which time it was common in the industry. The Court found that there was no material change in 1951, the only later year for which there was data. It concluded that, taking the effects of classified and general together, the Item's revenue had declined by less than one percent.

Had this effect been larger, the unit rule could have harmed newspaper competition and, with it, the dissemination of news and advertising. However, as an exclamation mark on this analysis, the Court noted that, "The Item, the alleged victim of the Times-Picayune Company's challenged trade practices appeared, in short to be doing well."[152] It flourished in the decade before the trial in terms of expanding advertising, reaching record circulation, and in recent years had made a profit. The Court concluded there was no violation of Section 1.

The Court then turned to the Section 2 attempted monopolization claim. It noted that most of the attempted monopolization case had failed in the District Court, including the claim that "the Company deliberately operated the evening States at a financial loss to the detriment of the competing Item." Only the unit rates remained and, since the Court found that they advanced legitimate business aims, the Court rejected the Section 2 claim as well.

The Court never considered the Government's original claims that the Company had tried to monopolize dissemination of news, or newspapers overall, since they didn't survive the District Court decision. Readers didn't come up except whether they were the source of monopoly power for the morning newspaper over advertisers. And the record is silent on whether readers care about advertising, and therefore whether there's a feedback from advertisers to readers.[153]

## E.  *Times-Picayune* and *American Express*

By the time *Times-Picayune* made it to the Supreme Court it was mainly about whether certain advertising contracts were *per se* violations of Section 1. Consumers of news weren't the subject of the dispute. Caution signs thus abound for those seeking to place the weight of all subsequent rule of reason analysis for two-sided platform cases, or for ad-supported media, on this foundation.

However, upon a close read, there isn't actually much tension between *American Express* and *Times-Picayune*. To see why, we need to replay the movie, despite having seen its ending.

---

152   *Times-Picayune Publishing Co. v. United States*, 345 U.S. 594, 621 (1953).

153   The Item was sold to the Times-Picayune Publishing Company five years after the Supreme Court's decision. It lived on another two decades as the Daily States-Item. The afternoon paper was closed in 1980. The Times-Picayune briefly stopped daily publication in October 2012 making New Orleans one of the few major cities without a daily newspaper. It resumed the next year and folded into a regional newspaper group in 2015.

## 1.   *Times-Picayune* and the Rule of Reason

Throughout the case, the courts, and the parties themselves, recognized that the newspaper business was about readers and advertisers.  One couldn't be in the newspaper business without providing readers for advertisers, and without securing advertising which was essential for funding the paper. Those business realities, properly, colored everything.

The Government claimed that the Company had engaged in a series of practices, beginning with the purchase of the States in 1933, to establish monopoly control over the daily newspaper business, and the dissemination of news and advertising, in New Orleans. The alleged competitive harm wasn't limited to an advertising market. It was about destroying a competing two-sided platform and thus necessarily harming competition for both readers and advertisers.

The Government's predation case was premised on the newspapers providing a joint product for readers and advertisers. It didn't posit that the Company had lowed advertising prices to monopolize an advertising market. It claimed that the Company was operating the States at a financial loss to drive a competing platform out of business. That harmed newspaper competition and, with it, competition for the dissemination of news and advertising.

The Government, and the trial judge, examined the financials of the newspaper as a whole.  That is essentially the two-sided analysis required by *American Express*. It aggregates the revenues received from both sides and costs incurred on both sides to determine whether the challenged conduct restrained competition at the platform level.  If the Government could have shown that the States was operating at a financial loss overall, it would have had support for its claim that the Company was monopolizing the dissemination of news and advertising. The trial judge was firm that there no evidence to support these predation claims.

There was another opportunity for the trial judge to consider competitive harm to the dissemination of news.  He examined whether the advertising contracts were an unreasonable restraint of trade under Section 1.  He found that they were when it came to advertising, but was silent on the impact on the dissemination of news.

Since the Government didn't appeal the District Court's dismissal of their claims, when the case got to the Supreme Court there wasn't much of a rule of reason case. Furthermore, harm to newspaper competition overall, or for the dissemination of news, wasn't on the table.

The Court's rule of reason analysis of harm to competition in advertising sales, however, at least touches on the impact of the unit rule on newspapers overall. It noted that the Item was profitable and mentioned its circulation, as well as its advertising. It also gave a nod to the District Court's finding that the States was operating profitably overall as well.  Most of its analysis concerns showing that the advertising contracts had a negligible effect on newspaper revenue. Since it recognized that advertising revenue was essential to the operation of newspapers these findings demonstrated, though the Court did not say, that the advertising contracts could not have harmed newspaper competition overall, or the dissemination of news. Since there were no claimed feedbacks between advertising and readers, and no meaningful jeopardy to funding content, that one-sided analysis of the importance of advertising revenue was dispositive.

On a different record the Court could have found that the Company had been running the States at a loss as a result of low advertising rates and that this practice would destroy the Company's only newspaper rival. There is nothing in the majority decision that suggests that the Court would have, if this were the case, limited its analysis to harm in the newspaper advertising market that was the subject of the challenged conduct. It had gone out of its way to emphasize that newspapers couldn't survive, and implicitly provide content to readers, without advertising. Nothing in the decision suggests that, just because the challenged conduct related to advertising, the Court would have rejected the Government's claim that the challenged conduct was harming competition in the dissemination of news. It understood well that, without advertising, there would be no newspaper and no dissemination of news for readers.

## 2. *Times-Picayune* and the *Per Se* Tying Analysis

The Court did say that the case "concerns solely one of the markets" and that "dominance in the advertising market, not in readership, must be decisive in gauging the legality of the Company's unit plan."[154] This language specifically referred to the analysis of whether the unit rule was an unlawful *per se* tie under *International Salt* and the related tying cases. It came between the Court's review of the tying cases and its lengthy analysis of tying in the matter at hand.

The issue was whether the morning newspaper had leverage over advertisers. It may be possible to conduct a sound economic analysis of that particular question without defining a single platform market or considering the interrelated pricing and feedback issues raised by *American Express*.[155] It is not possible, however, to conduct a sound economic analysis without considering how two-sided platform businesses operate.

Here the Court recognized that the analysis had to consider the relationship between the two sides to assess whether there was an unlawful tie. It found that advertisers wanted readers. But it didn't have any basis for finding that advertisers cared whether people saw their classified and general ads in the morning or evening papers. And where they might—as with local displays—there was no tie. That demolished the tying case.

---

154   *Times-Picayune Publishing Co. v. United States*, 345 U.S. 594, 610 (1953).

155   Generally, the courts would have to consider whether there were significant feedback effects between advertisers and readers, but none were claimed here.

The Court could have reached the same conclusion based upon a substantive examination of newspaper competition. Starting with the challenged conduct a court would have had to decide whether the morning and evening newspapers—the two-sided platforms at issue—were in one relevant antitrust market or two. Evidence that advertisers cared about whether readers were morning or evening would have led to separate newspaper markets while evidence that advertisers found readers fungible would have led to a single newspaper market.

As a general matter there are good economic reasons for considering competition among newspapers overall since advertisers may care about who readers are; readers may care about what the type of content that is attracting them as well as the amount and type of advertising. So long as economic analysis can fully account for inter-relationships, it can get to the right answers on substantive questions regardless of whether newspapers are analyzed in a single newspaper market or interdependent advertiser and reader ones.

### 3. *American Express* Discussion of *Times-Picayune*

The *American Express* dissent said that the *Times-Picayune* Court held that "an antitrust court should begin its definition of a relevant market by focusing narrowly on the good or service affected by a challenged restraint."[156] This claim is based on the Court's statement that "dominance in the advertising market, not in readership, must be decisive in gauging the legality of the Company's unit plan." The dissent goes on to say that the Government had claimed that the newspaper's advertising policy was unlawful under the rule of reason. But, as noted above, the Court's statement about focusing on dominance in the advertising market was made in the middle of its *per se* tying analysis.

The Court's rule of reason analysis at least touches on whether the Company had harmed newspaper competition through the unit rule and operating the evening newspaper at loss. The Court didn't need to go further because if newspaper advertiser competition was not harmed, it follows immediately that competition in the dissemination of news wasn't harmed. If the unit rule and low advertising rates had diminished the Item, it is hard to see why the Court would have stopped at the boundaries of an advertising market and not crossed over into newspapers and their readers; or why it should have taken such a restrictive view.

Faced with a different record the *Times-Picayune* Court would have had to grapple with similar issues raised in *American Express*. Suppose consumers value classified advertising. That's likely the case based on common experience and given that people patronize classified ad services such as Craigslist. If this is the case, then the Company could have provided more value to their readers by imposing the unit rule on advertisers. That could have increased the circulation of the Company's newspapers, which could have benefited its advertisers.

---

156  *Ohio v. Am. Express Co.*, 138 S. Ct. 2274, 2295 (2018) (Breyer dissenting opinion).

Depending on the facts, it is possible in this hypothetical case that the unit rule could have increased newspaper circulation and advertising in the market overall.[157] It is also possible that benefits to readers outweighed any costs to advertisers. It would therefore not have made economic sense to analyze harm solely in an advertising market for the reasons given in *AmEx*.

Of course, we can't know what the *Times-Picayune* Court would have done with that hypothetical case. But its brief rule of reason discussion does not show, at least not clearly, that it would have focused on an advertising market rather than assessing the overall impact of the challenged practices on newspaper competition.

The *American Express* majority opinion gave newspaper advertising as an example of a platform in which indirect network effects were minor because readers do not value advertising. It said, citing *Times-Picayune,* that "the market for newspaper advertising behaves much like a one-sided market and should be analyzed as such." [158] The economic theory of two-sided platforms, which leads to the pricing and market power issues the *American Express* majority decision was concerned with, does not require positive indirect network effects in both directions. In fact, much of the theoretical and empirical literature concerns two-sided advertising platforms, for which there are possibly negative indirect effects of advertisers on readers. There may well be cases in which the feedback effects between the two-sides are immaterial, or in which they are not relevant to the question at hand. However, there is no economic basis for concluding that is commonly the situation for newspapers or other ad-supported media platforms.

## F.  Conclusion

The Court's decisions in *American Express* and *Times-Picayune* share common ground. Both recognized the two-sided nature of the businesses under consideration and the interdependence of the two groups of customers. Each adhered to the two-sided business realities for the claims and facts before the Court.

The claimed tension between the two cases is overstated. The lengthy discussion of *per se* tying in *Times-Picayune* was based on the interaction between the two sides of the platform. The Court could then dispense with the *per se* tying claim by showing there was no separate tied product. In analyzing whether the challenged conduct restricted competition, it didn't need to go further than showing the negligible economic effect of the advertising contracts at issue.

---

157  If the Court was correct that the unit rule didn't materially reduce classified advertising in the Item, then it is plausible that the unit rule could have resulted in delivering more classified ads that readers valued. Nevertheless, there are certainly other circumstances in which the unit rule could have reduced newspaper competition to the detriment of readers and advertisers.

158  *Ohio v. Am. Express Co.*, 138 S. Ct. 2274, 2286 (2018).

The Court did not clearly limit the rule of reason analysis of competitive harm to a market restricted to the side of the platform on which the challenged conduct occurred. The very brief discussion in *Times-Picayune* is not inconsistent with looking at harm to platform competition overall.[159] Thus, it is quite a stretch to suggest that *Times-Picayune* established the rule of reason framework for two-sided platforms generally and concluded that courts should limit their analysis to the side on which the challenged conduct applied.

---

159  Even if it had, the courts have, of course, repeatedly modified their approach to antitrust analysis of conduct under *per se* and rule of reason based on economic learning. There has been an explosive growth in the theoretical and empirical learning on two-sided platforms, including credit card networks and newspapers, in the last 20 years. The Court relied on that learning in developing the fulsome approach towards applying the rule of reason to two-sided platforms with significant indirect network effects.

**APPENDIX 1:**

# Supreme Court Decision

Syllabus

NOTE: Where it is feasible, a syllabus (headnote) will be released, as is being done in connection with this case, at the time the opinion is issued. The syllabus constitutes no part of the opinion of the Court but has been prepared by the Reporter of Decisions for the convenience of the reader. See *United States v. Detroit Timber & Lumber Co.*, 200 U. S. 321, 337.

# SUPREME COURT OF THE UNITED STATES

Syllabus

## OHIO ET AL. *v.* AMERICAN EXPRESS CO. ET AL.

### CERTIORARI TO THE UNITED STATES COURT OF APPEALS FOR THE SECOND CIRCUIT

No. 16–1454. Argued February 26, 2018—Decided June 25, 2018

Respondent credit card companies American Express Company and American Express Travel Related Services Company (collectively, AmEx) operate what economists call a "two-sided platform," providing services to two different groups (cardholders and merchants) who depend on the platform to intermediate between them. Because the interaction between the two groups is a transaction, credit card networks are a special type of two-sided platform known as a "transaction" platform. The key feature of transaction platforms is that they cannot make a sale to one side of the platform without simultaneously making a sale to the other. Unlike traditional markets, two-sided platforms exhibit "indirect network effects," which exist where the value of the platform to one group depends on how many members of another group participate. Two-sided platforms must take these effects into account before making a change in price on either side, or they risk creating a feedback loop of declining demand. Thus, striking the optimal balance of the prices charged on each side of the platform is essential for two-sided platforms to maximize the value of their services and to compete with their rivals.

Visa and Mastercard—two of the major players in the credit card market—have significant structural advantages over AmEx. AmEx competes with them by using a different business model, which focuses on cardholder spending rather than cardholder lending. To encourage cardholder spending, AmEx provides better rewards than the other credit card companies. AmEx must continually invest in its cardholder rewards program to maintain its cardholders' loyalty. But to fund those investments, it must charge merchants higher fees than its rivals. Although this business model has stimulated competitive innovations in the credit card market, it sometimes causes friction with merchants. To avoid higher fees, merchants sometimes attempt to dissuade cardholders from using AmEx cards at the point of sale— a practice known as "steering." AmEx places antisteering provisions in its contracts with merchants to combat this.

In this case, the United States and several States (collectively, plaintiffs) sued AmEx, claiming that its antisteering provisions violate §1 of the Sherman Antitrust Act. The District Court agreed, finding that the credit card market should be treated as two separate markets—one for merchants and one for cardholders—and that AmEx's antisteering provisions are anticompetitive because they result in higher merchant fees. The Second Circuit reversed. It determined that the credit card market is one market, not two. And it concluded that AmEx's antisteering provisions did not violate §1.

*Held:* AmEx's antisteering provisions do not violate federal antitrust law. Pp. 8–20.

(a) Section 1 of the Sherman Act prohibits "unreasonable restraints" of trade. *State Oil Co. v. Khan*, 522 U. S. 3, 10. Restraints may be unreasonable in one of two ways—unreasonable *per se* or unreasonable as judged under the "rule of reason." *Business Electronics Corp. v. Sharp Electronics Corp.*, 485 U. S. 717, 723. The parties agree that AmEx's antisteering provisions should be judged under the rule of reason using a three-step burden-shifting framework. They ask this Court to decide whether the plaintiffs have satisfied the first step in that framework—*i.e.*, whether they have proved that AmEx's antisteering provisions have a substantial anticompetitive effect that harms consumers in the relevant market. Pp. 8–10.

(b) Applying the rule of reason generally requires an accurate definition of the relevant market. In this case, both sides of the two-sided credit card market—cardholders and merchants—must be considered. Only a company with both cardholders and merchants willing to use its network could sell transactions and compete in the credit card market. And because credit card networks cannot make a sale unless both sides of the platform simultaneously agree to use their services, they exhibit more pronounced indirect network effects and interconnected pricing and demand. Indeed, credit card networks are best understood as supplying only one product—the transaction—that is jointly consumed by a cardholder and a merchant. Accordingly, the two-sided market for credit card transactions should be analyzed as a whole. Pp. 10–15.

(c) The plaintiffs have not carried their burden to show anticompetitive effects. Their argument—that AmEx's antisteering provisions increase merchant fees—wrongly focuses on just one side of the market. Evidence of a price increase on one side of a two-sided transaction platform cannot, by itself, demonstrate an anticompetitive exercise of market power. Instead, plaintiffs must prove that AmEx's antisteering provisions increased the cost of credit card transactions above a competitive level, reduced the number of credit card transactions, or otherwise stifled competition in the two-sided credit card market. They failed to do so. Pp. 15–20.

(1) The plaintiffs offered no evidence that the price of credit card transactions was higher than the price one would expect to find in a competitive market. AmEx's increased merchant fees reflect increases in the value of its services and the cost of its transactions, not an ability to charge above a competitive price. It uses higher merchant fees to offer its cardholders a more robust rewards program, which is necessary to maintain cardholder loyalty and encourage the level of spending that makes it valuable to merchants. In addition, the evidence that does exist cuts against the plaintiffs' view that AmEx's antisteering provisions are the cause of any increases in merchant fees: Visa and Mastercard's merchant fees have continued to increase, even at merchant locations where AmEx is not accepted. Pp. 16–17.

(2) The plaintiffs' evidence that AmEx's merchant-fee increases between 2005 and 2010 were not entirely spent on cardholder rewards does not prove that AmEx's antisteering provisions gave it the power to charge anticompetitive prices. This Court will "not infer competitive injury from price and output data absent some evidence that tends to prove that output was restricted or prices were above a competitive level." *Brooke Group Ltd. v. Brown & Williamson Tobacco Corp.*, 509 U. S. 209, 237. There is no such evidence here. Output of credit card transactions increased during the relevant period, and the plaintiffs did not show that AmEx charged more than its competitors. P. 17.

(3) The plaintiffs also failed to prove that AmEx's antisteering provisions have stifled competition among credit card companies. To the contrary, while they have been in place, the market experienced expanding output and improved quality. Nor have AmEx's antisteering provisions ended competition between credit card networks with respect to merchant fees. AmEx's competitors have exploited its higher merchant fees to their advantage. Lastly, there is nothing inherently anticompetitive about the provisions. They actually stem negative externalities in the credit card market and promote inter- brand competition. And they do not prevent competing credit card networks from offering lower merchant fees or promoting their broader merchant acceptance. Pp. 18–20.

838 F. 3d 179, affirmed.

THOMAS, J., delivered the opinion of the Court, in which ROBERTS, C. J., and KENNEDY, ALITO, and GORSUCH, JJ., joined. BREYER, J., filed a dissenting opinion, in which GINSBURG, SOTOMAYOR, and KAGAN, JJ., joined.

Opinion of the Court

**NOTICE:** This opinion is subject to formal revision before publication in the preliminary print of the United States Reports. Readers are requested to notify

# SUPREME COURT OF THE UNITED STATES

No. 16–1454

OHIO, ET AL., PETITIONERS *v.* AMERICAN EXPRESS COMPANY, ET AL.

ON WRIT OF CERTIORARI TO THE UNITED STATES COURT OF APPEALS FOR THE SECOND CIRCUIT

[June 25, 2018]

JUSTICE THOMAS delivered the opinion of the Court.

American Express Company and American Express Travel Related Services Company (collectively, AmEx) provide credit card services to both merchants and card- holders. When a cardholder buys something from a merchant who accepts AmEx credit cards, AmEx processes the transaction through its network, promptly pays the merchant, and subtracts a fee. If a merchant wants to accept AmEx credit cards—and attract AmEx cardholders to its business—AmEx requires the merchant to agree to an antisteering contractual provision. The antisteering pro- vision prohibits merchants from discouraging customers from using their AmEx card after they have already entered the store and are about to buy something, thereby avoiding AmEx's fee. In this case, we must decide whether AmEx's antisteering provisions violate federal antitrust law. We conclude they do not.

## I

### A

Credit cards have become a primary way that consumers in the United States purchase goods and services. When a cardholder uses a credit card to buy something from a merchant, the transaction is facilitated by a credit card network. The network provides separate but interrelated services to both cardholders and merchants. For cardholders, the network extends them credit, which allows them to make purchases without cash and to defer payment until later. Cardholders also can receive rewards based on the amount of money they spend, such as airline miles, points for travel, or cash back. For merchants, the network allows them to avoid the cost of processing transactions and offers them quick, guaranteed payment. This saves merchants the trouble and risk of extending credit to customers, and it increases the number and value of sales that they can make.

By providing these services to cardholders and merchants, credit card companies bring these parties together, and therefore operate what economists call a "two-sided platform." As the name implies, a two-sided platform offers different products or services to two different groups who both depend on the platform to intermediate between them. See Evans & Schmalensee, Markets With Two- Sided Platforms, 1 Issues in Competition L. & Pol'y 667 (2008) (Evans & Schmalensee); Evans & Noel, Defining Antitrust Markets When Firms Operate Two-Sided Plat- forms, 2005 Colum. Bus. L. Rev. 667, 668 (Evans & Noel); Filistrucchi, Geradin, Van Damme, & Affeldt, Market Definition in Two-Sided Markets: Theory and Practice, 10 J. Competition L. & Econ. 293, 296 (2014) (Filistrucchi). For credit cards, that interaction is a transaction. Thus, credit card networks are a special type of two-sided platform known as a "transaction" platform. See id., at 301, 304, 307; Evans & Noel 676–678. The key feature of transaction platforms is that they cannot make a sale to one side of the platform without simultaneously making a sale to the other. See Klein, Lerner, Murphy, & Plache, Competition in Two-Sided Markets: The Antitrust Economics of Payment Card Interchange Fees, 73 Antitrust L. J. 571, 580, 583 (2006) (Klein). For example, no credit card transaction can occur unless both the merchant and the cardholder simultaneously agree to use the same credit card network. See Filistrucchi 301.

Two-sided platforms differ from traditional markets in important ways. Most relevant here, two-sided platforms often exhibit what economists call "indirect network effects." Evans & Schmalensee 667. Indirect network effects exist where the value of the two-sided platform to one group of participants depends on how many members of a different group participate. D. Evans & R. Schmalensee, Matchmakers: The New Economics of Multisided Platforms 25 (2016). In other words, the value of the services that a two-sided platform provides increases as the number of participants on both sides of the platform increases. A credit card, for example, is more valuable to cardholders when more merchants accept it, and is more valuable to merchants when more cardholders use it. See Evans & Noel 686–687; Klein 580, 584. To ensure sufficient participation, two-sided platforms must be sensitive to the prices that they charge each side. See Evans & Schmalensee 675; Evans & Noel 680; Muris, Payment Card Regulation and the (Mis)Application of the Economics of Two-Sided Markets, 2005 Colum. Bus. L. Rev. 515, 532– 533 (Muris); Rochet & Tirole, Platform Competition in Two-Sided Markets, 1 J. Eur. Econ. Assn. 990, 1013 (2003). Raising the price on side A risks losing participation on that side, which decreases the value of the plat- form to side B. If participants on side B leave due to this loss in value, then the platform has even less value to side A—risking a feedback loop of declining demand. See Evans & Schmalensee 675; Evans & Noel 680–681. Two-sided platforms therefore must take these indirect network effects into account before making a change in price on either side. See Evans & Schmalensee 675; Evans & Noel 680–681.[160]

Sometimes indirect network effects require two-sided platforms to charge one side much more than the other. See Evans & Schmalensee 667, 675, 681, 690–691; Evans & Noel 668, 691; Klein 585; Filistrucchi 300. For two-sided platforms, " 'the [relative] price structure matters, and platforms must design it so as to bring both sides on board.'" Evans & Schmalensee 669 (quoting Rochet & Tirole, Two-Sided Markets: A Progress Report, 37 RAND J. Econ. 645, 646 (2006)). The optimal price might require charging the side with more elastic demand a below-cost (or even negative) price. See Muris 519, 550; Klein 579; Evans & Schmalensee 675; Evans & Noel 681. With credit cards, for example, networks often charge cardholders a lower fee than merchants because cardholders are more price sensitive.[161] See Muris 522; Klein 573–574, 585, 595. In fact, the network might well *lose* money on the card-holder side by offering rewards such as cash back, airline miles, or gift cards. See Klein 587; Evans & Schmalensee 672. The network can do this because increasing the number of cardholders increases the value of accepting the card to merchants and, thus, increases the number of merchants who accept it. Muris 522; Evans & Schmalensee 692. Networks can then charge those merchants a fee for every transaction (typically a percentage of the purchase price). Striking the optimal balance of the prices charged on each side of the platform is essential for two-sided platforms to maximize the value of their services and to compete with their rivals.

## B

AmEx, Visa, Mastercard, and Discover are the four dominant participants in the credit card market. Visa, which is by far the largest, has 45% of the market as measured by transaction volume.[162] AmEx and Mastercard trail with 26.4% and 23.3%, respectively, while Discover has just 5.3% of the market.

Visa and Mastercard have significant structural ad-vantages over AmEx. Visa and Mastercard began as bank cooperatives and thus almost every bank that offers credit cards is in the Visa or Mastercard network. This makes it very likely that the average consumer carries, and the average merchant accepts, Visa or Mastercard. As

---

160  In a competitive market, indirect network effects also encourage companies to take increased profits from a price increase on side A and spend them on side B to ensure more robust participation on that side and to stem the impact of indirect network effects. See Evans & Schmalensee 688; Evans & Noel 670–671, 695. Indirect network effects thus limit the platform's ability to raise overall prices and impose a check on its market power. See Evans & Schmalensee 688; Evans & Noel 695.

161  "Cardholders are more price-sensitive because many consumers have multiple payment methods, including alternative payment cards. Most merchants, by contrast, cannot accept just one major card because they are likely to lose profitable incremental sales if they do not take [all] the major payment cards. Because most consumers do not carry all of the major payment cards, refusing to accept a major card may cost the merchant substantial sales." Muris 522.

162  All figures are accurate as of 2013.

a result, the vast majority of AmEx cardholders have a Visa or Mastercard, but only a small number of Visa and Mastercard cardholders have an AmEx. Indeed, Visa and Mastercard account for more than 432 million cards in circulation in the United States, while AmEx has only 53 million. And while 3.4 million merchants at 6.4 million locations accept AmEx, nearly three million more locations accept Visa, Mastercard, and Discover.[163]

AmEx competes with Visa and Mastercard by using a different business model. While Visa and Mastercard earn half of their revenue by collecting interest from their cardholders, AmEx does not. AmEx instead earns most of its revenue from merchant fees. AmEx's business model thus focuses on cardholder spending rather than card-holder lending. To encourage cardholder spending, AmEx provides better rewards than other networks. Due to its superior rewards, AmEx tends to attract cardholders who are wealthier and spend more money. Merchants place a higher value on these cardholders, and AmEx uses this advantage to recruit merchants.

AmEx's business model has significantly influenced the credit card market. To compete for the valuable cardholders that AmEx attracts, both Visa and Mastercard have introduced premium cards that, like AmEx, charge merchants higher fees and offer cardholders better rewards. To maintain their lower merchant fees, Visa and Master-Card have created a sliding scale for their various cards— charging merchants less for low-reward cards and more for high-reward cards. This differs from AmEx's strategy, which is to charge merchants the same fee no matter the rewards that its card offers. Another way that AmEx has influenced the credit card market is by making banking and card-payment services available to low-income individuals, who otherwise could not qualify for a credit card and could not afford the fees that traditional banks charge. See 2 Record 3835–3837, 4527–4529. In sum, AmEx's business model has stimulated competitive innovations in the credit card market, increasing the volume of transactions and improving the quality of the services.

Despite these improvements, AmEx's business model sometimes causes friction with merchants. To maintain the loyalty of its cardholders, AmEx must continually invest in its rewards program. But, to fund those investments, AmEx must charge merchants higher fees than its rivals. Even though AmEx's investments benefit merchants by encouraging cardholders to spend more money, merchants would prefer not to pay the higher fees. One way that merchants try to avoid them, while still enticing AmEx's cardholders to shop at their stores, is by dissuading cardholders from using AmEx at the point of sale. This practice is known as "steering."

---

163 Discover entered the credit card market several years after AmEx, Visa, and Mastercard. It nonetheless managed to gain a foothold because Sears marketed Discover to its already significant base of private-label cardholders. Discover's business model shares certain features with AmEx, Visa, and Mastercard. Like AmEx, Discover interacts directly with its cardholders. But like Visa and Mastercard, Discover uses banks that cooperate with its network to interact with merchants.

AmEx has prohibited steering since the 1950s by placing antisteering provisions in its contracts with merchants. These antisteering provisions prohibit merchants from implying a preference for non-AmEx cards; dissuading customers from using AmEx cards; persuading customers to use other cards; imposing any special restrictions, conditions, disadvantages, or fees on AmEx cards; or promoting other cards more than AmEx. The antisteering provisions do not, however, prevent merchants from steering customers toward debit cards, checks, or cash.

### C

In October 2010, the United States and several States (collectively, plaintiffs) sued AmEx, claiming that its antisteering provisions violate §1 of the Sherman Act, 26 Stat. 209, as amended, 15 U. S. C. §1.[164] After a 7-week trial, the District Court agreed that AmEx's antisteering provisions violate §1. *United States v. American Express Co.*, 88 F. Supp. 3d 143, 151–152 (EDNY 2015). It found that the credit card market should be treated as two separate markets—one for merchants and one for card-holders. See *id.*, at 171–175. Evaluating the effects on the merchant side of the market, the District Court found that AmEx's antisteering provisions are anticompetitive because they result in higher merchant fees. See *id.*, at 195–224.

The Court of Appeals for the Second Circuit reversed. *United States v. American Express Co.*, 838 F. 3d 179, 184 (2016). It concluded that the credit card market is one market, not two. *Id.*, at 196–200. Evaluating the credit card market as a whole, the Second Circuit concluded that AmEx's antisteering provisions were not anticompetitive and did not violate §1. See *id.*, at 200–206.

We granted certiorari, 583 U. S. _____ (2017), and now affirm.

### II

Section 1 of the Sherman Act prohibits "[e]very contract, combination in the form of trust or otherwise, or conspiracy, in restraint of trade or commerce among the several States." 15 U. S. C. §1. This Court has long recognized that, "[i]n view of the common law and the law in this country" when the Sherman Act was passed, the phrase "restraint of trade" is best read to mean "undue restraint." *Standard Oil Co. of N. J. v. United States*, 221 U. S. 1, 59– 60 (1911). This Court's precedents have thus understood §1 "to outlaw only *unreasonable* restraints." *State Oil Co. v. Khan*, 522 U. S. 3, 10 (1997) (emphasis added).

Restraints can be unreasonable in one of two ways. A small group of restraints are unreasonable *per se* because they """"always or almost always tend to restrict competition and decrease output."" *Business Electronics Corp. v. Sharp Electronics Corp.*, 485 U. S. 717, 723 (1988). Typically only "horizontal" restraints—restraints "imposed

---

164   Plaintiffs also sued Visa and Mastercard, claiming that their anti-steering provisions violated §1. But Visa and Mastercard voluntarily revoked their antisteering provisions and are no longer parties to this case.

by agreement between competitors"—qualify as unreasonable *per se*. *Id.*, at 730. Restraints that are not unreasonable *per se* are judged under the "rule of reason." *Id.*, at 723. The rule of reason requires courts to conduct a fact-specific assessment of "market power and market structure . . . to assess the [restraint]'s actual effect" on competition. *Copperweld Corp. v. Independence Tube Corp.*, 467 U. S. 752, 768 (1984). The goal is to "distinguis[h] between restraints with anticompetitive effect that are harmful to the consumer and restraints stimulating competition that are in the consumer's best interest." *Leegin Creative Leather Products, Inc. v. PSKS, Inc.*, 551 U. S. 877, 886 (2007).

In this case, both sides correctly acknowledge that AmEx's antisteering provisions are vertical restraints— *i.e.*, restraints "imposed by agreement between firms at different levels of distribution." *Business Electronics, supra*, at 730. The parties also correctly acknowledge that, like nearly every other vertical restraint, the anti- steering provisions should be assessed under the rule of reason. See *Leegin, supra*, at 882; *State Oil, supra*, at 19; *Business Electronics, supra*, at 726; *Continental T. V., Inc. v. GTE Sylvania Inc.*, 433 U. S. 36, 57 (1977).

To determine whether a restraint violates the rule of reason, the parties agree that a three-step, burdenshifting framework applies. Under this framework, the plaintiff has the initial burden to prove that the challenged restraint has a substantial anticompetitive effect that harms consumers in the relevant market. See 1 J. Kalinowski, Antitrust Laws and Trade Regulation §12.02[1] (2d ed. 2017) (Kalinowski); P. Areeda & H. Hovenkamp, Fundamentals of Antitrust Law §15.02[B] (4th ed. 2017) (Areeda & Hovenkamp); *Capital Imaging Assoc., P. C. v. Mohawk Valley Medical Associates, Inc.*, 996 F. 2d 537, 543 (CA2 1993). If the plaintiff carries its burden, then the burden shifts to the defendant to show a procompetitive rationale for the restraint. See 1 Kalinowski §12.02[1]; Areeda & Hovenkamp §15.02[B]; *Capital Imaging Assoc., supra*, at 543. If the defendant makes this showing, then the burden shifts back to the plaintiff to demonstrate that the procompetitive efficiencies could be reasonably achieved through less anticompetitive means. See 1 Kalinowski §12.02[1]; *Capital Imaging Assoc., supra*, at 543.

Here, the parties ask us to decide whether the plaintiffs have carried their initial burden of proving that AmEx's antisteering provisions have an anticompetitive effect. The plaintiffs can make this showing directly or indirectly. Direct evidence of anticompetitive effects would be " 'proof of actual detrimental effects [on competition],' " *FTC v. Indiana Federation of Dentists*, 476 U. S. 447, 460 (1986), such as reduced output, increased prices, or decreased quality in the relevant market, see 1 Kalinowski §12.02[2]; *Craftsman Limousine, Inc. v. Ford Motor Co.*, 491 F. 3d 381, 390 (CA8 2007); *Virginia Atlantic Airways Ltd. v. British Airways PLC*, 257 F. 3d 256, 264 (CA2 2001). Indirect evidence would be proof of market power plus some evidence that the challenged restraint harms competition. See 1 Kalinowski §12.02[2]; *Tops Markets, Inc. v. Quality Markets, Inc.*, 142 F. 3d 90, 97 (CA2 1998); *Spanish Broadcasting System of Fla. v. Clear Channel Communications, Inc.*, 376 F. 3d 1065, 1073 (CA11 2004).

Here, the plaintiffs rely exclusively on direct evidence to prove that AmEx's antisteering provisions have caused anticompetitive effects in the credit card market.[165] To assess this evidence, we must first define the relevant market. Once defined, it becomes clear that the plaintiffs' evidence is insufficient to carry their burden.

## A

Because "[l]egal presumptions that rest on formalistic distinctions rather than actual market realities are generally disfavored in antitrust law," *Eastman Kodak Co. v. Image Technical Services, Inc.*, 504 U. S. 451, 466–467 (1992), courts usually cannot properly apply the rule of reason without an accurate definition of the relevant market.[166] "Without a definition of [the] market there is no way to measure [the defendant's] ability to lessen or destroy competition." *Walker Process Equipment, Inc. v. Food Machinery & Chemical Corp.*, 382 U. S. 172, 177 (1965); accord, 2 Kalinowski §24.01[4][a]. Thus, the relevant market is defined as "the area of effective competition." *Ibid.* Typically this is the "arena within which significant substitution in consumption or production occurs." Areeda & Hovenkamp §5.02; accord, 2 Kalinowski §24.02[1]; *United States v. Grinnell Corp.*, 384 U. S. 563, 571 (1966). But courts should "combin[e]" different products or services into "a single market" when "that combination reflects commercial realities." *Id.*, at 572; see also *Brown Shoe Co. v. United States*, 370 U. S. 294, 336– 337 (1962) (pointing out that "the definition of the relevant market" must " 'correspond to the commercial realities' of the industry").

As explained, credit card networks are two-sided platforms. Due to indirect network effects, two-sided platforms cannot raise prices on one side without risking

---

165  Although the plaintiffs relied on indirect evidence below, they have abandoned that argument in this Court. See Brief for United States 23, n. 4 (citing Pet. for Cert. i, 18–25).

166  The plaintiffs argue that we need not define the relevant market in this case because they have offered actual evidence of adverse effects on competition—namely, increased merchant fees. See Brief for United States 40–41 (citing *FTC v. Indiana Federation of Dentists*, 476 U. S. 447 (1986), and *Catalano, Inc. v. Target Sales, Inc.*, 446 U. S. 643 (1980) (*per curiam*)). We disagree. The cases that the plaintiffs cite for this proposition evaluated whether horizontal restraints had an adverse effect on competition. See *Indiana Federation of Dentists, supra*, at 450–451, 459 (agreement between competing dentists not to share X rays with insurance companies); *Catalano, supra*, at 644–645, 650 (agreement among competing wholesalers not to compete on extending credit to retailers). Given that horizontal restraints involve agreements between competitors not to compete in some way, this Court concluded that it did not need to precisely define the relevant market to conclude that these agreements were anticompetitive. See *Indiana Federation of Dentists, supra*, at 460–461; *Catalano, supra*, at 648–649. But vertical restraints are different. See *Arizona v. Maricopa County Medical Soc.*, 457 U. S. 332, 348, n. 18 (1982); *Leegin Creative Leather Products, Inc. v. PSKS, Inc.*, 551 U. S. 877, 888 (2007). Vertical restraints often pose no risk to competition unless the entity imposing them has market power, which cannot be evaluated unless the Court first defines the relevant market. See *id.*, at 898 (noting that a vertical restraint "may not be a serious concern unless the relevant entity has market power"); Easterbrook, Vertical Arrangements and the Rule of Reason, 53 Antitrust L. J. 135, 160 (1984) ("[T]he possibly anticompetitive manifestations of vertical arrangements can occur only if there is market power").

a feedback loop of declining demand. See Evans & Schmalensee 674–675; Evans & Noel 680–681. And the fact that two-sided platforms charge one side a price that is below or above cost reflects differences in the two sides' demand elasticity, not market power or anticompetitive pricing. See Klein 574, 595, 598, 626. Price increases on one side of the platform likewise do not suggest anticompetitive effects without some evidence that they have increased the overall cost of the platform's services. See *id.*, at 575, 594, 626. Thus, courts must include both sides of the platform—merchants and cardholders—when defining the credit card market.

To be sure, it is not always necessary to consider both sides of a two-sided platform. A market should be treated as one sided when the impacts of indirect network effects and relative pricing in that market are minor. See Filistrucchi 321–322. Newspapers that sell advertisements, for example, arguably operate a two-sided platform because the value of an advertisement increases as more people read the newspaper. *Id.*, at 297, 315; Klein 579. But in the newspaper-advertisement market, the indirect networks effects operate in only one direction; newspaper readers are largely indifferent to the amount of advertising that a newspaper contains. See Filistrucchi 321, 323, and n. 99; Klein 583. Because of these weak indirect network effects, the market for newspaper advertising behaves much like a one-sided market and should be analyzed as such. See Filistrucchi 321; *Times-Picayune Publishing Co. v. United States*, 345 U. S. 594, 610 (1953).

But two-sided transaction platforms, like the credit card market, are different. These platforms facilitate a single, simultaneous transaction between participants. For credit cards, the network can sell its services only if a merchant and cardholder both simultaneously choose to use the network. Thus, whenever a credit card network sells one transaction's worth of card-acceptance services to a merchant it also must sell one transaction's worth of card-payment services to a cardholder. It cannot sell transaction services to either cardholders or merchants individually. See Klein 583 ("Because cardholders and merchants jointly consume a single product, payment card transactions, their consumption of payment card transactions must be directly proportional"). To optimize sales, the network must find the balance of pricing that encourages the greatest number of matches between cardholders and merchants.

Because they cannot make a sale unless both sides of the platform simultaneously agree to use their services, two-sided transaction platforms exhibit more pronounced indirect network effects and interconnected pricing and demand. Transaction platforms are thus better understood as "suppl[ying] only one product"—transactions. Klein 580. In the credit card market, these transactions "are jointly consumed by a cardholder, who uses the payment card to make a transaction, and a merchant, who accepts the payment card as a method of payment." *Ibid.* Tellingly, credit cards determine their market share by measuring the volume of transactions they have sold.[167]

Evaluating both sides of a two-sided transaction platform is also necessary to accurately assess competition. Only other two-sided platforms can compete with a two-sided platform for transactions. See Filistrucchi 301. A credit card company that processed transactions for merchants, but that had no cardholders willing to use its card, could not compete with AmEx. See *ibid.* Only a company that had both cardholders and merchants willing to use its network could sell transactions and compete in the credit card market. Similarly, if a merchant accepts the four major credit cards, but a cardholder only uses Visa or AmEx, only those two cards can compete for the particular transaction. Thus, competition cannot be accurately assessed by looking at only one side of the platform in isolation.[168]

For all these reasons, "[i]n two-sided transaction markets, only one market should be defined." *Id.*, at 302; see also Evans & Noel 671 ("[F]ocusing on one dimension of . . . competition tends to distort the competition that actually exists among [two-sided platforms]"). Any other analysis would lead to ""mistaken inferences"" of the kind that could ""chill the very conduct the antitrust laws are designed to protect."" *Brooke Group Ltd. v. Brown & Williamson Tobacco Corp.*, 509 U. S. 209, 226 (1993); see also *Matsushita Elec. Industrial Co. v. Zenith Radio Corp.*, 475 U. S. 574, 594 (1986) (" '[W]e must be concerned lest a rule or precedent that authorizes a search for a particular type of undesirable pricing behavior end up by discouraging legitimate price competition' "); *Leegin*, 551 U. S., at 895 (noting that courts should avoid "increas[ing] the total cost of the antitrust system by prohibiting procompetitive conduct the antitrust laws should encourage"). Accordingly, we will analyze the two-sided market for credit card transactions as a whole to determine whether the plaintiffs have shown that AmEx's antisteering provisions have anticompetitive effects.

## B

The plaintiffs have not carried their burden to prove anticompetitive effects in the relevant market. The plaintiffs stake their entire case on proving that AmEx's agreements increase merchant fees. We find this argument unpersuasive.

---

167 Contrary to the dissent's assertion, *post*, at 11–12, merchant services and cardholder services are not complements. See Filistrucchi 297 ("[A] two-sided market [is] different from markets for complementary products, in which both products are bought by the same buyers, who, in their buying decisions, can therefore be expected to take into account both prices"). As already explained, credit card companies are best understood as supplying only one product—transactions—which is jointly consumed by a cardholder and a merchant. See Klein 580. Merchant services and cardholder services are both inputs to this single product. See *ibid.*

168 Nontransaction platforms, by contrast, often do compete with companies that do not operate on both sides of their platform. A newspaper that sells advertising, for example, might have to compete with a television network, even though the two do not meaningfully compete for viewers. See Filistrucchi 301.

As an initial matter, the plaintiffs' argument about merchant fees wrongly focuses on only one side of the two-sided credit card market. As explained, the credit card market must be defined to include both merchants and cardholders. Focusing on merchant fees alone misses the mark because the product that credit card companies sell is transactions, not services to merchants, and the competitive effects of a restraint on transactions cannot be judged by looking at merchants alone. Evidence of a price in- crease on one side of a two-sided transaction platform cannot by itself demonstrate an anticompetitive exercise of market power. To demonstrate anticompetitive effects on the two-sided credit card market as a whole, the plaintiffs must prove that AmEx's antisteering provisions increased the cost of credit card transactions above a competitive level, reduced the number of credit card transactions, or otherwise stifled competition in the credit card market. See 1 Kalinowski §12.02[2]; *Craftsman Limousine, Inc.*, 491 F. 3d, at 390; *Virginia Atlantic Airways Ltd.*, 257 F. 3d, at 264. They failed to do so.

1

The plaintiffs did not offer any evidence that the price of credit card transactions was higher than the price one would expect to find in a competitive market. As the District Court found, the plaintiffs failed to offer any reliable measure of AmEx's transaction price or profit margins. 88 F. Supp. 3d, at 198, 215. And the evidence about whether AmEx charges more than its competitors was ultimately inconclusive. *Id.*, at 199, 202, 215.

AmEx's increased merchant fees reflect increases in the value of its services and the cost of its transactions, not an ability to charge above a competitive price. AmEx began raising its merchant fees in 2005 after Visa and Mastercard raised their fees in the early 2000s. *Id.*, at 195, 199–200. As explained, AmEx has historically charged higher merchant fees than these competitors because it delivers wealthier cardholders who spend more money. *Id.*, at 200–201. AmEx's higher merchant fees are based on a careful study of how much additional value its cardholders offer merchants. See *id.*, at 192–193. On the other side of the market, AmEx uses its higher merchant fees to offer its cardholders a more robust rewards program, which is necessary to maintain cardholder loyalty and encourage the level of spending that makes AmEx valuable to merchants. *Id.*, at 160, 191–195. That AmEx allocates prices between merchants and cardholders differently from Visa and Mastercard is simply not evidence that it wields market power to achieve anticompetitive ends. See Evans & Noel 670–671; Klein 574–575, 594–595, 598, 626.

In addition, the evidence that does exist cuts against the plaintiffs' view that AmEx's antisteering provisions are the cause of any increases in merchant fees. Visa and Master- Card's merchant fees have continued to increase, even at merchant locations where AmEx is not accepted and, thus, AmEx's antisteering provisions do not apply. See 88 F. Supp. 3d, at 222. This suggests that the cause of increased merchant fees is not AmEx's antisteering provisions, but rather increased competition for cardholders and a corresponding market wide adjustment in the relative price charged to merchants. See Klein 575, 609.

2

The plaintiffs did offer evidence that AmEx increased the percentage of the purchase price that it charges merchants by an average of 0.09% between 2005 and 2010 and that this increase was not entirely spent on cardholder rewards. See 88 F. Supp. 3d, at 195–197, 215. The plaintiffs believe that this evidence shows that the price of AmEx's transactions increased.

Even assuming the plaintiffs are correct, this evidence does not prove that AmEx's antisteering provisions gave it the power to charge anticompetitive prices. "Market power is the ability to raise price profitably by *restricting output*." Areeda & Hovenkamp §5.01 (emphasis added); accord, *Kodak*, 504 U. S., at 464; *Business Electronics*, 485 U. S., at 723. This Court will "not infer competitive injury from price and output data absent some evidence that tends to prove that output was restricted or prices were above a competitive level." *Brooke Group Ltd.*, 509 U. S., at 237. There is no such evidence in this case. The output of credit card transactions grew dramatically from 2008 to 2013, increasing 30%. See 838 F. 3d, at 206. "Where . . . output is expanding at the same time prices are increasing, rising prices are equally consistent with growing product demand." *Brooke Group Ltd., supra*, at 237. And, as previously explained, the plaintiffs did not show that AmEx charged more than its competitors.

The plaintiffs also failed to prove that AmEx's antisteering provisions have stifled competition among credit card companies. To the contrary, while these agreements have been in place, the credit card market experienced expanding output and improved quality. AmEx's business model spurred Visa and Mastercard to offer new premium card categories with higher rewards. And it has increased the availability of card services, including free banking and card-payment services for low-income customers who otherwise would not be served. Indeed, between 1970 and 2001, the percentage of households with credit cards more than quadrupled, and the proportion of households in the bottom-income quintile with credit cards grew from just 2% to over 38%. See D. Evans & R. Schmalensee, Paying With Plastic: The Digital Revolution in Buying and Borrowing 88–89 (2d ed. 2005) (Paying With Plastic).

Nor have AmEx's antisteering provisions ended competition between credit card networks with respect to merchant fees. Instead, fierce competition between networks has constrained AmEx's ability to raise these fees and has, at times, forced AmEx to lower them. For instance, when AmEx raised its merchant prices between 2005 and 2010, some merchants chose to leave its network. 88 F. Supp. 3d, at 197. And when its remaining merchants complained, AmEx stopped raising its merchant prices. *Id.*, at 198. In another instance in the late 1980s and early 1990s, competition forced AmEx to offer lower merchant fees to "everyday spend" merchants—supermarkets, gas stations, pharmacies, and the like—to persuade them to accept AmEx. See *id.*, at 160–161, 202.

In addition, AmEx's competitors have exploited its higher merchant fees to their advantage. By charging lower merchant fees, Visa, Mastercard, and Discover have achieved broader merchant acceptance—approximately 3 million more locations than AmEx. *Id.*, at 204. This broader merchant acceptance is a major advantage for these networks and a significant challenge for AmEx, since consumers prefer cards that will be accepted everywhere. *Ibid.* And to compete even further with AmEx, Visa and Mastercard charge different merchant fees for different types of cards to maintain their comparatively lower merchant fees and broader acceptance. Over the long run, this competition has created a trend of declining merchant fees in the credit card market. In fact, since the first credit card was introduced in the 1950s, merchant fees— including AmEx's merchant fees—have decreased by more than half. See *id.*, at 202–203; Paying With Plastic 54, 126, 152.

Lastly, there is nothing inherently anticompetitive about AmEx's antisteering provisions. These agreements actually stem negative externalities in the credit card market and promote interbrand competition. When merchants steer cardholders away from AmEx at the point of sale, it undermines the cardholder's expectation of "welcome acceptance"—the promise of a frictionless transaction. 88 F. Supp. 3d, at 156. A lack of welcome acceptance at one merchant makes a cardholder less likely to use AmEx at all other merchants. This externality endangers the viability of the entire AmEx network. And it undermines the investments that AmEx has made to encourage increased cardholder spending, which discourages investments in rewards and ultimately harms both cardholders and merchants. Cf. *Leegin*, 551 U. S., at 890–891 (recognizing that vertical restraints can prevent retailers from free riding and thus increase the availability of "tangible or intangible services or promotional efforts" that enhance competition and consumer welfare). Perhaps most importantly, antisteering provisions do not prevent Visa, Mastercard, or Discover from competing against AmEx by offering lower merchant fees or promoting their broader merchant acceptance.[169]

In sum, the plaintiffs have not satisfied the first step of the rule of reason. They have not carried their burden of proving that AmEx's antisteering provisions have anticompetitive effects. AmEx's business model has spurred robust interbrand competition and has increased the quality and quantity of credit card transactions. And it is "[t]he promotion of interbrand competition," after all, that "is . . . 'the primary purpose of the antitrust laws.'" *Id.*, at 890.

---

169 The plaintiffs argue that *United States v. Topco Associates, Inc.*, 405 U. S. 596, 610 (1972), forbids any restraint that would restrict competition in part of the market—here, for example, merchant steering. See Brief for Petitioners and Respondents Nebraska, Tennessee, and Texas 30, 42. *Topco* does not stand for such a broad proposition. *Topco* concluded that a horizontal agreement between competitors was unreasonable *per se*, even though the agreement did not extend to every competitor in the market. See 405 U. S., at 599, 608. A horizontal agreement between competitors is markedly different from a vertical agreement that incidentally affects one particular method of competition. See *Leegin*, 551 U. S., at 888; *Maricopa County Medical Soc.*, 457 U. S., at 348, n. 18.

*    *    *

Because AmEx's antisteering provisions do not unreasonably restrain trade, we affirm the judgment of the Court of Appeals.

*It is so ordered.*

# SUPREME COURT OF THE UNITED STATES

No. 16–1454

OHIO, ET AL., PETITIONERS v. AMERICAN EXPRESS COMPANY, ET AL.

ON WRIT OF CERTIORARI TO THE UNITED STATES COURT

OF APPEALS FOR THE SECOND CIRCUIT

[June 25, 2018]

JUSTICE BREYER, with whom JUSTICE GINSBURG, JUSTICE SOTO-MAYOR, and JUSTICE KAGAN join, dissenting.

For more than 120 years, the American economy has prospered by charting a middle path between pure *lassez-faire* and state capitalism, governed by an antitrust law "dedicated to the principle that *markets*, not individual firms and certainly not political power, produce the optimal mixture of goods and services." 1 P. Areeda & H. Hovenkamp, Antitrust Law ¶100b, p. 4 (4th ed. 2013) (Areeda & Hovenkamp). By means of a strong antitrust law, the United States has sought to avoid the danger of monopoly capitalism. Long gone, we hope, are the days when the great trusts presided unfettered by competition over the American economy.

This lawsuit is emblematic of the American approach. Many governments around the world have responded to concerns about the high fees that credit card companies often charge merchants by regulating such fees directly. See GAO, Credit and Debit Cards: Federal Entities Are Taking Actions to Limit Their Interchange Fees, but Additional Revenue Collection Cost Savings May Exist 31–35 (GAO–08–558, 2008). The United States has not followed that approach. The Government instead filed this lawsuit, which seeks to restore market competition over credit card merchant fees by eliminating a contractual barrier with anticompetitive effects. The majority rejects that effort. But because the challenged contractual term clearly has serious anticompetitive effects, I dissent.

I

I agree with the majority and the parties that this case is properly evaluated under the three-step "rule of reason" that governs many antitrust lawsuits. *Ante*, at 9–10. Under that approach, a court looks first at the agreement or restraint at issue to assess whether it has had, or is likely to have, anticompetitive effects. *FTC v. Indiana*

*Federation of Dentists*, 476 U. S. 447, 459 (1986). In doing so, the court normally asks whether the restraint may tend to impede competition and, if so, whether those who have entered into that restraint have sufficient economic or commercial power for the agreement to make a negative difference. See *id.*, at 459–461. Sometimes, but not al ways, a court will try to determine the appropriate market (the market that the agreement affects) and determine whether those entering into that agreement have the power to raise prices above the competitive level in that market. See *ibid.*

It is important here to understand that in cases under §1 of the Sherman Act (unlike in cases challenging a merger under §7 of the Clayton Act, 15 U. S. C. §18), it may well be unnecessary to undertake a sometimes complex, market power inquiry:

"Since the purpose [in a Sherman Act §1 case] of the inquiries into . . . market power is [simply] to deter mine whether an arrangement has the potential for genuine adverse effects on competition, 'proof of actual detrimental effects, such as a reduction in output,' can obviate the need for an inquiry into market power, which is but a 'surrogate for detrimental effects.' " *Indiana Federation of Dentists, supra*, at 460–461 (quoting 7 P. Areeda, Antitrust Law ¶1511, p. 429 (3d ed. 1986)).

Second (as treatise writers summarize the case law), if an antitrust plaintiff meets the initial burden of showing that an agreement will likely have anticompetitive effects, normally the "burden shifts to the defendant to show that the restraint in fact serves a legitimate objective." 7 Areeda & Hovenkamp ¶1504b, at 415; see *California Dental Assn. v. FTC*, 526 U. S. 756, 771 (1999); *id.*, at 788 (BREYER, J., dissenting).

Third, if the defendant successfully bears this burden, the antitrust plaintiff may still carry the day by showing that it is possible to meet the legitimate objective in less restrictive ways, or, perhaps by showing that the legitimate objective does not outweigh the harm that competition will suffer, *i.e.*, that the agreement "on balance" re mains unreasonable. 7 Areeda & Hovenkamp ¶1507a, at 442.

Like the Court of Appeals and the parties, the majority addresses only the first step of that three-step framework. *Ante*, at 10.

## II

### A

This case concerns the credit card business. As the majority explains, *ante*, at 2, that business involves the selling of two different but related card services. First, when a shopper uses a credit card to buy something from a participating merchant, the credit card company pays the merchant the amount of money that the merchant's customer has charged to his card and charges the merchant a fee, say 5%, for that speedy-payment service. I shall refer to that kind of transaction as a merchant-related card service. Second, the credit card company then sends a bill to the merchant's customer, the shopper who holds the card; and the shopper pays the card company the sum that merchant charged the shopper for the goods or services he or she bought.

The cardholder also often pays the card company a fee, such as an annual fee for the card or an interest charge for delayed payment. I shall call that kind of transaction a shopper-related card service. The credit- card company can earn revenue from the sale (directly or indirectly) of each of these services: (1) speedy payment for merchants, and (2) credit for shoppers. (I say "indirectly" to reflect the fact that card companies often create or use networks of banks as part of the process—but I have found nothing here suggesting that that fact makes a significant difference to my analysis.)

Sales of the two basic card services are related. A shop per can pay for a purchase with a particular credit card only if the merchant has signed up for merchant-related card services with the company that issued the credit card that the shopper wishes to use. A firm in the credit card business is therefore unlikely to make money unless quite a few merchants agree to accept that firm's card and quite a few shoppers agree to carry and use it. In general, the more merchants that sign up with a particular card company, the more useful that card is likely to prove to shoppers and so the more shoppers will sign up; so too, the more shoppers that carry a particular card, the more useful that card is likely to prove to merchants (as it obviously helps them obtain the shoppers' business) and so the more merchants will sign up. Moreover, as a rough rule of thumb (and assuming constant charges), the larger the networks of paying merchants and paying shoppers that a card firm maintains, the larger the revenues that the firm will likely receive, since more payments will be processed using its cards. Thus, it is not surprising that a card company may offer shoppers incentives (say, points redeemable for merchandise or travel) for using its card or that a firm might want merchants to accept its card exclusively.

**B**

This case focuses upon a practice called "steering." American Express has historically charged higher merchant fees than its competitors. App. to Pet. for Cert. 173a–176a. Hence, fewer merchants accept American Express' cards than its competitors'. *Id.*, at 184a–187a. But, perhaps because American Express cardholders are, on average, wealthier, higher-spending, or more loyal to American Express than other cardholders, vast numbers of merchants still accept American Express cards. See *id.*, at 156a, 176a–177a, 184a–187a. Those who do, however, would (in order to avoid the higher American Express fee) often prefer that their customers use a different card to charge a purchase. Thus, the merchant has a monetary incentive to "steer" the customer towards the use of a different card. A merchant might tell the customer, for example, "American Express costs us more," or "please use Visa if you can," or "free shipping if you use Discover." See *id.*, at 100a–102a.

Steering makes a difference, because without it, the shopper does not care whether the merchant pays more to American Express than it would pay to a different card company—the shopper pays the same price either way. But if steering works, then American Express will find it more difficult to charge more than its competitors for merchant-related services, because merchants will respond by steering their customers, encouraging them to use other cards. Thus, American Express dislikes steering; the merchants like it; and the shoppers may benefit from it, whether because merchants will offer them incentives to use less expensive cards or in the form of lower retail prices overall. See *id.*, at 92a, 97a–104a.

In response to its competitors' efforts to convince merchants to steer shoppers to use less expensive cards, American Express tried to stop, or at least to limit, steering by placing antisteering provisions in most of its contracts with merchants. It called those provisions "nondiscrimination provisions." They prohibited steering of the forms I have described above (and others as well). See *id.*, at 95a–96a, 100a–101a. After placing them in its agreements, American Express found it could maintain, or even raise, its higher merchant prices without losing too many transactions to other firms. *Id.*, at 195a–198a. These agreements—the "nondiscrimination provisions"—led to this lawsuit.

## C

In 2010 the United States and 17 States brought this antitrust case against American Express. They claimed that the "nondiscrimination provisions" in its contracts with merchants created an unreasonable restraint of trade. (Initially Visa and Mastercard were also defend ants, but they entered into consent judgments, dropping similar provisions from their contracts with merchants). After a 7-week bench trial, the District Court entered judgment for the Government, setting forth its findings of fact and conclusions of law in a 97-page opinion. 88 F. Supp. 3d 143 (EDNY 2015).

Because the majority devotes little attention to the District Court's detailed factual findings, I will summarize some of the more significant ones here. Among other things, the District Court found that beginning in 2005 and during the next five years, American Express raised the prices it charged merchants on 20 separate occasions. See *id.*, at 195–196. In doing so, American Express did not take account of the possibility that large merchants would respond to the price increases by encouraging shoppers to use a different credit card because the nondiscrimination provisions prohibited any such steering. *Id.*, at 215. The District Court pointed to merchants' testimony stating that, had it not been for those provisions, the large merchants would have responded to the price increases by encouraging customers to use other, less-expensive cards. *Ibid.*

The District Court also found that even though American Express raised its merchant prices 20 times in this 5-year period, it did not lose the business of any large merchant. *Id.*, at 197. Nor did American Express increase benefits (or cut credit card prices) to American Express cardholders in tandem with the merchant price increases. *Id.*, at 196. Even had there been no direct evidence of injury to competition, American Express' ability to raise merchant prices without losing any meaningful market share, in the District Court's view, showed that American Express possessed power in the relevant market. See *id.*, at 195.

The District Court also found that, in the absence of the provisions, prices to merchants would likely have been lower. *Ibid.* It wrote that in the late 1990's, Discover, one of American Express' competitors, had tried to develop a business model that involved charging lower prices to merchants than the other companies charged. *Id.*, at 213. Discover then invited each "merchant to save money by shifting volume to Discover," while simultaneously offering merchants additional discounts "if they would steer customers to Discover." *Ibid.* The court determined that these efforts failed because of American Express' (and the other card companies') "nondiscrimination provisions." These provisions, the court found, "denied merchants the ability to express a preference for Discover or to employ any other tool by which they might steer share to Discover's lower-priced network." Id., at 214. Because the provisions eliminated any advantage that lower prices might produce, Discover "abandoned its low-price business model" and raised its merchant fees to match those of its competitors. *Ibid.* This series of events, the court concluded was "emblematic of the harm done to the competitive process" by the "nondiscrimination provisions." *Ibid.* jᴜtev

The District Court added that it found no offsetting pro- competitive benefit to shoppers. *Id.*, at 225–238. Indeed, it found no offsetting benefit of any kind. See *ibid.*

American Express appealed, and the U. S. Court of Appeals for the Second Circuit held in its favor. 838 F. 3d 179 (2016). The Court of Appeals did not reject any fact found by the District Court as "clearly erroneous." See Fed. Rule Civ. Proc. 52(a)(6). Rather, it concluded that the District Court had erred in step 1 of its rule of reason analysis by failing to account for what the Second Circuit called the credit card business's "two-sided market" (or "two-sided platform"). 838 F. 3d, at 185–186, 196–200.

### III

The majority, like the Court of Appeals, reaches only step 1 in its "rule of reason" analysis. *Ante*, at 10. To repeat, that step consists of determining whether the challenged "nondiscrimination provisions" have had, or are likely to have, anticompetitive effects. See *Indiana Federation of Dentists*, 476 U. S., at 459. Do those provisions tend to impede competition? And if so, does American Express, which imposed that restraint as a condition of doing business with its merchant customers, have sufficient economic or commercial power for the provision to make a negative difference? See *id.*, at 460–461.

### A

Here the District Court found that the challenged provisions have had significant anticompetitive effects. In particular, it found that the provisions have limited or prevented price competition among credit card firms for the business of merchants. 88 F. Supp. 3d, at 209. That conclusion makes sense: In the provisions, American Express required the merchants to agree not to encourage customers to use American Express'

101

competitors' credit cards, even cards from those competitors, such as Discover, that intended to charge the merchants lower prices. See *id.*, at 214. By doing so, American Express has "disrupt[ed] the normal price-setting mechanism" in the market. *Id.*, at 209. As a result of the provisions, the District Court found, American Express was able to raise merchant prices repeatedly without any significant loss of business, because merchants were unable to respond to such price increases by encouraging shoppers to pay with other cards. *Id.*, at 215. The provisions also meant that competitors like Discover had little incentive to lower their merchant prices, because doing so did not lead to any additional market share. *Id.*, at 214. The provisions thereby "suppress[ed] [American Express'] . . . competitors' incentives to offer lower prices . . . resulting in higher profit-maximizing prices across the network services market." *Id.*, at 209. Consumers throughout the economy paid higher retail prices as a result, and they were denied the opportunity to accept incentives that merchants might otherwise have offered to use less-expensive cards. *Id.*, at 216, 220. I should think that, considering step 1 alone, there is little more that need be said. **STOP HERE — "inter"**

The majority, like the Court of Appeals, says that the District Court should have looked not only at the market for the card companies' merchant-related services but also at the market for the card companies' shopper-related services, and that it should have combined them, treating them as a single market. *Ante*, at 14–15; 838 F. 3d, at 197. But I am not aware of any support for that view in antitrust law. Indeed, this Court has held to the contrary.

In *Times-Picayune Publishing Co. v. United States*, 345 U. S. 594, 610 (1953), the Court held that an antitrust court should begin its definition of a relevant market by focusing narrowly on the good or service directly affected by a challenged restraint. The Government in that case claimed that a newspaper's advertising policy violated the Sherman Act's "rule of reason." See *ibid.* In support of that argument, the Government pointed out, and the District Court had held, that the newspaper dominated the market for the sales of newspapers to readers in New Orleans, where it was the sole morning daily newspaper. *Ibid.* But this Court reversed. We explained that "every newspaper is a dual trader in separate though interdependent markets; it sells the paper's news and advertising content to its readers; in effect that readership is in turn sold to the buyers of advertising space." *Ibid.* We then added:

"This case concerns solely one of those markets. The Publishing Company stands accused not of tying sales to its readers but only to buyers of general and classified space in its papers. For this reason, dominance in the advertising market, not in readership, must be decisive in gauging the legality of the Company's unit plan." *Ibid.*

Here, American Express stands accused not of limiting or harming competition for shopper-related card services, but only of merchant-related card services, because the challenged contract provisions appear only in American Express' contracts with merchants. That is why the District Court was correct in considering, at step 1, simply whether the agreement had diminished competition in merchant-related services.

## B

The District Court did refer to market definition, and the majority does the same. *Ante*, at 11–15. And I recognize that properly defining a market is often a complex business. Once a court has identified the good or service directly restrained, as *Times-Picayune Publishing Co.* requires, it will sometimes add to the relevant market what economists call "substitutes": other goods or services that are reasonably substitutable for that good or service. See, *e.g.*, *United States v. E. I. du Pont de Nemours & Co.*, 351 U. S. 377, 395–396 (1956) (explaining that cellophane market includes other, substitutable flexible wrapping materials as well). The reason that substitutes are included in the relevant market is that they restrain a firm's ability to profitably raise prices, because customers will switch to the substitutes rather than pay the higher prices. See 2B Areeda & Hovenkamp ¶561, at 378.

But while the market includes substitutes, it does not include what economists call complements: goods or services that are used together with the restrained product, but that cannot be substituted for that product. See *id.*, ¶565a, at 429; *Eastman Kodak Co. v. Image Technical Services, Inc.*, 504 U. S. 451, 463 (1992). An example of complements is gasoline and tires. A driver needs both gasoline and tires to drive, but they are not substitutes for each other, and so the sale price of tires does not check the ability of a gasoline firm (say a gasoline monopolist) to raise the price of gasoline above competitive levels. As a treatise on the subject states: "Grouping complementary goods into the same market" is "economic nonsense," and would "undermin[e] the rationale for the policy against monopolization or collusion in the first place." 2B Areeda & Hovenkamp ¶565a, at 431.

Here, the relationship between merchant-related card services and shopper-related card services is primarily that of complements, not substitutes. Like gasoline and tires, both must be purchased for either to have value. Merchants upset about a price increase for merchant-related services cannot avoid that price increase by becoming cardholders, in the way that, say, a buyer of newspaper advertising can switch to television advertising or direct mail in response to a newspaper's advertising price increase. The two categories of services serve fundamentally different purposes. And so, also like gasoline and tires, it is difficult to see any way in which the price of shopper-related services could act as a check on the card firm's sale price of merchant-related services. If anything, a lower price of shopper-related card services is likely to cause more shoppers to use the card, and increased shop per popularity should make it *easier* for a card firm to raise prices to merchants, not *harder*, as would be the case if the services were substitutes. Thus, unless there is something unusual about this case—a possibility I discuss below, see *infra*, at 13–20—there is no justification for treating shopper-related services and merchant-related services as if they were part of a single market, at least not at step 1 of the "rule of reason."

It is power over c/h that mattered. [Not on in T-P.]

## C

Regardless, a discussion of market definition was legally unnecessary at step 1. That is because the District Court found strong *direct* evidence of anticompetitive effects flowing from the challenged restraint. 88 F. Supp. 3d, at 207–224.

As I said, *supra*, at 7, this evidence included Discover's efforts to break into the credit card business by charging lower prices for merchant-related services, only to find that the "nondiscrimination provisions," by preventing merchants from encouraging shoppers to use Discover cards, meant that lower merchant prices did not result in any additional transactions using Discover credit cards. 88 F. Supp. 3d, at 213–214. The direct evidence also included the fact that American Express raised its merchant prices 20 times in five years without losing any appreciable market share. *Id.*, at 195–198, 208–212. It also included the testimony of numerous merchants that they would have steered shoppers away from American Express cards in response to merchant price increases (thereby checking the ability of American Express to raise prices) had it not been for the nondiscrimination provisions. See *id.*, at 221–222. It included the factual finding that American Express "did not even account for the possibility that [large] merchants would respond to its price increases by attempting to shift share to a competitor's network" because the nondiscrimination provisions prohibited steering. *Id.*, at 215. It included the District Court's ultimate finding of fact, not overturned by the Court of Appeals, that the challenged provisions "were integral to" American Express' "[price] increases and thereby caused merchants to pay higher prices." *Ibid.*

As I explained above, this Court has stated that "[s]ince the purpose of the inquiries into market definition and market power is to determine *whether an arrangement has the potential for* genuine adverse effects on competition, proof of actual detrimental effects . . . can obviate the need for" those inquiries. *Indiana Federation of Dentists*, 476 U. S., at 460–461 (internal quotation marks omitted). That statement is fully applicable here. Doubts about the District Court's market-definition analysis are beside the point in the face of the District Court's findings of actual anticompetitive harm.

The majority disagrees that market definition is irrelevant. See *ante*, at 11–12, and n. 7. The majority explains that market definition is necessary because the nondiscrimination provisions are "vertical restraints" and "[v]ertical restraints often pose no risk to competition unless the entity imposing them has market power, which cannot be evaluated unless the Court first determines the relevant market." *Ante*, at 11, n. 7. The majority thus, in a footnote, seems categorically to exempt vertical restraints from the ordinary "rule of reason" analysis that has applied to them since the Sherman Act's enactment in 1890. The majority's only support for this novel exemption is *Leegin Creative Leather Products, Inc. v. PSKS, Inc.*, 551 U. S. 877 (2007). But *Leegin* held that the "rule of reason" *applied* to the vertical restraint at issue in that case. See *id.*, at 898–899. It said nothing to suggest that vertical restraints are not subject to the usual "rule of reason" analysis. See also *infra*, at 24.

One critical point that the majority's argument ignores is that proof of actual adverse effects on competition *is, a fortiori*, proof of market power. Without such power, the restraints could not have brought about the anticompetitive effects that the plaintiff proved. See *Indiana Federation of Dentists, supra*, at 460 ("[T]he purpose of the inquiries into market definition and market power is to determine *whether an arrangement has the potential for* genuine adverse effects on competition" (emphasis added)). The District Court's findings of actual anticompetitive harm from the non-discrimination provisions thus showed that, whatever the relevant market might be, American Express had enough power in that market to cause that harm. There is no reason to require a separate showing of market definition and market power under such circumstances. And so the majority's extensive discussion of market definition is legally unnecessary.

## D

The majority's discussion of market definition is also wrong. Without raising any objection in general with the longstanding approach I describe above, *supra*, at 10–11, the majority agrees with the Court of Appeals that the market for American Express' card services is special because it is a "two-sided transaction platform." *Ante*, at 2–5, 12–15. The majority explains that credit card firms connect two distinct groups of customers: First, merchants who accept credit cards, and second, shoppers who use the cards. *Ante*, at 2; accord, 838 F. 3d, at 186. The majority adds that "no credit card transaction can occur unless both the merchant and the cardholder simultaneously agree to use to the same credit card network." *Ante*, at 3. And it explains that the credit card market involves "indirect network effects," by which it means that shoppers want a card that many merchants will accept and merchants want to accept those cards that many customers have and use. *Ibid.* From this, the majority concludes that "courts must include both sides of the platform—merchants and cardholders—when defining the credit card market." *Ante*, at 12; accord, 838 F. 3d, at 197.

### 1

Missing from the majority's analysis is any explanation as to *why*, given the purposes that market definition serves in antitrust law, the fact that a credit card firm can be said to operate a "two-sided transaction platform" means that its merchant-related and shopper-related services should be combined into a single market. The phrase "two-sided transaction platform" is not one of antitrust art—I can find no case from this Court using those words. The majority defines the phrase as covering a business that "offers different products or services to two different groups who both depend on the platform to intermediate between them," where the business "cannot make a sale to one side of the platform without simultaneously making a sale to the other" side of the platform. *Ante*, at 2. I take from that definition that there are four relevant features of such businesses on the majority's account: they (1) offer different products or services, (2) to different groups of customers, (3) whom the "platform" connects, (4) in simultaneous transactions. See *ibid.*

What is it about businesses with those four features that the majority thinks justifies a special market-definition approach for them? It cannot be the first two features—that the company sells different products to different groups of customers. Companies that sell multiple products to multiple types of customers are common—place. A firm might mine for gold, which it refines and sells both to dentists in the form of fillings and to investors in the form of ingots. Or, a firm might drill for both oil and natural gas. Or a firm might make both ignition switches inserted into auto bodies and tires used for cars. I have already explained that, ordinarily, antitrust law will not group the two nonsubstitutable products together for step 1 purposes. *Supra*, at 10–11.

Neither should it normally matter whether a company sells related, or complementary, products, *i.e.*, products which must both be purchased to have any function, such as ignition switches and tires, or cameras and film. It is well established that an antitrust court in such cases looks at the product where the attacked restraint has an anticompetitive effect. *Supra*, at 9; see *Eastman Kodak*, 504 U. S., at 463. The court does not combine the customers for the separate, nonsubstitutable goods and see if "over all" the restraint has a negative effect. See *ibid.*; 2B Areeda & Hovenkamp ¶565a. That is because, as I have explained, the complementary relationship between the products is irrelevant to the purposes of market-definition. See *supra*, at 10–11.

The majority disputes my characterization of merchant-related and shopper-related services as "complements." See *ante*, at 14, n. 8. The majority relies on an academic article which devotes one sentence to the question, saying that "a two-sided market [is] different from markets for complementary products [*e.g.*, tires and gas], in which both products are bought by the same buyers, who, in their buying decisions, can therefore be expected to take into account both prices." Filistrucchi, Geradin, Van Damme, & Affeldt, Market Definition in Two-Sided Markets: Theory and Practice, 10 J. Competition L. & Econ. 293, 297 (2014) (Filistrucchi). I agree that two-sided platforms—at least as some academics define them, but see *infra*, at 19–20—may be distinct from some types of complements in the respect the majority mentions (even though the services resemble complements because they must be used together for either to have value). But the distinction the majority mentions has nothing to do with the relevant question. The relevant question is whether merchant-related and shopper-related services are *substitutes*, one for the other, so that customers can respond to a price increase for one service by switching to the other service. As I have explained, the two types of services are not substitutes in this way. *Supra*, at 11–12. And so the question remains, just as before: What is it about the economic relationship between merchant-related and shopper-related services that would justify the majority's novel approach to market definition?

What about the last two features—that the company connects the two groups of customers to each other, in simultaneous transactions? That, too, is commonplace. Consider a farmers' market. It brings local farmers and local shoppers together, and transactions will occur only if a farmer and a shopper simultaneously agree to engage

in one. Should courts abandon their ordinary step 1 inquiry if several competing
farmers' markets in a city agree that only certain kinds of farmers can participate, or
if a farmers' market charges a higher fee than its competitors do and prohibits participating farmers from raising their prices to cover it? Why? If farmers' markets are
special, what about travel agents that connect airlines and passengers? What about
internet retailers, who, in addition to selling their own goods, allow (for a fee) other
goods- producers to sell over their networks? Each of those businesses seems to meet
the majority's four-prong definition.

*with*
*when*
*if*
*only*

→ *St. Louis Terminal!*

Apparently as its justification for applying a special market-definition rule
to "two-sided transaction plat forms," the majority explains that such platforms "often exhibit" what it calls "indirect network effects." *Ante*, at 3. By this, the majority means that sales of merchant-related card services and (different) shopper-related
card services are interconnected, in that increased merchant-buyers mean increased
shopper-buyers (the more stores in the card's network, the more customers likely to
use the card), and vice versa. See *ibid.* But this, too, is commonplace. Consider, again,
a farmers' market. The more farmers that participate (within physical and esthetic
limits), the more customers the market will likely attract, and vice versa. So too with
travel agents: the more airlines whose tickets a travel agent sells, the more potential
passengers will likely use that travel agent, and the more potential passengers that use
the travel agent, the easier it will likely be to convince airlines to sell through the travel
agent. And so forth. Nothing in antitrust law, to my knowledge, suggests that a court,
when presented with an agreement that restricts competition in any one of the markets my examples suggest, should abandon traditional market-definition approaches
and include in the relevant market services that are complements, not substitutes, of
the restrained good. See *supra*, at 10–11.

*Can not fit pica*

*tonatoo*

*Farmers' Mkt = interesting. FM*
*2 pays shoppers to go there.*

To justify special treatment for "two-sided transaction platforms," the majority relies on the Court's decision in *United States v. Grinnell Corp.*, 384 U. S. 563, 571–
572 (1966). In Grinnell, the Court treated as a single market several different "central
station services," including burglar alarm services and fire alarm services. *Id.*, at 571.
It did so even though, for *consumers*, "burglar alarm services are not interchangeable
with fire alarm services." *Id.*, at 572. But that is because, for *producers*, the services
were indeed interchangeable: A company that offered one could easily offer the other,
because they all involve "a single basic service—the protection of property through use
of a central service station." *Ibid.* Thus, the "commercial realit[y]" that the Grinnell
Court relied on, *ibid.*, was that the services being grouped were what economists call
"producer substitutes." See 2B Areeda & Hovenkamp ¶561, at 378. And the law is
clear that "two products produced interchangeably from the same production facili-
ties are presumptively in the same market," even if they are not "close substitutes for
each other on the demand side." *Ibid.* That is because a firm that produces one such
product can, in response to a price increase in the other, easily shift its production and
thereby limit its competitor's power to impose the higher price. See *id.*, ¶561a, at 379.

*That is just a price cut. Would want to compile that if claim was that*

*changed farmers more for space.*

107

Unlike the various types of central station services at issue in Grinnell Corp., however, the shopper-related and merchant-related services that American Express provides are not "producer substitutes" any more than they are traditional substitutes. For producers as for consumers, the services are instead complements. Credit card companies must sell them together for them to be useful. As a result, the credit card companies cannot respond to, say, merchant-related price increases by shifting production away from shopper-related services to merchant-related services. The relevant "commercial realities" in this case are thus completely different from those in Grinnell Corp. (The majority also cites *Brown Shoe Co. v. United States*, 370 U. S. 294, 336–337 (1962), for this point, but the "commercial realities" considered in that case were that "shoe stores in the outskirts of cities compete effectively with stores in central downtown areas," and thus are part of the same market. *Id.*, at 338–339. Here, merchant-related services do not, as I have said, compete with shopper-related services, and so *Brown Shoe Co.* does not support the majority's position.) Thus, our precedent provides no support for the majority's special approach to defining markets involving "two-sided transaction platforms."

### 3

What about the academic articles the majority cites? The first thing to note is that the majority defines "two-sided transaction platforms" much more broadly than the economists do. As the economists who coined the term explain, if a "two-sided market" meant simply that a firm connects two different groups of customers via a platform, then "pretty much any market would be two-sided, since buyers and sellers need to be brought together for markets to exist and gains from trade to be realized." Rochet & Tirole, Two-Sided Markets: A Progress Report, 37 RAND J. Econ. 645, 646 (2006). The defining feature of a "two- sided market," according to these economists, is that "the platform can affect the volume of transactions by charging more to one side of the market and reducing the price paid by the other side by an equal amount." *Id.*, at 664–665; accord, Filistrucchi 299. That requirement appears no where in the majority's definition. By failing to limit its definition to platforms that economists would recognize as "two sided" in the relevant respect, the majority carves out a much broader exception to the ordinary antitrust rules than the academic articles it relies on could possibly support.

Even as limited to the narrower definition that economists use, however, the academic articles the majority cites do not support the majority's flat rule that firms operating "two-sided transaction platforms" should always be treated as part of a single market for all antitrust purposes. *Ante*, at 13–15. Rather, the academics explain that for market-definition purposes, "[i]n some cases, the fact that a business can be thought of as two-sided may be irrelevant," including because "nothing in the analysis of the practices [at issue] really hinges on the linkages between the demands of participating groups." Evans & Schmalensee, Markets With Two-Sided Platforms, 1 Issues in Competition L. & Pol'y 667, 689 (2008). "In other cases, the fact that a business is two-sided will prove important both by identifying the real dimensions of competition and focusing on sources of constraints." *Ibid.* That flexible approach, however, is precisely the one the District Court followed in this case, by considering the effects of "[t]he two-sided nature of the . . . card industry" throughout its analysis. 88 F. Supp. 3d, at 155.

Neither the majority nor the academic articles it cites offer any explanation for why the features of a "two-sided transaction platform" justify always treating it as a single antitrust market, rather than accounting for its economic features in other ways, as the District Court did. The article that the majority repeatedly quotes as saying that "'[i]n two-sided transaction markets, only one market should be defined,'" *ante*, at 14–15 (quoting Filistrucchi 302), justifies that conclusion only for purposes of assessing the effects of a merger. In such a case, the article explains, "[e]veryone would probably agree that a payment card company such as American Express is either in the relevant market on both sides or on neither side . . . . The analysis of a merger between two payment card platforms should thus consider . . . both sides of the market." *Id.*, at 301. In a merger case this makes sense, but is also meaningless, because, whether there is one market or two, a reviewing court will consider both sides, because it must examine the effects of the merger in each affected market and submarket. See *Brown Shoe Co.*, 370 U. S., at 325. As for a nonmerger case, the article offers only *United States v. Grinnell* as a justification, see Filistrucchi 303, and as I have already explained, *supra*, at 16–18, Grinnell does not support this proposition.

### E

Put all of those substantial problems with the majority's reasoning aside, though. Even if the majority were right to say that market definition was relevant, and even if the majority were right to further say that the District Court should have defined the market in this case to include shopper-related services as well as merchant-related services, that *still* would not justify the majority in affirming the Court of Appeals. That is because, as the majority is forced to admit, the plaintiffs *made* the factual showing that the majority thinks is required. See *ante*, at 17.

Recall why it is that the majority says that market definition matters: because if the relevant market includes both merchant-related services and card-related services, then the plaintiffs had the burden to show that as a result of the nondiscrimination provisions, "the price of credit card transactions"—considering both fees charged to merchants and rewards paid to cardholders—"was higher than the price one would expect to find in a competitive market." *Ante*, at 16. This mirrors the Court of Appeals' holding that the Government had to show that the "non discrimination provisions" had "made *all* [American Ex press] customers on both sides of the platform—*i.e.*, both merchants and cardholders—worse off overall." 838 F. 3d, at 205.

The problem with this reasoning, aside from it being wrong, is that the majority admits that the plaintiffs *did* show this: they "offer[ed] evidence" that American Express "increased the percentage of the purchase price that it charges merchants ... and that this increase was not entirely spent on cardholder rewards." *Ante*, 17 (citing 88 F. Supp. 3d, at 195–197, 215). Indeed, the plaintiffs did not merely "offer evidence" of this—they persuaded the District Court, which made an unchallenged factual finding that the merchant price increases that resulted from the nondiscrimination provisions "were not wholly offset by additional rewards expenditures or otherwise passed through to cardholders, and *resulted in a higher net price.*" *Id.*, at 215 (emphasis added).

In the face of this problem, the majority retreats to saying that even net price increases do not matter after all, absent a showing of lower output, because if output is increasing, "'rising prices are equally consistent with growing product demand.'" *Ante*, at 18 (quoting *Brooke Group Ltd. v. Brown & Williamson Tobacco Corp.*, 509 U. S. 209, 237 (1993)). This argument, unlike the price argument, has nothing to do with the credit card market being a "two-sided transaction platform," so if this is the basis for the majority's holding, then nearly all of the opinion is dicta. The argument is also wrong. It is true as an economic matter that a firm exercises market power by restricting output in order to raise prices. But the relevant restriction of output is as compared with a hypothetical world in which the restraint was not present and prices were lower. The fact that credit card use in general has grown over the last decade, as the majority says, see *ante*, at 17–18, says nothing about whether such use would have grown more or less without the nondiscrimination provisions. And because the relevant question is a comparison between reality and a hypothetical state of affairs, to require actual proof of reduced output is often to require the impossible—tantamount to saying that the Sherman Act does not apply at all.

In any event, there are features of the credit card market that may tend to limit the usual relationship between price and output. In particular, merchants generally spread the costs of credit card acceptance across all their customers (whatever payment method they may use), while the benefits of card use go only to the cardholders. See, *e.g.*, 88 F. Supp. 3d, at 216; Brief for John M. Connor et al. as *Amici Curiae* 34–35. Thus, higher credit card merchant fees may have only a limited effect on credit-card transaction volume, even as they disrupt the market place by extracting anticompetitive profits.

### 4

### A

For the reasons I have stated, the Second Circuit was wrong to lump together the two different services sold, *at step 1*. But I recognize that the Court of Appeals has not yet considered whether the relationship between the two services might make a difference at steps 2 and 3. That is to say, American Express might wish to argue that the nondiscrimination provisions, while anticompetitive in respect to merchant-related services, nonetheless have an adequate offsetting procompetitive benefit in respect to its shopper-related services. I believe that American Express should have an opportunity to ask the Court of Appeals to consider that matter.

American Express might face an uphill battle. A Sher man Act §1 defendant can rarely, if ever, show that a procompetitive benefit in the market for one product offsets an anticompetitive harm in the market for another. In *United States v. Topco Associates, Inc.*, 405 U. S. 596, 611 (1972), this Court wrote:

"If a decision is to be made to sacrifice competition in one portion of the economy for greater competition in another portion, this . . . is a decision that must be made by Congress and not by private forces or by the courts. Private forces are too keenly aware of their own interests in making such decisions and courts are ill-equipped and ill-situated for such decision making."

American Express, pointing to vertical price-fixing cases like our decision in *Leegin*, argues that comparing competition-related pros and cons is more common than I have just suggested. See 551 U. S., at 889–892. But *Leegin* held only that vertical price fixing is subject to the "rule of reason" instead of being *per se* unlawful; the "rule of reason" still applies to vertical agreements just as it applies to horizontal agreements. See *id.*, at 898–899.

Moreover, the procompetitive justifications for vertical price-fixing agreements are not apparently applicable to the distinct types of restraints at issue in this case. A vertically imposed price-fixing agreement typically involves a manufacturer controlling the terms of sale for its own product. A television set manufacturer, for example, will insist that its dealers not cut prices for the manufacturer's own televisions below a particular level. Why might a manufacturer want its dealers to refrain from price competition in the manufacturer's own products? Perhaps because, for example, the manufacturer wants to encourage the dealers to develop the market for the manufacturer's brand, thereby increasing *interbrand* competition for the same ultimate product, namely a television set. This type of reasoning does not appear to apply to American Express' nondiscrimination provisions, which seek to control the terms on which merchants accept *other brands'* cards, not merely American Express' own.

Regardless, I would not now hold that an agreement such as the one before us can never be justified by procompetitive benefits of some kind. But the Court of Appeals would properly consider procompetitive justifications not at step 1, but at steps 2 and 3 of the "rule of reason" inquiry. American Express would need to show just how this particular anticompetitive merchant-related agreement has procompetitive benefits in the shopper-related market. In doing so, American Express would need to overcome the District Court's factual findings that the agreement had no such effects. See 88 F. Supp. 3d, at 224–238.

### B

The majority charts a different path. Notwithstanding its purported acceptance of the three-step, burden-shifting framework I have described, *ante*, at 9–10, the majority addresses American Express' procompetitive justifications now, at step 1 of the analysis, see *ante*, at 18–20. And in doing so, the majority inexplicably ignores the District Court's factual findings on the subject.

The majority reasons that the challenged nondiscrimination provisions "stem negative externalities in the creditcard market and promote interbrand competition." *Ante*, at 19. The "negative externality" the majority has in mind is this: If one merchant persuades a shopper not to use his American Express card at that merchant's store, that shopper becomes less likely to use his American Express card at other merchants' stores. *Ibid.* The majority worries that this "endangers the viability of the entire [American Express] network," *ibid.*, but if so that is simply a consequence of American Express' merchant fees being higher than a competitive market will support. "The antitrust laws were enacted for 'the protection of *competition*, not *competitors*.'" *Atlantic Richfield Co. v. USA Petroleum Co.*, 495 U. S. 328, 338 (1990). If American Express' merchant fees are so high that merchants successfully induce their customers to use other cards, American Express can remedy that problem by lowering those fees or by spending more on cardholder rewards so that cardholders decline such requests. What it may not do is demand contractual protection from price competition.

In any event, the majority ignores the fact that the District Court, in addition to saying what I have just said, also rejected this argument on independent factual grounds. It explained that American Express "presented no expert testimony, financial analysis, or other direct evidence establishing that without its [nondiscrimination provisions] it will, in fact, be unable to adapt its business to a more competitive market." 88 F. Supp. 3d, at 231. It further explained that the testimony that was provided on the topic "was notably inconsistent," with some of American Express' witnesses saying only that invalidation of the provisions "would require American Express to adapt its current business model." *Ibid.* After an extensive discussion of the record, the District Court found that "American Express possesses the flexibility and expertise necessary to adapt its business model to suit a market in which it is required to compete on both the cardholder and merchant sides of the [credit card] platform." *Id.*, at 231–232. The majority evidently rejects these factual findings, even though no one has challenged them as clearly erroneous.

Similarly, the majority refers to the nondiscrimination provisions as preventing "free riding" on American Express' "investments in rewards" for cardholders. *Ante*, at 19–20; see also *ante*, at 7 (describing steering in terms suggestive of free riding). But as the District Court explained, "[p]lainly . . . investments tied to card use (such as Membership Rewards points, purchase protection, and the like) are not subject to free-riding, since the network does not incur any cost if the cardholder is successfully steered away from using his or her American Express card." 88 F. Supp. 3d, at 237. This, I should think, is an unassailable conclusion: American Express pays rewards to cardholders only for transactions in which cardholders use their American Express cards, so if a steering effort succeeds, no rewards are paid. As for concerns about free riding on American Express' fixed expenses, including its investments in its brand, the District Court acknowledged that free-riding was in theory possible, but explained that American Express "ma[de] no effort to identify the fixed expenses to which its experts referred or to explain how they are subject to free riding." *Ibid.*; see also *id.*, at 238 (American Express' own data showed "that the network's ability to confer a credentialing benefit trails that of its competitors, casting doubt on whether there is in fact any particular benefit associated with accepting [American Express] that is subject to free riding"). The majority does not even acknowledge, much less reject, these factual findings, despite coming to the contrary conclusion.

Finally, the majority reasons that the nondiscrimination provisions "do not prevent Visa, Mastercard, or Discover from competing against [American Express] by offering lower merchant fees or promoting their broader merchant acceptance." *Ante*, at 20. But again, the District Court's factual findings were to the contrary. As I laid out above, the District Court found that the nondiscrimination provisions *in fact did prevent* Discover from pursuing a low merchant-fee business model, by "den[ying] merchants the ability to express a preference for Discover or to employ any other tool by which they might steer share to Discover's lower-priced network." 88 F. Supp. 3d, at 214; see *supra*, at 7. The majority's statements that the nondiscrimination provisions are procompetitive are directly contradicted by this and other factual findings.

\*   \*   \*

For the reasons I have explained, the majority's decision in this case is contrary to basic principles of antitrust law, and it ignores and contradicts the District Court's detailed factual findings, which were based on an extensive trial record. I respectfully dissent.

# APPENDIX 2:

# Brief for the United States as Respondent Supporting Petitioners

No. 16-1454

# In the Supreme Court of the United States

STATE OF OHIO, ET AL., PETITIONERS

*v.*

AMERICAN EXPRESS COMPANY, ET AL.

*ON WRIT OF CERTIORARI*
*TO THE UNITED STATES COURT OF APPEALS FOR*
*THE SECOND CIRCUIT*

**BRIEF FOR THE UNITED STATES**
**AS RESPONDENT SUPPORTING PETITIONERS**

NOEL J. FRANCISCO
*Solicitor General Counsel of Record*

MAKAN DELRAHIM
*Assistant Attorney General*

MALCOLM L. STEWART
*Deputy Solicitor General*

BRIAN H. FLETCHER
*Assistant to the Solicitor General*

WILLIAM J. RINNER
*Counsel to the Assistant*
*Attorney General*

KRISTEN C. LIMARZI

ROBERT B. NICHOLSON

JAMES J. FREDRICKS

CRAIG W. CONRATH

JOHN R. READ

NICKOLAI G. LEVIN

ANDREW J. EWALT
*Attorneys*

*Department of Justice Washington, D.C. 20530-0001*
*SupremeCtBriefs@usdoj.gov (202) 514-2217*

## QUESTION PRESENTED

In this antitrust enforcement action, the United States and a group of States challenged "anti-steering" rules that American Express imposes on the merchants that accept its credit cards. The rules prohibit merchants from encouraging their customers to use other credit cards that charge the merchants lower fees, or even truthfully disclosing to customers the relative cost of different cards. Applying the rule of reason, the District Court held that the anti-steering rules violate Section 1 of the Sherman Act, 15 U.S.C. 1 *et seq.* The court found that the rules stifle price competition among credit card networks, allowing all major networks to raise their merchant fees, blocking low-fee rivals, and inflating retail prices. The question presented is as follows:

Whether the District Court's findings that the anti-steering rules stifle price competition, block low-fee rivals, raise merchant fees, and inflate retail prices were sufficient to establish a prima facie case that the rules unreasonably restrain trade.

# Contents

Opinions below...........................................................................................................122

Jurisdiction ..............................................................................................................122

Statutory provision involved ..................................................................................122

**Statement:**

    **A.** Credit card networks compete for both cardholders and merchants ..................123

    **B.** AmEx strengthens its anti-steering rules in response to price competition from Visa and Mastercard ....................................................................................................124

    **C.** The District Court holds that AmEx's anti-steering rules unreasonably restrain trade...125

    **D.** The court of appeals reverses ........................................................................128

Summary of argument .............................................................................................129

**Argument:**

    The facts found by the District Court establish a prima facie case that the anti-steering rules unreasonably restrain trade ......................................................................131

        **A.** A plaintiff may carry its initial burden in a rule of reason case with direct evidence that a restraint has an actual adverse effect on competition ...................................132

        **B.** The facts found by the District Court establish that the anti-steering rules have severely impaired competition among credit card networks ......................................134

            **1.** The anti-steering rules stifle price competition ...........................................134

            **2.** The anti-steering rules raise merchant fees and inflate retail prices..............135

            **3.** The anti-steering rules block low-fee rivals and suppress the development of innovative payment models ....................................................................139

**C.** The court of appeals' alternative market definition departed from established anti-trust principles and provided no sound basis for reversal in any event .................... 140

    **1.** Services to merchants and services to cardholders do not belong in the same antitrust market because they are not substitutes ....................................... 141

    **2.** The facts found by the District Court established a prima facie case even under the court of appeals' market definition ....................................................... 143

**D.** The additional showings demanded by the court of appeals were not required.....145

    **1.** The United States and the States were not required to negate the anti-steering rules' potential benefits for cardholders in order to establish a prima facie case...........145

    **2.** The United States and the States were not required to calculate AmEx's "two-sided" price in order to establish a prima facie case.................................... 147

**E.** The District Court properly considered and rejected, at the second step of the burden shifting inquiry, AmEx's arguments about the benefits of the anti-steering rules for cardholders ............................................................................................149

Conclusion    .................................................................................................151

# Table of Authorities

## Cases

*American Needle, Inc.* v. *NFL*, 560 U.S. 183 (2010)..................................................133

*Board of Trade of Chicago* v. *United States*, 246 U.S. 231 (1918)................................133

*Broadcast Music, Inc.* v. *CBS, Inc.*, 441 U.S. 1 (1979)............................................140

*Brown Shoe Co.* v. *United States*, 370 U.S. 294 (1962)...........................................142

*California Dental Ass'n* v. *FTC*, 526 U.S. 756 (1999)....................................126, 129, 133, 145

*Catalano, Inc.* v. *Target Sales, Inc.*, 446 U.S. 643 (1980) ......................................144

*Clamp-All Corp.* v. *Cast Iron Soil Pipe Inst.*, 851 F.2d 478 (1st Cir. 1988), cert. denied, 488 U.S. 1007   (1989)..................................................................146

*Continental T.V., Inc.* v. *GTE Sylvania, Inc.*, 433 U.S. 36 (1977) ...............................135

*Eastman Kodak Co.* v. *Image Technical Servs., Inc.*, 504 U.S. 451 (1992).............133, 141, 142

*FTC* v. *Actavis, Inc.*, 133 S. Ct. 2223 (2013)..............................................133, 145

*FTC* v. *Indiana Fed'n of Dentists*, 476 U.S. 447 (1986)....................129, 130, 133, 134, 144

*Geneva Pharms. Tech. Corp.* v. *Barr Labs. Inc.*, 386 F.3d 485 (2d Cir. 2004) ......................147

*K.M.B. Warehouse Distribs., Inc.* v. *Walker Mfg. Co.*, 61 F.3d 123 (2d Cir. 1995)...................146

*Leegin Creative Leather Prods., Inc.* v. *PSKS, Inc.*, 551 U.S. 877 (2007)......................... passim

*Major League Baseball Props., Inc.* v. *Salvino, Inc.*, 542 F.3d 290 (2d Cir. 2008) ...............150

*National Soc'y of Prof'l Eng'rs* v. *United States*, 435 U.S. 679 (1978)........................128, 133

*NCAA* v. *Board of Regents*, 468 U.S. 85 (1984) .........................................133, 144, 148, 150

*North Carolina State Bd. of Dental Exam'rs* v. *FTC*, 135 S. Ct. 1101 (2015) .......................132

*Northern Pac. Ry. Co.* v. *United States*, 356 U.S. 1 (1958) ......................................132

*NYNEX Corp.* v. *Discon, Inc.*, 525 U.S. 128 (1998) ......................................146, 147, 148

*O'Bannon* v. *NCAA*, 802 F.3d 1049 (9th Cir. 2015), cert. denied, 137 S. Ct. 277 (2016) ...144, 148, 150

*Reiter* v. *Sonotone Corp.*, 442 U.S. 330 (1979) .................................................146

*Rothery Storage & Van Co.* v. *Atlas Van Lines, Inc.*, 792 F.2d 210 (D.C. Cir. 1986), cert. denied, 479 U.S. 1033 (1987) ...........................................................141, 150

*Schering-Plough Corp.* v. *FTC*, 402 F.3d 1056 (11th Cir. 2005), cert. denied, 548 U.S. 919 (2006)..................................................................150

*Smith* v. *United States*, 568 U.S. 106 (2013) ...................................................134

*State Oil Co.* v. *Khan*, 522 U.S. 3 (1997)..................................................135, 140

*Sullivan* v. *NFL*, 34 F.3d 1091 (1st Cir. 1994), cert. denied, 513 U.S. 1190 (1995) ............150

*Times-Picayune Publ'g Co.* v. *United States*, 345 U.S. 594 (1953)..............................141, 142

*Texaco, Inc.* v. *Dagher*, 547 U.S. 1 (2006) ........................................................................150

*Todd* v. *Exxon Corp.*, 275 F.3d 191 (2d Cir. 2001) ............................................................133

*Toys "R" Us, Inc.* v. *FTC*, 221 F.3d 928 (7th Cir. 2000) ......................................................133

*United States* v. *Continental Can Co.*, 378 U.S. 441 (1964)...............................................141

*United States* v. *E. I. du Pont de Nemours & Co.*, 351 U.S. 377 (1956)...............................126

*United States* v. *E. I. du Pont de Nemours & Co.*, 353 U.S. 586 (1957)...............................141

*United States* v. *Grinnell Corp.*, 384 U.S. 563 (1966) .........................................................143

*United States* v. *Socony-Vacuum Oil Co.*, 310 U.S. 150 (1940)...............................140, 144

*Verizon Commc'ns Inc.* v. *Law Offices of Curtis V. Trinko, LLP*, 540 U.S. 398 (2004) ............150

**Statutes:**

Clayton Act, 15 U.S.C. 18 ...............................................................................................141

Sherman Act, 15 U.S.C. 1 *et seq.*:

15 U.S.C. 1................................................................................................ *passim*

15 U.S.C. 2................................................................................................................141

**Miscellaneous:**

Philip E. Areeda & Herbert Hovenkamp, *Antitrust Law: An Analysis of Antitrust Principles and Their Application*:

Vol. 2B (4th ed. 2014) ..............................................................................................141

Vol. 7 (4th ed. 2017) ................................................................................................133

(Supp. 2017).............................................................................. 134, 142, 145, 146

Robert H. Bork, *The Antitrust Paradox: A Policy at War with Itself* (1978)............................146

Kate Collyer et al., *Measuring Market Power in Multi-Sided Markets*, Antitrust Chronicle (Sept. 2017), https://www.competitionpolicyinternational.com/wp-content/uploads/2017/09/CPI-Collyer-Mullan-Timan.pdf ...................................................................................................149

Robert H. Jackson, *Should the Antitrust Laws Be Revised?*, 71 U.S. L. Rev. 575 (1937) .........146

Jean-Charles Rochet & Jean Tirole, *Two-Sided Markets: A Progress Report*, 37 RAND J. Econ. 645 (2006) ......................................................................................................................149

# In the Supreme Court of the United States

## No. 16-1454

### STATE OF OHIO, ET AL., PETITIONERS

v.

### AMERICAN EXPRESS COMPANY, ET AL.

*ON WRIT OF CERTIORARI*
*TO THE UNITED STATES COURT OF APPEALS FOR THE SECOND CIRCUIT*

## BRIEF FOR THE UNITED STATES AS RESPONDENT
## SUPPORTING PETITIONERS

### OPINIONS BELOW

The opinion of the court of appeals (Pet. App. 1a-58a) is reported at 838 F.3d 179. The decision of the District Court (Pet. App. 63a-259a) is report ed at 88 F. Supp. 3d 143.

### JURISDICTION

The judgment of the court of appeals was entered on September 26, 2016. A petition for rehearing was denied on January 5, 2017 (Pet. App. 324a-326a). On March 24, 2017, Justice Ginsburg extended the time within which to file a petition for a writ of certiorari to and including May 5, 2017. On April 24, 2017, Justice Ginsburg further extended the time within which to file a petition to and including June 2, 2017, and the petition was filed on that date. The petition was granted on October 16, 2017. The jurisdiction of this Court rests on 28 U.S.C. 1254(1).

### STATUTORY PROVISION INVOLVED

Section 1 of the Sherman Act, 15 U.S.C. 1 *et seq.*, provides in relevant part: "Every contract, combination in the form of trust or otherwise, or conspiracy, in restraint of trade or commerce among the several States, or with foreign nations, is declared to be illegal."

### STATEMENT

This case is an antitrust enforcement action brought by the United States and a group of States against American Express (AmEx). The suit challenges "anti-steering" rules that AmEx imposes on merchants that accept its credit cards. Those rules bar merchants from encouraging their customers to use other credit cards that charge the merchants lower fees—by, for example, offering a discount, stating a preference, or even truthfully disclosing the relative costs of different cards. The District Court found that the anti-steering rules have stifled price competition among the major credit card networks, blocked low-fee rivals, raised merchant fees, and inflated retail prices. The question presented is whether those undisturbed factual findings suffice to make out a prima facie case that the anti-steering rules unreasonably restrain trade.

## A. Credit Card Networks Compete For Both Cardholders And Merchants

1. AmEx and other credit card networks provide different bundles of services to "two distinct sets of consumers," cardholders and merchants. Pet. App. 69a. Cardholders receive the convenience of making purchases without cash and deferring payment until their monthly bills are due. *Id.* at 75a. They may also receive other benefits, such as access to a line of credit, fraud protection, and frequent-flier miles or other rewards based on their spending. *Id.* at 74a-75a, 89a-90a. In exchange, cardholders may pay annual or other fees, as well as interest on any balance that is carried past their monthly billing cycle. *Ibid.*

Merchants that accept AmEx cards receive a guarantee of payment from AmEx, as well as related payment processing services. Pet. App. 82a-84a. In exchange, merchants pay AmEx a "merchant discount fee" based on a percentage of each transaction. *Id.* at 82a-83a. For example, a drugstore that accepts an AmEx card for a $100 purchase might receive only $97 from AmEx—the purchase price less a three percent fee.

AmEx operates a vertically integrated system and usually provides services directly to both cardholders and merchants. Pet. App. 83a-84a. Visa and Mastercard, in contrast, deal with cardholders and merchants through third-party banks known as issuers and acquirers. *Id.* at 81a-83a. Issuers like Citibank, Chase, and Capital One issue cards and provide services to card-holders; acquirers serve merchants. *Id.* at 81a-84a. Visa and Mastercard facilitate the interaction between issuers and acquirers and set the rules for the system. Ibid. In that role, they "establish nearly all elements of the price charged to merchants" by Visa and Mastercard affiliated acquirers. *Id.* at 82a.[1]

The credit card business involves a "two-sided" platform, in which the value of a network to customers on each side depends in part on the number of customers on the other. Pet. App. 77a (citation omitted). A card "is more valuable to the cardholder when there are more merchants willing to accept that card." *Id.* at 79a. Conversely, "the value to merchants of accepting [a network's] cards increases with the number of cards on that network in circulation." *Ibid.* Other familiar businesses with the same feature include "[n]ewspapers and other advertising-based forms of media," which "sell distinct products and services to subscribers and advertisers," as well as "a seemingly endless array of Internet companies like eBay, OpenTable, eHarmony, and

---

1 AmEx has begun to rely on third-party issuers and acquirers, but those entities still account for only a small fraction of its business. Pet. App. 84a-86a. The fourth major network, Discover, has a hybrid system. It issues cards directly to cardholders, but deals with merchants through acquirers. *Id.* at 86a.

Groupon," all of which serve to "facilitate some form of value-generating interaction between distinct sets of consumers." *Id.* at 77a-78a.

2. Credit cards "have become a principal means by which consumers in the United States purchase goods and services." Pet. App. 73a-74a. In 2013, the four major networks charged merchants more than $50 billion in fees to process nearly $2.4 trillion in transactions. *Id.* at 74a. AmEx was the second-largest network, capturing 26.4% of that volume. *Id.* at 151a. The rest was divided among Visa (45%), Mastercard (23.3%), and Discover (5.3%). *Ibid.*

Because of AmEx's business model, including its direct merchant relationships and its "premium pricing," its cards are accepted by fewer merchants than are the cards of its competitors. Pet. App. 186a. Roughly 6.4 million merchant locations accept AmEx cards, in comparison to more than 9 million locations for Visa, Mastercard, and Discover. *Id.* at 184a-185a. But AmEx cards are accepted by virtually all of the Nation's largest merchants, and the merchants that accept AmEx cards account for more than 90% of credit card transactions by dollar volume. *Id.* at 188a, 224a & n.48; C.A. App. 1457-1458, 1475, 1728.

## B. AmEx Strengthens Its Anti-Steering Rules In Response To Price Competition From Visa And Mastercard

AmEx has long charged merchants higher fees than its competitors. Pet. App. 174a-177a. In the 1990s, Visa launched a marketing campaign that highlighted AmEx's "significantly higher" fees and urged merchants to save money by encouraging their customers to pay with Visa cards instead. *Id.* at 91a-92a. Visa suggested that merchants could use " 'inoffensive, yet effective' " methods to steer their customers to use lower-fee Visa cards—by, for example, displaying "We Prefer Visa" signs. *Id.* at 199a (citation omitted); see *id.* at 92a. Visa also distributed a "profit improvement calculator" that allowed merchants to determine exactly how much they would save by shifting transactions from AmEx to Visa. J.A. 101-104, 207-210. Mastercard engaged in a similar campaign. Pet. App. 92a. Those efforts "were remarkably effective" and caused a substantial shift in transaction volume from AmEx to Visa and Mastercard. *Ibid.*

AmEx considered responding to this price competition by "reducing [its] discount rate" or "better communicat[ing] to merchants the value they received for the premium price charged." Pet. App. 200a. But rather than relying on those strategies, AmEx chose to "stifle any further steering or preference campaigns" by strengthening the anti-steering rules in its merchant contracts. *Ibid.*; see id. at 93a. As modified, AmEx's anti-steering rules prohibit merchants from offering customers discounts or other incentives to use other cards, expressing a preference for another card, or even truthfully disclosing the relative costs of different cards. *Id.* at 95a-96a.

Under the anti-steering rules, a merchant may not, for example:

- Offer "free shipping," "free checked bags," or "any other monetary incentive for using [a] Discover card."

- Offer a "designated checkout lane," "priority boarding," or "any other non-monetary incentive [for] using a Mastercard."

- Post a sign disclosing "the merchant's actual cost of accepting each network's cards."

- Inform customers that its "retail prices might be lower if it were better able to control its credit card costs."

- Respond to "a customer's inquiry into its credit card costs."

Pet. App. 100a-101a. The anti-steering rules prohibit merchants from taking any of these actions "even when American Express is not mentioned," and even when the affected customer does not have an AmEx card. *Id.* at 101a-102a.[2]

The "vast majority" of merchants are bound by AmEx's "standard card acceptance agreement," including its standard anti-steering rules. Pet. App. 94a-95a. Some large merchants—fewer than 1000—have negotiated contracts that depart from the standard agreement. *Id.* at 95a. Even within that group, the anti-steering rules "are only rarely subject to negotiation." *Id.* at 97a. Although "many" large merchants have asked AmEx to remove the rules from their contracts, AmEx has granted only a few, limited exceptions, such as temporary promotions and "co-brand[ed]" cards like the Southwest Airlines Visa card. *Id.* at 97a-98a. AmEx "actively monitors" compliance with the anti-steering rules and "vigorously enforces" the rules to prevent merchants from encouraging their consumers to use less expensive cards. *Id.* at 102a-103a; see *id.* at 104a & n.6.

### C. The District Court Holds That AmEx's Anti-Steering Rules Unreasonably Restrain Trade

In 2010, the United States and a group of States sued AmEx, as well as Visa and Mastercard, which had adopted their own anti-steering rules. The suit alleged that the anti-steering rules unreasonably restrained trade, in violation of Section 1 of the Sherman Act, 15 U.S.C. 1 *et seq.* Pet. App. 21a-22a. Visa and Mastercard entered into consent judgments and rescinded their anti-steering rules. *Id.* at 22a. AmEx proceeded to trial.

The District Court held a seven-week bench trial, which included testimony from four experts, "nearly twenty merchant witnesses representing a selection of the nation's largest retailers, airlines, and hotels," and executives from AmEx, Visa,

---

2   The United States and the States have not challenged provisions of the anti-steering rules that prohibit merchants from imposing special fees on customers paying with AmEx cards, mischaracterizing AmEx, or otherwise harming AmEx's brand. Pet. App. 96a-97a.

Mastercard, and Discover. Pet. App. 72a. The trial record included nearly 7000 transcript pages and more than 1000 exhibits. *Ibid.* Based on that record, the court held that the anti-steering rules violate Section 1 because they have "short-circuit[ed] the ordinary price-setting mechanism" in the credit card industry, causing "an absence of price competition" and "dramatically" higher merchant fees. *Id.* at 71a; see *id.* at 63a-259a.

1. The District Court analyzed the anti-steering rules under the rule of reason, "the most searching form of antitrust analysis." Pet. App. 107a. The rule of reason requires the factfinder to "weigh all of the circumstances of a case" in order to determine "whether the challenged agreement is one that promotes competition or one that suppresses competition." *Id.* at 107a-108a (brackets and citation omitted). Courts applying the rule of reason follow "a three-step burden shifting framework." *Id.* at 108a. The plaintiff bears the initial burden to show that the challenged restraint is "*prima facie* anticompetitive." *California Dental Ass'n* v. *FTC*, 526 U.S. 756, 771 (1999). If the plaintiff makes that showing, the burden shifts to the defendant to establish a "procompetitive justification." *Ibid.*; see Pet. App. 110a. If the defendant does so, the burden shifts back to the plaintiff to show that the " 'legitimate competitive benefits' proffered by [the defendant] could have been achieved through less restrictive means." Pet. App. 110a (citation omitted).

2. The District Court began its rule of reason analysis by defining the relevant market. Pet. App. 111a-148a. An antitrust market consists of products "that have reasonable interchangeability for the purposes for which they are produced," such that customers would switch from one product to another if faced with a price increase. *United States* v. *E. I. du Pont de Nemours & Co.*, 351 U.S. 377, 404 (1956). Here, the court concluded that the market restrained by the anti-steering rules is the market for "general purpose credit and charge card network services" of the type that AmEx provides to merchants. Pet. App. 112a-113a.

The District Court rejected AmEx's contention that the market must be defined to include services to cardholders as well as merchants. Pet. App. 114a-122a. The court recognized that the credit card industry is "two-sided," and that networks compete for both merchants and cardholders. *Id.* at 121a-122a; see *id.* at 77a-78a. The court explained, however, that the two markets are "distinct" because they involve "different sets of rivals and the sale of separate, though interrelated, products and services to separate groups of customers." *Id.* at 119a.

Although the District Court rejected AmEx's proposed market definition, it noted that the "two-sided" nature of a credit card platform is relevant to the Section 1 analysis because "the antitrust significance of a restraint that nominally affects conduct on only one side of [a credit card] platform cannot be assessed without considering its impact on the other side of the platform." Pet. App. 121a-122a. The court thus recognized that standard antitrust principles "must be applied in a manner that carefully accounts for the competitive realities in multi-sided platforms." *Id.* at 122a.

3. The plaintiff in a rule of reason case may establish a prima facie case either indirectly or directly. Pet. App. 108a-109a. Under the indirect method, the court infers the existence of anticompetitive effects from proof that the defendant has "sufficient market power to cause an adverse effect on competition" and the existence of "grounds to believe that the defendant's behavior will harm competition marketwide." *Id.* at 109a (citations omitted). The direct method requires proof of an actual "adverse effect on competition." *Id.* at 108a (citation omitted). The District Court held that the United States and the States had established a prima facie case under both methods. *Id.* at 148a-228a.

a. The District Court first held that AmEx has market power. Pet. App. 148a-191a. The court explained that AmEx captures 26.4% of a concentrated market with significant barriers to entry. *Id.* at 150a-156a. The court noted that AmEx's market power is magnified by "cardholder insistence," the term AmEx uses to describe the fact that many merchants cannot realistically refuse to accept AmEx cards because too many of their customers would shop elsewhere if they did. *Id.* at 156a-165a. The court also relied on AmEx's demonstrated ability to significantly increase its fees without causing merchants to stop accepting its cards. *Id.* at 165a-180a. The court further found that the anti-steering rules were likely to harm competition market-wide. *Id.* at 193a-194a.

b. The District Court separately held that the anti-steering rules have caused "actual, sustained adverse effects on competition." Pet. App. 193a (citation omitted); see *id.* at 191a-228a. The court found that "[p]rice competition is a critical avenue of horizontal interbrand competition, and yet it is frustrated to the point of near irrelevance" by the anti-steering rules. *Id.* at 195a. The court explained that, once a merchant identifies the set of networks from which it will accept cards, the cardholder decides which of those cards to use for a particular transaction. *Id.* at 196a. By barring merchants from encouraging cardholders to use lower-fee cards, the rules impede merchants' ability to control their consumption of a network's services in response to changes in the network's price. *Ibid.* As a result, "there is virtually no check on the networks' incentive or ability to charge higher prices to merchants, so long as the network's pricing is below the level at which a rational merchant would drop acceptance entirely." *Id.* at 197a.

The District Court also found that the anti-steering rules "render it nearly impossible" for a new network to enter the market "by offering merchants a low-cost alternative to the existing networks." Pet. App. 203a. The court observed that Discover had tried to pursue that strategy in the 1990s and had been thwarted by the anti-steering rules, which "denied merchants the ability to * * * steer share to Discover's lower-priced network." *Id.* at 205a. Discover therefore had "abandoned its low-price business model" and had "radically increase[d]" its merchant fees to align with those charged by Visa and Mastercard. *Id.* at 206a, 210a.

The District Court further found that, by stifling price competition, the anti-steering rules "allowed all four networks to raise their [merchant] fees more easily and more profitably." Pet. App. 207a. For example, the rules were "integral" to AmEx's ability to increase its fees repeatedly between 2005 and 2010 in order to restore its premium over its rivals' elevated rates. *Id.* at 208a-209a. Starting from fees "already at or above the competitive level," AmEx had imposed at least twenty "Value Recapture" price increases on more than a million merchants, "without any meaningful merchant attrition." *Id.* at 150a, 167a.

The District Court found that the higher merchant fees made possible by the anti-steering rules had "resulted in increased prices for consumers" because merchants "pass most, if not all, of their additional costs along to their consumers in the form of higher retail prices." Pet. App. 210a-211a. Those higher prices "affect not only those customers who use American Express cards, but also shoppers who instead prefer to pay using a lower-rewards [credit] card, debit card, check, or cash." *Id.* at 211a.

4. Having concluded that the United States and the States had established a prima facie case under both the indirect and direct methods, the District Court shifted the burden to AmEx to show that its anti-steering rules had redeeming procompetitive effects. Pet. App. 228a. The court held that AmEx had failed to make that showing. *Id.* at 228a-258a. *Inter alia*, the court rejected AmEx's contention that the rules are justified because they protect its "differentiated business model," which relies on charging higher merchant fees to offer more generous cardholder rewards. *Id.* at 229a; see id. at 229a-236a. The court held that, to find the anti-steering rules reasonable "because they shield [AmEx's] preferred business strategy from a legitimate form of interbrand competition, especially competition on the basis of price, would amount to 'nothing less than a frontal assault on the basic policy of the Sherman Act.' " *Id.* at 235a (quoting *National Soc'y of Prof 'l Eng'rs v. United States*, 435 U.S. 679, 695 (1978)).

## D. The Court Of Appeals Reverses

The court of appeals reversed and directed entry of judgment for AmEx. Pet. App. 1a-58a. The court did not overturn any of the District Court's factual findings as clearly erroneous. Instead, it held that those findings were legally insufficient to establish a prima facie case that the anti-steering rules unreasonably restrain trade.

1. The court of appeals first held that the District Court had "erred in excluding the market for cardholders from its relevant market definition." Pet. App. 32a; see *id.* at 31a-40a. The court emphasized the "interdependence" of credit card networks' competition for merchants and their competition for cardholders, and it stated that separating those two avenues of competition into different antitrust markets could allow "legitimate competitive activities in the market for [cardholders] to be penalized no matter how output-expanding such activities would be." *Id.* at 35a.

2. The court of appeals next held that the District Court had erred in holding that AmEx has market power. Pet. App. 40a-48a. It concluded that the District Court should not have focused on increases in AmEx's merchant fees because AmEx uses a portion of those fees to provide cardholder rewards (which are functionally

equivalent to reduced prices for cardholders). *Id.* at 43a-44a. The court stated that the District Court should have calculated AmEx's "two-sided price"—that is, the aggregate amount charged to both merchants and card-holders. *Id.* at 44a (citation omitted). The court also held that the District Court had erred in relying on "cardholder insistence" as evidence of market power. *Id.* at 45a-48a. The court reasoned that, "so long as AmEx's market share is derived from cardholder satisfaction, there is no reason to intervene." *Id.* at 48a.

3. Finally, the court of appeals overturned the District Court's holding that the United States and the States had made a prima facie case that the anti-steering rules have an actual adverse effect on competition. Pet. App. 49a-53a. The court did not question the District Court's findings that the anti-steering rules stifle price competition and thereby cause merchants (and their customers) to pay more. The court held, however, that those findings were insufficient to establish a prima facie case because the District Court had "failed to consider the two-sided net price accounting for the effects of the [anti-steering rules] on both merchants and card-holders." *Id.* at 49a. To prove anticompetitive effects using higher prices, the court stated, the United States and the States were required to provide at minimum a "reliable measure of American Express's two-sided price that appropriately account[ed] for the value or cost of the rewards paid to cardholders." *Id.* at 53a (citation omitted). The court also stated that the United States and the States bore the "initial burden" to show that the anti-steering rules "made *all* AmEx consumers on both sides of the platform—*i.e.,* both merchants and cardholders—worse off overall." *Id.* at 51a.

## SUMMARY OF ARGUMENT

The District Court found that AmEx's anti-steering rules have stifled price competition among credit card networks, blocked low-fee rivals, raised fees for millions of merchants, and inflated the retail prices paid by hundreds of millions of consumers. Those undisturbed findings established a prima facie case that the anti-steering rules unreasonably restrain trade.

A. The plaintiff in a rule of reason case bears the initial burden to show that the challenged restraint is "*prima facie* anticompetitive." *California Dental Ass'n* v. *FTC*, 526 U.S. 756, 771 (1999). If it does so, "the burden of procompetitive justification" shifts to the defendant. *Ibid.* A plaintiff may establish a prima facie case with direct evidence that the restraint has "actual detrimental effects" on competition. *FTC* v. *Indiana Fed'n of Dentists*, 476 U.S. 447, 460 (1986) (*Indiana Dentists*).

B. The United States and the States carried their initial burden by introducing overwhelming proof that the anti-steering rules impose "actual, sustained adverse effects on competition." *Indiana Dentists*, 476 U.S. at 461. As the District Court found, steering is an essential prerequisite for meaningful competition on merchant fees because it is the way merchants control their consumption of—and expenditures on—a network's services. The purpose and effect of the anti-steering rules is to prevent merchants from altering their consumption of AmEx's services in response to changes in price by AmEx *or by other networks*—and thus to suppress interbrand price competition between AmEx and its rivals. Indeed the District Court found that the anti-steering rules "create a competitive environment in which there is virtually no check on the networks' incentive or ability to charge higher prices to merchants, so long as the network's pricing is below the level at which a rational merchant would drop acceptance entirely." Pet. App. 197a.

The District Court thus found that the rules have "allowed all four networks to raise their swipe fees more easily and more profitably," Pet. App. 207a, leading to higher merchant fees—and, ultimately, to higher retail prices for all consumers. The court also found that the anti-steering rules make it "nearly impossible" for a new firm to enter the concentrated network-services market by offering merchants a low-cost alternative—a point that was vividly illustrated by the failure of Discover's low-cost strategy in the late 1990s. *Id.* at 203a.

C. The court of appeals did not purport to overturn any of those factual findings as clearly erroneous. Nonetheless, it held that the District Court had fatally erred by defining the relevant market to include only services to merchants, not services to cardholders. That is incorrect for two reasons.

First, this Court has repeatedly instructed that an antitrust market should be defined to include only products that are reasonable substitutes for each other. The court of appeals acknowledged that standard, but it never explained how the services that AmEx provides to merchants are reasonably interchangeable with the services it provides to cardholders. In fact, they are not. Those two sets of services are undoubtedly related, and both are used when an AmEx cardholder makes a purchase from an AmEx-accepting merchant. But the two bundles of services are not substitutes in any sense.

Second, and in any event, the District Court's findings that the anti-steering rules stifle price competition, inflate merchant fees, and block low-fee rivals were sufficient to establish a prima facie case even under the court of appeals' definition of the market. Indeed, when a court finds that a restraint has had "actual, sustained adverse effects on competition," "specific findings * * * concerning the definition of the market" are unnecessary. *Indiana Dentists*, 476 U.S. at 460-461. This Court thus need not resolve the market-definition question in order to hold that the United States and the States carried their initial burden.

D. The court of appeals deemed the District Court's findings legally insufficient to establish even a prima facie case because—in the court of appeals' view—the District Court did not adequately account for the anti-steering rules' purported benefits to AmEx cardholders. At times, the court appeared to fault the United States and the States for failing to identify and negate *all* possible benefits of the anti-steering rules at the first step of the burden-shifting framework. To treat such a showing as an essential element of a Section 1 plaintiff's prima facie case would seriously distort the applicable burden shifting framework. It is the defendant's burden to establish a challenged restraint's procompetitive benefits, not the plaintiff's initial burden to anticipate and refute them.

At other times, the court of appeals appeared to hold that the United States and the States were required to provide a precise calculation of AmEx's "two-sided" price, taking into account both its merchant fees and its cardholder rewards. That is incorrect for at least three reasons. First, restraints that prevent market forces from determining pricing in a two-sided business reflect a serious distortion of the competitive process even if the *sum* of the prices on both sides of the business does not increase. Second, and in any event, the District Court found that the anti-steering rules *did* allow AmEx to increase its two-sided, net price. Under the circumstances, a precise calculation of that price—something that AmEx itself was not able to provide—was not necessary. Third, the court of appeals erred in focusing exclusively on *AmEx's* pricing. The District Court found that the anti-steering rules have allowed *all* networks to charge higher merchant fees and blocked low-fee rivals. Restraints that enable such unfettered price increases would properly be deemed prima facie anticompetitive even if (counterfactually) they had not increased *AmEx's* two-sided price.

E. The court of appeals' approach to this case appears to have been driven in part by its recognition that antitrust analysis of the anti-steering rules should take account of the "two-sided" nature of AmEx's platform. The court's concern about the interdependence of the two sides of AmEx's platform was appropriate. But the court erred in requiring the United States and the States to negate AmEx's claim that the anti-steering rules have procompetitive benefits in the market for cardholders at the first (*i.e.*, prima facie case) step of the rule of reason analysis. Instead, AmEx's asserted procompetitive justifications are properly considered (as the District Court considered them) at the second step of the burden-shifting inquiry. This Court should thus vacate the judgment below, which held that the United States and the States failed to establish a prima facie case. On remand, the court of appeals can consider any challenges that AmEx has properly preserved to the District Court's holding that AmEx had failed to establish sufficient procompetitive justifications for the anti-steering rules.

## ARGUMENT

## THE FACTS FOUND BY THE DISTRICT COURT ESTABLISH A PRIMA FACIE CASE THAT THE ANTI-STEERING RULES UNREASONABLY RESTRAIN TRADE

The District Court found that AmEx's anti-steering rules have stifled price competition among the major credit card networks, blocked low-fee rivals, raised fees for millions of merchants, and inflated the retail prices paid by hundreds of millions of consumers. Those findings were based on an unusually robust evidentiary record, and the court of appeals did not purport to overturn any of them as clearly erroneous. The question presented in this Court is whether the District Court's undisturbed factual findings established a prima facie case that the anti-steering rules unreasonably restrain trade.

The answer to that question is yes. This Court has instructed time and again that the central concern of the antitrust laws is the preservation of interbrand price competition. Restraints that stifle that competition and disrupt the free market's price-setting mechanism are properly deemed (at least) prima facie anticompetitive— especially where, as here, they have demonstrably inflated prices and blocked low-priced rivals.

The court of appeals believed that AmEx's use of a portion of its inflated fees to fund rewards for its card- holders justifies its suppression of interbrand competition on merchant fees. That is not so. AmEx is free to pursue a strategy that relies on charging high merchant fees to fund especially generous cardholder rewards. Under the Sherman Act, however, AmEx is not entitled to protect its preferred business model through restraints that effectively force the *entire industry* to forgo competition on merchant fees in favor of competition on cardholder rewards.

In any event, the court of appeals erred by requiring the United States and the States to prove, as an element of their prima facie case, that the harms to competition in the network-services market caused by AmEx's anti-steering rules outweigh any benefits to cardholders that those rules may produce. The court was correct to recognize that the two-sided nature of the credit card business affects the appropriate rule of reason analysis, and that benefits to cardholders should be considered in determining whether the anti-steering rules are lawful. In light of the abundant evidence that the rules harmed competition in the network-services market, however, the court of appeals should have affirmed the District Court's holding that the United States and the States had established a prima facie case. This Court should vacate the Second Circuit's contrary holding, and should remand the case to allow the court of appeals to consider, at the second step of the three-step framework, any challenges that AmEx has properly preserved to the District Court's holding that it failed to establish sufficient procompetitive justifications for the anti-steering rules.

## A. A Plaintiff May Carry Its Initial Burden In A Rule of reason Case With Direct Evidence That A Restraint Has An Actual Adverse Effect On Competition

1. "Federal antitrust law is a central safeguard for the Nation's free market structures." *North Carolina State Bd. of Dental Exam'rs* v. *FTC*, 135 S. Ct. 1101, 1109 (2015). "The Sherman Act was designed to be a comprehensive charter of economic liberty aimed at preserving free and unfettered competition as the rule of trade." *Northern Pac. Ry.* v. *United States*, 356 U.S. 1, 4 (1958). "It rests on the premise that the unrestrained interaction of competitive forces will yield the best allocation of our economic resources, the lowest prices, the highest quality and the greatest material progress." *Ibid*.

Section 1 of the Sherman Act implements that fundamental policy by prohibiting unreasonable restraints of trade. *Leegin Creative Leather Prods., Inc.* v. *PSKS, Inc.*, 551 U.S. 877, 885 (2007) (*Leegin*). Some restraints, such as "horizontal agreements among competitors to fix prices," are deemed *per se* unreasonable because of their " 'manifestly anticompetitive' " character. *Id.* at 886 (citation omitted). Most restraints are analyzed under "[t]he rule of reason," which is "the accepted standard for testing whether a practice restrains trade in violation of [Section] 1." *Id.* at 885.

The "classic formulation" of the rule of reason, *American Needle, Inc.* v. *NFL*, 560 U.S. 183, 203 n.10 (2010), was articulated by Justice Brandeis nearly a century ago: "The true test of legality is whether the restraint imposed is such as merely regulates and perhaps thereby promotes competition or whether it is such as may suppress or even destroy competition." *Board of Trade of Chicago* v. *United States*, 246 U.S. 231, 238 (1918). The trier of fact ordinarily must consider all relevant circumstances, including "the facts peculiar to the business to which the restraint is applied; its condition before and after the restraint was imposed; [and] the nature of the restraint and its effect." *Ibid.*; see *Leegin*, 551 U.S. at 885-886. In analyzing those circumstances, however, the "inquiry is confined to a consideration of [the restraint's] impact on competitive conditions." *National Soc'y of Prof'l Eng'rs* v. *United States*, 435 U.S. 679, 690 (1978). "[T]he criterion to be used in judging the validity of a restraint on trade is its impact *on competition.*" *NCAA* v. *Board of Regents*, 468 U.S. 85, 104 (1984) (emphasis added).

2. The plaintiff in a rule of reason case bears the initial burden to show that the challenged restraint is *"prima facie* anticompetitive." *California Dental Ass'n* v. *FTC*, 526 U.S. 756, 771 (1999); see 7 Philip E. Areeda & Herbert Hovenkamp, *Antitrust Law: An Analysis of Antitrust Principles and Their Application* ¶ 1502, at 398-399 (4th ed. 2017) (Areeda & Hovenkamp). A plain- tiff can make that showing indirectly, by establishing that the defendant has "[m]arket power"—that is, "the power 'to force a purchaser to do something that he would not do in a competitive market.' " *Eastman Kodak Co.* v. *Image Technical Servs., Inc.*, 504 U.S. 451, 464 (1992) (Kodak) (citation omitted). Market power is typically inferred from the defendant's market share and other relevant market conditions. *Ibid.*

Alternatively, a plaintiff may discharge its initial burden with *direct* evidence of the challenged restraint's anticompetitive effects. "[T]he purpose of the inquir[y] into * * * market power is to determine whether an arrangement has the potential for genuine adverse effects on competition." *FTC* v. *Indiana Fed'n of Dentists*, 476 U.S. 447, 460 (1986). Accordingly, " 'proof of *actual* detrimental effects' * * * can obviate the need for an inquiry into market power, which is but a 'surrogate for detrimental effects.' " *Id.* at 460-461 (citation omitted).[3]

A prima facie showing that the challenged restraint adversely affects competition "place[s] the burden of procompetitive justification on [the defendant]." *California Dental*, 526 U.S. at 771; accord *FTC* v. *Actavis, Inc.*, 133 S. Ct. 2223, 2236 (2013). That allocation follows the familiar rule that, " 'where the facts with regard

---

3 Indeed, proof "that a defendant's conduct exerted an actual adverse effect on competition * * * arguably is more direct evidence of market power than calculations of elusive market share figures." *Todd* v. *Exxon Corp.*, 275 F.3d 191, 206 (2d Cir. 2001) (Sotomayor, J.); see, *e.g.*, Kodak, 504 U.S. at 477; *Toys "R" Us, Inc.* v. *FTC*, 221 F.3d 928, 937 (7th Cir. 2000).

to an issue lie peculiarly in the knowledge of a party,' that party is best situated to bear the burden of proof." *Smith* v. *United States*, 568 U.S. 106, 112 (2013) (citation omitted). "The defendant, being the author of the restraints, is in a better position to explain why they are profitable and in consumers' best interests." Areeda & Hovenkamp ¶ 1505, at 171 (Supp. 2017).

If the defendant carries its burden, the plaintiff may prevail if it establishes that the restraint's objective "can be achieved by a substantially less restrictive alternative." 7 Areeda & Hovenkamp ¶ 1502, at 398-399. If the plaintiff fails to make that showing, the court must determine whether "the challenged behavior is, on balance, unreasonable." *Id.* at 399.

## B. The Facts Found By The District Court Establish That The Anti-Steering Rules Have Severely Impaired Competition Among Credit Card Networks

By introducing overwhelming proof that AmEx's anti-steering rules impose "actual, sustained adverse effects on competition," *Indiana Dentists*, 476 U.S. at 461, the United States and the States carried their initial burden to establish a prima facie case that the rules unreasonably restrain trade. Indeed, few rule of reason cases have involved such extensive direct evidence of anticompetitive effects. That evidence was contained in a voluminous documentary record and thousands of pages of testimony from economists and market participants, including some of the Nation's leading merchants. Pet. App. 72a. And it was confirmed by the District Court's findings that the anti-steering rules have stifled price competition in the network-services market, induced all networks to raise their merchant fees, blocked low-fee rivals, and inflated retail prices.[4]

### 1. The anti-steering rules stifle price competition

The anti-steering rules are subject to the rule of reason, rather than to the *per se* rule, because they are "vertical restraints between firms at different levels of production—namely, between [AmEx] and its merchant-consumers." Pet. App. 105a. But the rules are significantly different from the vertical restraints this Court has considered in other recent cases. The anti-steering rules do not limit *intra*brand competition among retailers selling a manufacturer's products in order to enhance *inter*brand competition between the manufacturer and its rivals. Instead, the natural and demonstrated effect of the rules is to block *inter*brand merchant-fee (*i.e.*, price) competition among AmEx and its rival networks. Indeed, the District Court found

---

4  The United States and the States made prima facie showings that AmEx's anti-steering rules harm competition using both the indirect and direct methods. Pet. App. 148a-221a. We address only the direct proof of anticompetitive effects because the States did not seek further review of the court of appeals' holding that the United States and the States had failed to establish a prima facie case under the indirect method. Pet. i, 18-25.

that the rules have "frustrated" that "critical avenue of horizontal interbrand competition * * * to the point of near irrelevance." *Id.* at 195a.[5]

a. In recent decades, this Court has held that a variety of "vertical restraints a manufacturer imposes on its distributors," including restraints on the prices that distributors may charge, should be evaluated under the rule of reason rather than declared *per se* unlawful. *Leegin*, 551 U.S. at 882 (minimum prices); see, *e.g.*, *State Oil Co.* v. *Khan*, 522 U.S. 3, 7-8 (1997) (maximum prices); *Continental T. V., Inc.* v. *GTE Sylvania, Inc.*, 433 U.S. 36, 58-59 (1977) (*Sylvania*) (exclusive territories). Each time, the Court has emphasized that the type of vertical restraint at issue was potentially procompetitive because it could "stimulate *inter*brand competition—the competition among manufacturers selling different brands of the same type of product— by reducing intrabrand competition—the competition among retailers selling the same brand." *Leegin*, 551 U.S. at 890 (emphasis added); see, e.g., *State Oil*, 522 U.S. at 14-15; *Sylvania*, 433 U.S. at 51-55.

For example, a manufacturer may set minimum retail prices for its products in order to "encourage[] retailers to invest in tangible or intangible services or promotional efforts that aid the manufacturer's position as against rival manufacturers." *Leegin*, 551 U.S. at 890. Without manufacturer-set minimum prices, a retailer might be reluctant to make those investments for fear of being undersold by rivals who free-ride on its efforts by selling the same manufacturer's goods at lower prices. *Ibid.* A manufacturer's use of vertical restraints to limit competition among its own retailers thus has "the potential to give consumers more options," allowing them to "choose among low-price, low-service brands; high-price, high-service brands, and brands that fall in between." *Ibid.* Restraints that limit intrabrand competition to promote interbrand competition are generally lawful because "the primary purpose of the antitrust laws is to protect interbrand competition." *State Oil*, 522 U.S. at 15; accord *Leegin*, 551 U.S. at 890.

b. Unlike the types of vertical restraints this Court addressed in *Leegin, State Oil,* and *Sylvania,* the anti-steering rules "do not purport to restrain intrabrand competition in favor of greater interbrand competition." Pet. App. 107a. That is, they do not limit competition among distributors of AmEx's services to enhance competition among AmEx and its rival networks. The merchants restrained by the anti-steering rules are AmEx's consumers, not its distributors (at least in any traditional sense). *Id.* at 74a n.4. The purpose and effect of the rules is to prevent those consumers from al-

---

5  During much of the period that AmEx's anti-steering rules were in place, Visa and Mastercard had anti-steering rules as well. As a result of this suit, Visa and Mastercard have now rescinded their rules. Pet. App. 21a-22a. But the District Court found that, because AmEx's anti-steering rules prohibit *all* steering by AmEx-accepting merchants, which account for more than 90% of credit card transactions by dollar volume, the effect of AmEx's rules by themselves is essentially the same as the previous combined effect of the three networks' rules. *Id.* at 180a, 206a-207a n.43. Thus, "AmEx has been able to perpetuate" the "absence of inter-network competition on the basis of price * * * even after Visa and Mastercard abandoned their anti-steering rules." *Id.* at 180a.

tering their consumption of AmEx's services in responses to changes in price by AmEx *or by other networks*—and thus to suppress *inter*brand price competition among and its rivals.

The ability of merchants to engage in steering is an essential prerequisite for meaningful competition on merchant fees because it is the way that merchants control their consumption of—and expenditures on—a network's services. In other contexts, "merchants routinely seek lower prices for necessary goods and services by promoting competition among multiple suppliers, often by rewarding competitive bidders with increased purchase volume." Pet. App. 216a. Merchants cannot *directly* control their consumption of a particular credit card network's services in response to changes in the network's price, because the cardholder chooses (from among the cards that a particular merchant has chosen to accept) the card to be used for any given transaction. But just as merchants often "attempt to influence customers' purchasing decisions" through product placement, discounts, or other inducements, merchants could attempt to reduce their credit card costs by encouraging their customers to use cards that charge the merchants lower fees. *Id.* at 67a.

Merchants have strong economic incentives to take that step because credit card fees are a significant cost. Pet. App. 216a, 221a-222a. In 2013, for example, Hilton paid "[b]etween a half a billion and a billion dollars" in fees. Tr. 1608. Home Depot paid "roughly half a billion dollars." Tr. 1222. Alaska Airlines' credit card costs are roughly double the cost of wages for its U.S. airport employees. Tr. 192. And the credit card costs for the Solitude ski resort exceed its costs for fuel to groom its slopes and power to run its lifts. Tr. 2523.

The District Court's findings confirm that, if allowed to do so, merchants would seek to minimize those substantial costs by steering their customers towards less expensive cards. In the 1990s, merchants participating in the "We Prefer Visa" campaign were "markedly successful at shifting spend to Visa's [lower-cost] network." Pet. App. 200a. And numerous merchants—including Enterprise, Sears, Home Depot, IKEA, Crate & Barrel, and Hilton—"testified that they would, in fact, steer if given the opportunity." *Id.* at 222a.; see *id.* at 208a, 219a; see also Tr. 408-409, 2328-2329 (describing specific steering proposals).

AmEx does not deny that it imposed its current anti-steering rules to "stifle any further steering or preference campaigns" after the success of the "We Prefer Visa" initiative. Pet. App. 200a. To be sure, AmEx's anti-steering rules do not *preclude* other networks from charging merchant fees that are substantially lower than AmEx's own. But by preventing merchants from shifting transactions to lower-cost (or otherwise preferred) networks, the rules largely eliminate any economic incentive for other networks to take that step. And the evidence before the District Court amply demonstrated that the rules have stifled price competition among the networks and increased the merchant fees charged by all four of them.

As the District Court found, "[s]teering is a lynchpin to inter-network competition on the basis of price," because a credit card network "cannot increase sales or gain market share by offering merchants a more attractive price than its competitors" unless merchants are capable of responding by "shift[ing] share in response to pricing differentials." Pet. App. 196a. The anti-steering rules therefore "create a competitive environment in which there is virtually no check on the networks' incentive or ability to charge higher prices to merchants, so long as the network's pricing is below the level at which a rational merchant would drop acceptance entirely." *Id.* at 197a.

c. The anti-steering rules' suppression of price competition would be mitigated if merchants could feasibly escape AmEx's prohibition on steering by "refus[ing] to accept AmEx cards altogether." Pet. App. 196a. But often that is not a realistic option, especially for large merchants. Many AmEx cardholders are, to use AmEx's term, "insistent" on using their AmEx cards, and will shop elsewhere if a merchant stops accepting AmEx. *Id.* at 156a-157a. Some AmEx cardholders—10% to 20%—hold or regularly carry *only* AmEx cards. *Id.* at 157a-158a. Others prefer to "consolidate their credit card spending on their American Express cards" to take advantage of AmEx's rewards. *Id.* at 158a. And still others are required by their employers "to use AmEx cards for business expenses." *Ibid.*

The District Court found that this cardholder insistence "effectively prevents merchants from dropping American Express." Pet. App. 158a; see *id.* at 129a. Enterprise, for example, "determined it could not drop AmEx because its 'corporate customers were not interested in paying for their rental [cars] with a different method of payment.' " *Id.* at 159a n.27 (quoting Tr. 492) (brackets omitted). IKEA, Best Buy, and Sprint likewise "analyzed the issue in detail" and concluded that they could not stop accepting AmEx. *Id.* at 158a-159a; see *id.* at 159a n.27. Other merchants, including Alaska Airlines, Sears, Crate & Barrel, and Hilton, have never seriously considered dropping AmEx because it would obviously be unprofitable to do so. *Id.* at 158a & n.26. And at least two large merchants that tried to stop accepting AmEx cards were "forced to retreat" in the face of resistance from their customers. *Id.* at 163a; see *id.* at 162a-163a (describing attempts by Walgreens and Murphy Oil).[6]

d. Because the anti-steering rules apply "even when American Express is not mentioned" or the customer being steered does not have an AmEx card, the effect of the rules is "inflicted across the [credit card] industry." Pet. App. 101a-102a. The 6.4 million merchant locations that accept AmEx cards cannot engage in steering efforts with respect to *any* brand of credit cards. Those locations account for more than 90% of all credit card spending. See p. 4, *supra*.

---

6 The court of appeals held that this "cardholder insistence" could not establish AmEx's market power under the indirect method of proving harm to competition. Pet. App. 45a-49a. Whatever the merits of that legal holding, the court did not question the District Court's factual finding that merchants' theoretical ability to stop accepting AmEx cards has not practically constrained AmEx's ability to raise merchant fees. That undisturbed factual finding confirms, under the direct method, the actual anticompetitive effects of the anti-steering rules.

The participants in the market "recognize the dysfunction" caused by the anti-steering rules. Pet. App. 198a. As a Southwest Airlines executive put it, "the market is broken" because the rules allow the networks to avoid competing on price. Ibid. (quoting Tr. 2440). AmEx, too, "recognizes the absence of competition on the basis of merchant pricing." Id. at 197a. In developing its pricing strategy, AmEx "does not account for any downward pressure associated with its competitors' swipe fees." Ibid. And an AmEx executive acknowledged at trial that, when it comes to merchant fees, it is not "anybody's business strategy" to be "cheaper than the next guy." Ibid. (quoting Tr. 2667-2668).

### 2. The anti-steering rules raise merchant fees and inflate retail prices

The District Court's findings confirm that AmEx's anti-steering rules have "allowed all four networks to raise their swipe fees more easily and more profitably than would have been possible were merchants permitted to influence their customers' payment decisions," leading to "higher all-in merchant prices across the network services market." Pet. App. 207a. Because merchants pass those higher fees on to their customers, the economic burden is ultimately borne by all Americans in the form of higher retail prices.

a. Between 1997 and 2009, Visa and Mastercard increased their average merchant rates "by more than 20%." Pet. App. 210a. Because of the anti-steering rules, they did so "without fear of other networks undercutting their prices." Ibid. Between 2000 and 2007, Discover "was able to radically increase its merchant pricing," raising its average fee by nearly 24%. Ibid.; see id. at 206a. It, too, did so "with virtual impunity, relying on the restraining effect of anti-steering rules to ensure that it would not be undercut by a competitor offering a lower price." Id. at 210a.

In the early 2000s, price increases by Visa and Mastercard had reduced AmEx's premium over the rates charged by its rivals. Pet. App. 166a. Although AmEx's merchant fees "were already at or above the competitive level," AmEx responded by further increasing its prices through the "Value Recapture" initiative. Id. at 167a. Between 2005 and 2010, AmEx "repeatedly and profitably raised its discount rates to millions of merchants across the United States * * * without losing a single large merchant and losing relatively few small merchants." Id. at 165a. The initiative included "at least twenty separate price increases," with several merchant segments "targeted for multiple rounds of price hikes." Id. at 167a.

Between 2007 and 2010, for example, AmEx increased the discount rate charged to airlines "between 7% and 15%," which produced "over $90 million in additional pre-tax income." Pet. App. 167a; see id. at 167a-168a (describing similar increases imposed on restaurants). The Value Recapture initiative led to "a 9 basis point improvement to AmEx's weighted average discount rate" and "$1.3 billion in incremental pre-tax income for AmEx." Id. at 170a. The District Court found that the anti-steering rules were "integral" to those price increases because they prevented merchants from responding to AmEx's higher rates by steering transactions to other networks, or by using their ability to steer to negotiate lower rates from AmEx. *Id.* at 208a-209a.

b. Retail consumers bear the ultimate economic burden of the anti-steering rules. The District Court found that "[m]erchants facing increased credit card acceptance costs will pass most, if not all, of their additional costs along to their customers in the form of higher retail prices." Pet. App. 210a-211a. Those higher prices "affect not only those customers who use American Express cards, but also shoppers who instead prefer to pay using a lower-rewards [credit] card, debit card, check, or cash." *Id.* at 211a. Those other customers bear a portion of the cost of AmEx's high-fees, high-rewards business model, "but do not receive any of the premium rewards or other benefits conferred by American Express on the cardholder side of its platform." *Ibid.*

### 3. *The anti-steering rules block low-fee rivals and suppress the development of innovative payment models*

The District Court further found that, by blocking price competition, the anti-steering rules make it "nearly impossible" for a new firm to enter the concentrated network-services market "by offering merchants a low-cost alternative to the existing networks" or an innovative alternative payment system. Pet. App. 203a.

a. Discover's experience vividly illustrates that point. Discover "launched in 1985 by offering a combination of breakthrough value propositions" for both cardholders and merchants. Pet. App. 203a. It charged no annual fee and was the first network to offer card-holder rewards, yet its merchant fees were "significantly below those of its competitors." *Id.* at 203a-204a; see *id.* at 154a n.24.

In 1999, "Discover saw an opportunity to leverage its position as the lowest-price network to gain share" from merchants who were dissatisfied because of "a series of price increases by its competitors." Pet. App. 204a. Discover launched "a 'major campaign' aimed at highlighting the pricing disparity between it and its competitors in order to persuade merchants to 'shift their business to Discover's lower-priced network.' " *Ibid.* (quoting Tr. 833) (brackets omitted). It "sent a letter to every merchant on its network, alerting them to their competitors' recent price increases and inviting the merchants to save money by shifting volume to Discover." *Ibid.* And Discover representatives "met with a number of larger merchants to offer discounts from the network's already lower prices if they would steer customers to Discover." *Ibid.*

The other networks' anti-steering rules thwarted Discover's attempt to translate its lower fees into greater market share. "In its conversations with a number of merchants, Discover learned that the [anti-steering rules] denied merchants the ability to express a preference for Discover or to employ any other tool by which they might steer share to Discover's lower-priced network." Pet. App. 205a. As a result, Discover's "major campaign" and significantly lower fees "failed to produce 'any significant movement in share.' " *Ibid.* (quoting Tr. 848).

In 2000, once it recognized the competitive environment created by the other networks' anti-steering rules, Discover "abandoned its low-price business model" and "began raising discount rates in order to more closely align its merchant pricing with that of Visa and Mastercard." Pet. App. 206a. As a Discover executive explained, the company had been "leaving money on the table" because "offering a lower price was not going to give Discover any business benefits." *Ibid.* (brackets and citation omitted). Discover thus increased its rates to match Visa's and Mastercard's—a correspondence that remains in effect today. *Ibid.*

b. More broadly, the District Court found that the anti-steering rules have "stunted innovation" by blocking new payment models. Pet. App. 213a. In the early 2000s, Discover proposed a new network venture in which "merchants would receive equity in the network and be able to directly control their payment costs by influencing future pricing decisions." *Ibid.* But Discover abandoned the project "when it became clear that merchant-investors would be unable to encourage customers to use the preferred cards by traditional forms of steering." *Ibid.* Similarly, a group of large retailers recently created a joint venture to develop a new mobile-device based payment platform that would "significantly reduce the participating merchants' payment processing costs." *Ibid.* But the venture's "capacity to develop a viable brand as the low-cost alternative to traditional [credit] cards is endangered by merchants' inability to 'compare and contrast' [the venture's] payment services with those offered by American Express." *Id.* at 214a (quoting Tr. 2436) (brackets omitted). The same would be true of other innovative alternative payment platforms. The District Court thus found that the anti-steering rules "are responsible for impeding development of novel payment solutions that would have injected or potentially may inject greater diversification into the network services industry." *Ibid.*

\*\*\*\*\*

Far from "stimulat[ing] interbrand competition," *Leegin*, 551 U.S. at 890, AmEx's anti-steering rules have had the opposite effect. After carefully examining "the relevant business," "its condition before and after the restraint was imposed," and "the restraint's history, nature, and effect," *State Oil*, 522 U.S. at 10, the District Court found that the anti-steering rules have stifled interbrand price competition among networks, increased merchant fees, blocked low-fee rivals, and inflated the retail prices paid by all Americans. Those are particularly serious anticompetitive effects because price is the "central nervous system of the economy," *United States* v. *Socony-Vacuum Oil Co.*, 310 U.S. 150, 226 n.59 (1940), and "competitive pricing [is] the free market's means of allocating resources," *Broadcast Music, Inc.* v. *CBS, Inc.*, 441 U.S. 1, 23 (1979). The rules therefore are (at least) prima facie anticompetitive.

## C. The Court Of Appeals' Alternative Market Definition Departed From Established Antitrust Principles And Provided No Sound Basis For Reversal In Any Event

The District Court defined the relevant market in this case as the "market for general purpose credit and charge card network services" of the type that AmEx provides to merchants. Pet. App. 112a. The court of appeals disagreed, holding that the market should include services to cardholders as well as services to merchants. *Id.* at 32a-33a. The court then held that the District Court's market definition was "fatal to its conclusion that AmEx violated [Section] 1." *Id.* at 31a. The court of appeals was mistaken on both counts.

As we explain below (see pp. 50-55, *infra*), the effects of the anti-steering rules on the related cardholder-services market are relevant to the ultimate determination whether the rules violate Section 1. Those effects are properly considered, however, not in deciding whether the United States and the States established a prima facie case, but in deciding whether AmEx rebutted that case by proving sufficient procompetitive impact in an interdependent market. Maintaining that distinction is important, both because different parties bear the burden at the first two steps of the rule of reason analysis, and because the principles governing identification of the relevant market must be applied in a variety of antitrust contexts.

### 1. Services to merchants and services to cardholders do not belong in the same antitrust market because they are not substitutes

a. In many antitrust cases, courts define the "market" affected by the challenged action. In a merger case, for example, courts define the market in which the challenged merger could "substantially lessen competition" in violation of the Clayton Act, 15 U.S.C. 18. *United States* v. *E. I. du Pont de Nemours & Co.*, 353 U.S. 586, 593 (1957). Defining the relevant market and measuring the defendant's market share is also the usual means of assessing market power under both Section 1 and Section 2 of the Sherman Act. See, *e.g.*, *Kodak*, 504 U.S. at 464 (Sections 1 and 2); *United States* v. *E.I. du Pont de Nemours & Co.*, 351 U.S. 377, 394 (1956) (*du Pont*) (Section 2).

In all of those contexts, the purpose of defining the market is to identify the products that compete with the defendant's products. Consistent with that purpose, an antitrust market consists of those products "that have reasonable interchangeability for the purposes for which they are produced," such that customers would switch from one to another if faced with a price increase. *du Pont*, 351 U.S. at 404; see, *e.g.*, *Kodak*, 504 U.S. at 482; *United States* v. *Continental Can Co.*, 378 U.S. 441, 449 (1964); *Times-Picayune Publ'g Co.* v. *United States*, 345 U.S. 594, 612 n.31 (1953) (*Times-Picayune*). In other words, "a relevant market consists only of goods that are reasonably close *substitutes* for one another." 2B Areeda & Hovenkamp ¶ 565a, at 430 (4th ed. 2014); accord *Rothery Storage & Van Co.* v. *Atlas Van Lines, Inc.*, 792 F.2d 210, 218 (D.C. Cir. 1986) (Bork, J.) ("[T]he definition of the 'relevant market' rests on a determination of available substitutes."), cert. denied, 479 U.S. 1033 (1987).

This Court's decision in *Continental Can* illustrates the application of the rule that market definition turns on the identification of substitutes. The United States challenged a merger between "the Nation's second largest producer of metal containers" and its "third largest producer of glass containers." 378 U.S. at 443. The District Court rejected the challenge, concluding that the merger would not substantially lessen competition in any market because metal and glass containers were, with one exception, separate markets. *Id.* at 448-449. This Court reversed, holding that metal and glass containers belonged in the same market because of the pervasive "competition between them for the same end uses" and evidence that many customers regarded them as "interchangeable." *Id.* at 453-456.

b. In this case, the court of appeals articulated the correct legal standard, stating that the market should be defined to include "products 'reasonably interchangeable by consumers for the same purposes.' " Pet. App. 32a (citation omitted). But the court never explained how the services that AmEx provides to merchants are "reasonably interchangeable" with the services it provides to cardholders. In fact, they are not.

AmEx enables cardholders to make purchases without cash and to defer payment, and it provides cardholders with related services such as credit, fraud protection, and rewards. Pet. App. 74a-75a, 89a-90a. In contrast, AmEx provides merchants with guaranteed payment and related payment-processing services. *Id.* at 82a-84a. Those two sets of services are undoubtedly related, and both sets are used when an AmEx cardholder makes a purchase from an AmEx-accepting merchant. But the two bundles of services are not substitutes in any sense. A beverage company facing an increase in the price of glass bottles could switch to metal cans, but a merchant facing an increase in AmEx's fees could not become an AmEx cardholder instead.

Rather than faithfully applying the "reasonably interchangeable" standard, the court of appeals emphasized that AmEx's competition for merchants and its competition for cardholders are interdependent. Thus, the court observed that "the price charged to merchants necessarily affects cardholder demand, which in turn has a feedback effect on merchant demand." Pet. App. 39a. But it is common for prices in one market to affect prices in another. That sort of indirect effect does not mean that the relevant products should be collapsed into a single market for purposes of antitrust analysis. See, *e.g., Kodak*, 504 U.S. at 463, 481-482 (distinguishing the markets for photocopier replacement parts and services from the market for photocopiers). The leading antitrust treatise thus specifically disapproves of the court of appeals' approach in this case, emphasizing that "the fact that a firm obtains its profits from two different, non-substitutable groups does not serve to place the two groups into the same market." Areeda & Hovenkamp ¶ 565, at 104 (Supp. 2017).[7]

The court of appeals also placed great weight on the fact that the credit card industry is two-sided. Pet. App. 39a-40a. But distinct competitions on different sides of a two-sided platform are properly analyzed as separate, albeit interdependent, antitrust markets. That point is well illustrated by this Court's decision in *Times-Picayune*,

_____

7 An antitrust case may implicate multiple, separate markets composed of products that are not substitutes. For example, a merger in the shoe industry could affect separate markets for "men's, women's, and children's shoes." Brown Shoe Co. v. United States, 370 U.S. 294, 326 (1962). But the proper course in such a circumstance is not to depart from settled market-definition principles by collapsing the affected markets; it is to consider the impact of the challenged action in each of the relevant markets. Id. at 325-326.

which involved a newspaper publisher's requirement that advertisements appear in both its morning and evening papers. The Court explained that "every newspaper is a dual trader in separate though interdependent markets" serving advertisers and readers. 345 U.S. at 610. But because the challenged restraint "concern[ed] solely one of these markets," the Court limited the relevant market to reasonable substitutes for newspaper advertising; it did not treat the two sides of the platform taken together as a single market. *Ibid.*; see id. at 612 & n.31.[8]

Like the markets for newspaper advertisers and readers, the markets for merchants and cardholders are distinct spheres of competition, "involving different sets of rivals and the sale of separate, though interrelated, products and services to separate groups of consumers." Pet. App. 119a. In the market for merchants, AmEx competes with the acquirers affiliated with Visa, Mastercard, and Discover (which offer merchants terms that are largely dictated by the networks). *Id.* at 81a-82a. In the market for cardholders, in contrast, AmEx competes with Discover and with Citibank, Chase, and the thousands of other banks that issue cards on the Visa and Mastercard networks. *Id.* at 84a. By collapsing those very different avenues of competition into a single market, the court of appeals severed market definition from its purpose and "prevent[ed] the relevant-market inquiry from accurately answering the questions for which it is asked." Antitrust Law Professors' Cert. Amicus Br. 5.

c. AmEx concedes (Br. in Opp. 16) that services to merchants and services to cardholders "cannot [be] substitute[d]" for one another. Instead, it asserts (*ibid.*) that those two sets of services are, in reality, "*part of the same product*," akin to "[m]atching left and right shoes." The court of appeals did not adopt that argument, and it is incorrect. AmEx relies on this Court's observation that it may be appropriate "to combin[e] in a single market a number of different products or services where that combination reflects commercial realities." *United States* v. *Grinnell Corp.*, 384 U.S. 563, 572 (1966) (brackets omitted). But that principle applies to related products and services that are offered *to the same consumers*—in *Grinnell*, centrally monitored "burglar alarm" and "fire alarm" services. *Ibid.* Here, in contrast, services to merchants and services to card-holders are sold separately to distinct groups of consumers. AmEx cites no precedent placing such services in a single antitrust market.

### 2. The facts found by the District Court established a prima facie case even under the court of appeals' market definition

In any event, the District Court's findings that the anti-steering rules stifle price competition, inflate merchant fees, and block low-fee rivals were sufficient to

---

8 The court of appeals stated that the District Court, in assessing the extent to which an increase in merchant fees would cause a shift to other forms of payment, had failed adequately to consider "feedback effect[s]" between the merchant and cardholder markets. Pet. App. 39a. In fact, the District Court did consider the possibility of such "cross-platform feedback effects." *Id.* at 126a. And in any event, the analysis at issue was relevant only to AmEx's argument that the relevant market should be defined to include debit-card services as well as credit card services—a contention that AmEx "abandoned" on appeal. *Id.* at 5a n.1.

establish a prima facie case even under the court of appeals' definition of the relevant market. When a court finds that a restraint has had "actual, sustained adverse effects on competition," "specific findings * * * concerning the definition of the market" are unnecessary. *Indiana Dentists*, 476 U.S. at 460-461. The Court thus need not resolve the market-definition question in order to hold that the United States and the States carried their initial burden.

The District Court found that AmEx's anti-steering rules have "frustrated [interbrand price competition] to the point of near irrelevance," inflating the merchant fees charged by all four networks. Pet. App. 195a. That distortion of competitive pricing, the "central nervous system of the economy," *Socony-Vacuum Oil*, 310 U.S. at 226 n.59, would be a matter of serious antitrust concern even if the networks competed for cardholders by expending all of their merchant fees on more generous cardholder rewards.

This Court made a version of the same point in *Catalano, Inc.* v. *Target Sales, Inc.*, 446 U.S. 643 (1980) (per curiam). There, a group of wholesalers had agreed among themselves to demand immediate payment from retailers, eliminating the practice of affording "short term trade credit" on negotiated terms. *Id.* at 643. The Court acknowledged that, "in a competitive market," the elimination of trade credit would, in theory, "ultimately lead * * * to corresponding decreases in the invoice price." *Id.* at 649. The Court nonetheless held that the agreement was *per se* unlawful because credit terms are "an inseparable part of the price," *id.* at 648, and the agreement "extinguish[ed] one form of competition among the sellers," *id.* at 649.

Although *Catalano* was a *per se* case, it illustrates that a restraint that extinguishes price competition can be anticompetitive even if "the agreement relates only to one component of an overall price." *O'Bannon* v. *NCAA*, 802 F.3d 1049, 1071 (9th Cir. 2015), cert. denied, 137 S. Ct. 277 (2016). "By effectively suppressing competition on merchant pricing," AmEx's anti-steering rules "shift the bulk of interbrand competition in the credit and charge card industry to the cardholder side of the platform." Pet. App. 238a. The anti-steering rules are analogous to "a decision made by [AmEx] on behalf of all participants in the network services market that networks will not compete * * * by lowering their merchant pricing" and will instead "focus their competitive efforts on cardholders." *Id.* at 240a.

Even with respect to the cardholder side of the platform, the anti-steering rules have the additional effect of limiting the *bases* on which the various networks can compete for cardholders. If steering were permitted, and if merchants adopted a widespread practice of offering more favorable terms of sale to cardholders who used lower-cost cards, the card issuers could compete for cardholder business by emphasizing that potential advantage. AmEx's preferred strategy is to charge high merchant fees and offer premium cardholder rewards. Pet. App. 238a-239a. But other networks might choose instead to compete for cardholders by encouraging merchant steering practices that will make their own cards more desirable. The anti-steering rules effectively preclude that form of competition.

There is, of course, nothing improper about AmEx's strategy of pairing high merchant fees with premium cardholder rewards. But the range of options available to both merchants and cardholders will be increased if other networks remain free to pursue a different strategy. Cf. *Leegin*, 551 U.S. at 890 (identifying, as one procompetitive effect of vertical resale price maintenance, that such price maintenance "has the potential to give consumers more options so that they can choose among low-cost, low-service brands; high-price, high-service brands; and brands that fall in between"). As the District Court correctly recognized, AmEx may not "decide on behalf of the entire market which legitimate forms of interbrand competition should be available and which should not." Pet. App. 240a.

## D. The Additional Showings Demanded By The Court Of Appeals Were Not Required

The court of appeals deemed the District Court's findings legally insufficient to establish even a prima facie case because—in the court of appeals' view—the district court did not adequately account for the anti-steering rules' purported benefits to AmEx cardholders. At times, the court appeared to fault the United States and the States for failing to identify and negate *all* possible benefits of the anti-steering rules at the first step of the burden-shifting framework. At other times, the court appeared to hold that the United States and the States were required to provide a precise calculation of AmEx's "two-sided" price, taking into account both its merchant fees and its cardholder rewards—something that even AmEx itself could not reliably do. Neither of those showings was required.

### 1. The United States and the States were not required to negate the anti-steering rules' potential benefits for cardholders in order to establish a prima facie case

The court of appeals stated that the United States and the States bore the "initial burden" of "show[ing] that the [anti-steering rules] made *all* AmEx consumers on both sides of the platform—*i.e.*, both merchants and cardholders—worse off overall." Pet. App. 51a. The court also stated that, in order to carry their initial burden, the United States and the States were required "to take into account offsetting benefits to cardholders" and "to prove net harm" to cardholders and merchants. *Id.* at 49a n.52, 54a. To treat such showings as essential elements of a Section 1 plaintiff's prima facie case would seriously distort the applicable burden-shifting framework and subvert fundamental antitrust principles.

a. A plaintiff's initial burden in a rule of reason case is to show that the challenged restraint is "*prima facie* anticompetitive." *California Dental*, 526 U.S. at 771. Such a showing "place[s] the burden of procompetitive justification on [the defendant]," *ibid.*, which is responsible for establishing any "legitimate justifications," *Actavis*, 133 S. Ct. at 2236; see Areeda & Hovenkamp ¶ 1505, at 171 (Supp. 2017). Whatever the merits of AmEx's claim that the anti-steering rules have "offsetting benefits to cardholders," Pet. App. 49a n.52, that argument is not relevant at the first step of the burden shifting inquiry. It is the defendant's burden to establish a challenged restraint's procompetitive benefits, not the plaintiff's initial burden to anticipate and refute them.[9]

b. The court of appeals' analysis also reflected a misunderstanding of the nature of the harm that the Sherman Act seeks to prevent. Although the Sherman Act is a "consumer welfare prescription," *Reiter* v. *Sonotone Corp.*, 442 U.S. 330, 343 (1979) (quoting Robert H. Bork, *The Antitrust Paradox: A Policy at War With Itself* 66 (1978)), courts do not enforce that prescription by making their own judgments about the allocation of resources that would best serve consumers' interests. Instead, consistent with the Sherman Act's fundamental policy of market competition, courts protect consumers by protecting the *competitive process*. As Robert H. (later Justice) Jackson explained while serving as the head of the Antitrust Division, "[t]he antitrust laws represent an effort to avoid detailed government regulation of business by keeping competition in control of prices." Robert H. Jackson, *Should the Antitrust Laws Be Revised?*, 71 U.S. L. Rev. 575, 576 (1937). Accordingly, antitrust law "assesses both harms and benefits in light of the [Sherman] Act's basic objective, the protection of a competitive process." *Clamp-All Corp.* v. *Cast Iron Soil Pipe Inst.*, 851 F.2d 478, 486 (1st Cir. 1988) (Breyer, J.), cert. denied, 488 U.S. 1007 (1989).

The court of appeals' reasoning reflects a serious departure from that fundamental principle. The court stated, for example, that the lower merchant fees that would result from eliminating the anti-steering rules could harm AmEx cardholders by decreasing AmEx's "optimal level of cardholder benefits." Pet. App. 50a. Under the Sherman Act, however, the optimal mix of goods and services is set through market competition, and the courts' role is to protect the competitive process. As the leading treatise explains, the Second Circuit erred in this case by failing to recognize that "under antitrust policy competition should choose the optimal mix of revenue as between the two sides" of AmEx's platform. Areeda & Hovenkamp ¶ 562e, at 101 (Supp. 2017).

c. The court of appeals appeared to base its contrary approach on circuit precedent stating that a rule of reason plaintiff must establish that the challenged restraints have "an actual adverse effect on competition *as a whole* in the relevant market." Pet. App. 49a-50a (quoting *K.M.B. Warehouse Distribs., Inc.* v. *Walker Mfg. Co.*, 61 F.3d 123, 127 (2d Cir. 1995)). But the court misunderstood the principle on which it relied. The statement that an antitrust plaintiff must demonstrate harm to competition "as a whole" simply means that a plaintiff "must allege and prove harm, not just to a single competitor, but to the competitive process, *i.e.*, to competition itself." *NYNEX Corp.* v. *Discon, Inc.*, 525 U.S. 128, 135 (1998). That requirement follows from the

---

9   In one sentence of its opinion, the court of appeals acknowledged that "[w]hether the [anti-steering rules] had pro-competitive effects on cardholders—let alone whether any alleged procompetitive effects on cardholders outweigh 'anticompetitive' effects on merchants—has no bearing on whether [the United States and the States] carried their initial burden." Pet. App. 51a. That statement, however, came only two sentences after the court's assertion that the United States and the States bore the "initial burden" of "show[ing] that the [anti-steering rules] made all AmEx consumers on both sides of the platform * * * worse off overall." *Ibid.*

axiom that "[t]he purpose of the antitrust laws * * * is 'the protection of *competition, not competitors.*'" *Leegin*, 551 U.S. at 906 (citation omitted). This Court has never suggested, however, that the Sherman Act requires a showing of "net harm" to all consumers in the market.[10] Instead, what is required is proof of harm "to the competitive process." *NYNEX*, 525 U.S. at 135. A showing that a restraint disrupts the market's price-setting mechanism, stifles interbrand price competition, and raises fees amply satisfies that standard.

### 2. The United States and the States were not required to calculate AmEx's "two-sided" price in order to establish a prima facie case

The court of appeals also deemed the District Court's findings insufficient to establish a prima facie case because the United States and the States had not provided "a reliable measure of [AmEx's] two-sided price that appropriately accounts for the value or cost of the rewards paid to cardholders." Pet. App. 53a (citation omitted). That is incorrect for at least three reasons.

First, proof of an increase in AmEx's "two-sided price" was not necessary to establish a prima facie case of anticompetitive effects. "Two-sided platforms compete, in part, via the prices offered by each platform to the two sides. For example, one hotel booking service may charge a high price to hotels and a relatively low price to travelers," while others may do the reverse. Economists Cert. Amicus Br. 11. "Competition is likely to result in competing platforms offering different price pairs, and those offering the price pairs that best satisfy consumer preferences will thrive." Ibid. The court of appeals committed "a fundamental economic error" by holding that the metric of competitive effects in such an industry is "whether the *sum* of the two prices increased." *Ibid.* Where, as here, restraints "prevent[] competitive market forces from determining the price pairs offered by the competing platforms," "anticompetitive harm" exists "regardless of whether the sum of the prices increases, decreases, or remains unchanged." *Id.* at 11-12. The harm is the distortion of the market process.

Second, and in any event, the District Court's findings *did* establish that AmEx's "two-sided" price was inflated above competitive levels. During the Value Recapture initiative, AmEx increased fees that were "already at or above the competitive level" to re-establish its price premium over its rivals' elevated rates. Pet. App. 167a; see *id.* at 167a-170a, 174a-176a. Because those increased fees "were not paired with offsetting adjustments on the cardholder side of the platform, the resulting increases in merchant pricing are properly viewed as changes to the net price charged across AmEx's integrated platform." *Id.* at 166a-167a. The court of appeals recognized, and "AmEx conceded," that "not all of AmEx's gains from increased merchant fees are passed along to cardholders in the form of rewards." *Id.* at 51a. In

---

10 Until this case, the Second Circuit had interpreted the requirement of a showing of harm to competition "as a whole" to mean simply that "evidence that plaintiffs have been harmed as individual competitors will not suffice." Geneva Pharms. Tech. Corp. v. Barr Labs. Inc., 386 F.3d 485, 507 (2004); see K.M.B. Warehouse Distribs., 61 F.3d at 127-128.

fact, AmEx spends less than half of its merchant fees on cardholder rewards. *Id.* at 210a-211a; see Tr. 3853.

The court of appeals did not question the District Court's conclusion that the anti-steering rules increased AmEx's two-sided price. Instead, the court faulted the United States and the States for failing to calculate "a reliable *measure* of [AmEx's] two-sided price." Pet. App. 51a (quoting *id.* at 174a n.30) (emphasis added). But the District Court found that, because of the complexity of AmEx's system of cardholder rewards and the difficulty of quantifying some of those rewards, "neither party" had provided a reliable measure of that two-sided price. *Id.* at 209a; see *id.* at 182a-186a. The United States and the States should not be faulted for failing to calculate with precision a measure of AmEx's pricing that AmEx itself could not reliably provide. To the contrary, because any procompetitive effects on the cardholder market are properly considered at the *second* step of the rule of reason analysis, at which AmEx bore the burden of rebutting the prima facie case, uncertainty as to the scope of those benefits must be resolved against AmEx.

Third, the court of appeals erred in focusing exclusively on *AmEx's* pricing. The District Court also found that the anti-steering rules have "enabled [AmEx's] competitors to charge higher * * * fees" and have blocked low-cost rivals. Pet. App. 210a. Most obviously, the rules thwarted Discover's low-fee strategy and then allowed Discover "to radically increase its merchant pricing over a relatively short period of time," *ibid.*, to avoid " 'leaving money on the table,' " *id.* at 206a (citation omitted). Restraints that enable such unfettered price increases would properly be deemed prima facie anticompetitive even if (counterfactually) they had not increased *AmEx's* two-sided price.

That is particularly true because supracompetitive prices are merely one means of establishing anticompetitive effects. The ultimate question is whether the challenged restraint has harmed "the competitive process." *NYNEX*, 525 U.S. at 135; accord *NCAA*, 468 U.S. at 104. The District Court's findings were more than sufficient to establish that the anti-steering rules have harmed the competitive process in the credit card industry.[11]

---

11 In addition to its focus on AmEx's two-sided price, the court of appeals deemed it significant that output in the credit card industry, as measured by the dollar value of credit card transactions, has increased. Pet. App. 52a. "[O]utput reductions are one common kind of anticompetitive effect in antitrust cases," but "a 'reduction in output is not the only measure of anticompetitive effect.' " O'Bannon, 802 F.3d at 1070 (citation omitted). Transaction volume is a particularly unilluminating metric here, because the anti-steering rules have severed the normal link between "merchants' demand for network services and the price charged," and thus have prevented volume from responding normally to price changes. Pet. App. 195a.

## E. The District Court Properly Considered And Rejected, At The Second Step Of The Burden-Shifting Inquiry, AmEx's Arguments About The Benefits Of The Anti-Steering Rules For Cardholders

The court of appeals' approach to this case appears to have been driven in part by its recognition that antitrust analysis of the anti-steering rules should take account of the "two-sided" nature of AmEx's platform. "In a two-sided platform, a single firm or collection of firms sells different products or services to two separate yet interrelated groups of customers who, in turn, rely on the platform to intermediate some type of interaction between them." Pet. App. 77a. Such two-sided platforms are not new, but their importance has grown in recent years as "a seemingly endless array of Internet companies" have developed to "facilitate some form of value-generating interaction between distinct sets of consumers." *Id.* at 77a-78a; see generally Jean-Charles Rochet & Jean Tirole, *Two-Sided Markets: A Progress Report*, 37 RAND J. Econ. 645 (2006); Kate Collyer et al., *Measuring Market Power in Multi-Sided Markets*, Antitrust Chronicle (Sept. 2017).

The court of appeals believed that excluding services to cardholders from the relevant market would allow "legitimate competitive activities in the market for [cardholders] to be penalized no matter how output-expanding such activities may be," so long as those activities had some anticompetitive effects in the market for merchants. *Id.* at 35a. The court's concern about the interdependence of the two sides of the credit card platform was appropriate. As we explain above (see pp. 43-46, *supra*), however, the court erred in requiring the United States and the States to negate AmEx's claim that the anti-steering rules have procompetitive benefits in the market for cardholders at the first (*i.e.*, prima facie case) step of the rule of reason analysis. Instead, AmEx's asserted procompetitive justifications are properly considered (as the District Court considered them) at the second step of the burden-shifting inquiry. This Court should vacate the judgment below, which held that the United States and the States failed to establish a prima facie case. On remand, the court of appeals can consider any challenges that AmEx has properly preserved to the District Court's holding that AmEx failed to establish sufficient procompetitive justifications for the anti-steering rules.

1. Although courts applying the rule of reason ordinarily confine their analysis of procompetitive benefits to the market in which the challenged restraint operates, this Court has not rigidly adhered to that limitation. In *NCAA*, for example, the Court recognized that "most of the regulatory controls of the NCAA are justifiable means of fostering competition among amateur athletic teams and therefore procompetitive because they enhance public interest in intercollegiate athletics," a product that competes with other forms of entertainment in markets that are distinct from the markets restrained by the NCAA's rules governing "the eligibility of participants" and other similar matters. *NCAA*, 468 U.S. at 117. The Court rejected the NCAA's defense of the restraint at issue—limits on televised football games—only because that restraint was "not even arguably tailored to serve such an interest" in competitive balance. *Id.* at 119. Other courts have likewise "balance[d] the anticompetitive

effects on competition in one market with certain procompetitive benefits in other markets." *Sullivan* v. *NFL*, 34 F.3d 1091, 1112 (1st Cir. 1994), cert. denied, 513 U.S. 1190 (1995); see, e.g., *O'Bannon*, 802 F.3d at 1057-1058, 1072-1074 (considering procompetitive justifications in other markets in assessing the reasonableness of an NCAA rule restricting the markets for "college education" and "group licensing" of the rights to use athletes' names, images, and likenesses).

2. A rigid rule holding that a court analyzing a restraint on one side of a two-sided platform is always barred from considering asserted procompetitive benefits on the other side of the platform would risk condemning as unlawful business practices that actually serve valid procompetitive purposes. Cf. *Leegin*, 551 U.S. at 875 (explaining that *per se* rules "can increase the total cost of the antitrust system by prohibiting procompetitive conduct the antitrust laws should encourage"); *Verizon Commc'ns Inc.* v. *Law Offices of Curtis V. Trinko, LLP*, 540 U.S. 398, 414 (2004) ("Mistaken inferences and the resulting false condemnations 'are especially costly, because they chill the very conduct the antitrust laws are designed to protect.' ") (citation omitted). Instead, a court should consider out-of-market effects at the second step of its rule of reason analysis if, but only if, the defendant shows that the challenged restraint is reasonably necessary to achieve legitimate procompetitive benefits in a closely related and interdependent market.

That standard is in some respects analogous to the ancillary-restraints doctrine, which "governs the validity of restrictions imposed by a legitimate business collaboration, such as a * * * joint venture, on nonventure activities." *Texaco, Inc.* v. *Dagher*, 547 U.S. 1, 7 (2006). When a restraint is ancillary to a legitimate collaboration, both are "typically evaluated as a whole under the rule of reason." *Major League Baseball Props., Inc.* v. *Salvino, Inc.*, 542 F.3d 290, 338 (2d Cir. 2008) (Sotomayor, J., concurring in the judgment). "To be ancillary," a restraint must be "subordinate and collateral to a separate, legitimate transaction," and *reasonably necessary* to "make the main transaction more effective in accomplishing its purpose." *Rothery Storage*, 792 F.2d at 224, 227. "Ancillary restraints are generally permitted if they are 'reasonably necessary' toward the contract's objective of utility and efficiency." *Schering-Plough Corp.* v. *FTC*, 402 F.3d 1056, 1072 (11th Cir. 2005), cert. denied, 548 U.S. 919 (2006). But when a restraint is "not reasonably necessary to achieve any of the efficiency-enhancing purposes of a joint venture, it will be evaluated apart from the rest of the venture." *Salvino*, 542 F.3d at 338 (Sotomayor, J., concurring in the judgment).

3. The District Court's analysis in this case was consistent with those principles. The court recognized the interdependence between the two sides of AmEx's platform. Pet. App. 121a-122a. And at the second step of the burden-shifting framework, the District Court considered all of AmEx's proffered procompetitive justifications for its anti-steering rules, including those in "the interrelated but distinct [card]issuing market." *Id.* at 239a. The court concluded, however, that AmEx had failed to carry its burden to show that the anti-steering rules were "reasonably necessary to robust competition on the cardholder side," or that "any such gains offset the harm done in

the network services market." *Id.* at 240a. The court found AmEx's procompetitive justifications to be legally invalid, factually unsupported, or both. *Id.* at 228a-258a.

The District Court considered in particular AmEx's argument that, if steering were permitted, AmEx's revenues would decline and the company would be less able to compete in the cardholder market. See Pet. App. 229a-233a. The court viewed it as inconsistent with the policies of the Sherman Act "[t]o find the [anti-steering rules] to be reasonable restraints on trade because they shield American Express's preferred business strategy from a legitimate form of interbrand competition." *Id.* at 235a. The court also stated that, assuming that benefits to competition in the cardholder market could be balanced against a loss of competition in the network-services market, AmEx had "failed to establish that [anti-steering rules] are reasonably necessary to robust competition on the cardholder side of the  * * * platform, or that any such gains offset the harm done in the network services market." *Id.* at 239a-240a. And the court also noted, at an earlier stage of its opinion, that the retail price increases caused by AmEx's anti-steering rules are borne by many consumers who are not AmEx card-holders and therefore derive no benefit from AmEx's more generous rewards program. *Id.* at 210a-212a.

4. With one exception not relevant here, all of AmEx's arguments on appeal focused on the first step of the burden-shifting process. AmEx C.A. Br. 37-79. The court of appeals agreed with AmEx that the United States and the States had failed to establish a prima facie case under Section 1. For the reasons set forth above, that holding was erroneous. Although benefits to cardholders are potentially relevant to the rule of reason analysis in this case, they are appropriately considered at the second rather than the first step of the burden-shifting framework. This Court therefore should vacate the court of appeals' judgment holding that the United States and the States failed to establish a prima facie case. On remand, the court of appeals may consider any properly preserved challenges to the District Court's holdings concerning procompetitive justifications.

## CONCLUSION

The judgment of the court of appeals should be vacated, and the case should be remanded to the court of appeals for further proceedings.

Respectfully submitted.

NOEL J. FRANCISCO
*Solicitor General*

MAKAN DELRAHIM
*Assistant Attorney General*

MALCOLM L. STEWART
*Deputy Solicitor General*

BRIAN H. FLETCHER
*Assistant to the Solicitor General*

WILLIAM J. RINNER
*Counsel to the Assistant Attorney General*

KRISTEN C. LIMARZI

ROBERT B. NICHOLSON

JAMES J. FREDRICKS

CRAIG W. CONRATH

JOHN R. READ

NICKOLAI G. LEVIN

ANDREW J. EWALT
*Attorneys*

**DECEMBER 2017**

# Brief of 28 Professors of Antitrust Law as *Amici Curiae* Supporting Petitioners

N0. 16-1454

IN THE

# SUPREME COURT OF THE UNITED STATES

STATE OF OHIO, ET AL.

*Petitioners,*

v.

AMERICAN EXPRESS COMPANY & AMERICAN EXPRESS TRAVEL RELATED
SERVICES COMPANY, INC.,

*Respondents.*

ON PETITION FOR A WRIT
OF CERTIORARI TO THE UNITED STATES COURT
OF APPEALS FOR THE SECOND CIRCUIT

BRIEF OF 28 PROFESSORS OF ANTITRUST LAW AS
*AMICI CURIAE* SUPPORTING PETITIONERS

ERIC F. CITRON
*Counsel of Record*
GOLDSTEIN & RUSSELL, P.C.
7475 Wisconsin Ave.
Suite 850
Bethesda, MD 20814
(202) 362-0636

*ec@goldsteinrussell.com*

# Table of Contents

INTEREST OF *AMICI*..............................................................................................................................158

SUMMARY OF ARGUMENT....................................................................................................................159

I. The District Court Correctly Applied Rule of reason Analysis To The Facts It Found.............160

    A.  How the rule of reason works.....................................................................................................160

        1. Step one and "marketpower"...................................................................................................160

        2. Step two.........................................................................................................................................163

        3. Step three.....................................................................................................................................163

    B.  The District Court's analysis.......................................................................................................164

II. The Second Circuit's "Two-Sided-Market" Innovations Are Fundamentally Unsound..........166

    A.  The relevant market cannot encompass both sides of AmEx's platform........................166

    B.  "Netting" or "balancing" competitive effects across both sides of a two-sided platform
is fundamentally unsound...............................................................................................................168

        1. The Second Circuit's "neting" exercise is erroneous....................................................168

        2. A special "net" price or benefit rule for two-sided platforms is an unnecessary invita-
tion to error in the lower courts.....................................................................................................171

CONCLUSION..........................................................................................................................................176

# Table of Authorities

**Cases**

*Brown Shoe Co. v. United States*, 370 U.S. 294 (1962) ........................................166, 175

*Cal. Dental Ass'n v. F.T.C.*, 526 U.S.756(1999)........................................................160

*Eastman Kodak v. Image Technical Servs., Inc.*, 504 U.S. 451 (1992) ..............161, 166

*F.T.C. v. Actavis*, 133S.Ct.2223 (2013)....................................................................158

*F.T.C. v. Indiana Fed'n of Dentists*, 476 U.S. 447 (1986) ...........................161, 164, 170

*F.T.C. v. Phoebe Putney Health Sys.*, 568 U.S.216 (2013)........................................158

*Hanover Shoe v. United Shoe Machinery Corp.*, 392 U.S.481 (1968)........................175

*Illinois Brick Co. v. Illinois*, 431 U.S.720(1977)........................................................175

*Illinois Tool Works v. Independent Ink*, 547 U.S.28 (2006)........................................162

*Kimble v. Marvel Entm't*, 135 S. Ct.2401 (2015)......................................................158

*Leegin Creative Prods. v. PSKS*, 551 U.S. 877 (2007) ......................................158, 166

*Nat'l Soc. of Prof. Eng'rs v. UnitedStates*, 435 U.S.679 (1978)................................163

*NCAA v. Bd. Of Regents of Univ. of Okla.*, 468 U.S. 85 (1984) ...............163, 170, 173, 175

*Novell, Inc. v. Microsoft Corp.*, 731 F.3d 1064 (10thCir.2013).................................158

*Pac. Bell Tel. Co. v. Linkline Commc'ns Inc.*, 555 U.S.438 (2009)...........................158

*Times-Picayune Publ'g Co. v. United States*, 345 U.S.594 (1953)...........................169

*Todd v. Exxon Corp.*, 275 F.3d 206 (2dCir.2001)....................................................161

*United States v. E.I. Du Pont de Nemours & Co.*, 351 U.S.377 (1956)......................164

*United States v. Microsoft*, 253 F.3d 34 (D.C.Cir.2001).........................................162

*United States v. Socony-Vacuum Oil Co.*, 310 U.S.150 (1940)................................170

*Verizon Commc'ns v. Law Offices of Curtis V. Trinko*, 540 U.S.398 (2004)................158

## Other Authorities

D.H. Ginsburg & J. Wright, *Dynamic Analysis and the Limits of Antitrust Institutions*, 78 Antitrust L.J.1(2012)................................................................................................................175

Evans & Schmalensee, *Industrial Organization of Markets with Two-Sided Platforms*, 3 COMPETITION POL'Y INT'L150 (2007)......................................................................................168

Frank Easterbrook, *The Limits of Antitrust*, 63 Tex. L. Rev.1 (1984).......................................172

Herbert Hovenkamp, *The Rule of Reason* (Fla. L. Rev. forthcoming 2018).......................................162

Louis Kaplow, *Why (Ever) Define Markets?*, 124 Harv. L. Rev.437 (2010)..........................................162

Michael Carrier, *The Rule of Reason: An Empirical Update For The 21st Century*, 16 Geo. Mason L. Rev. 827,827-29 (2009)..............................................................................................................160

Rochet & Tirole, *Two-Sided Markets: A Progress Report*, 37 RAND J. Econ.645(2006)................168

US DOJ & FTC, *Horizontal Merger Guidelines* (2010) ..............................................................164, 175

William Landes & Richard Posner, *Market Power in Antitrust Cases*, 94 Harv. L. Rev. 937 (1981) ..........................................................................................................................................161

## Treatises

Phillip Areeda & Herbert Hovenkamp, *Antitrust Law: An Analysis of Antitrust Principles and their Application* (4th ed. 2017)................................................................................. passim

# INTEREST OF *AMICI*

*Amici* are 28 antitrust scholars who write to share their disinterested perspective with the Court. Their respective backgrounds are compiled in the addendum, but it suffices to note that they include many leaders in the field, including the author of the treatise most often relied upon by this Court's anti-trust opinions. *See, e.g., Kimble v. Marvel Entm't*, 135 S. Ct. 2401, 2415 (2015) (Alito, J. dissenting);

*F.T.C. v. Actavis*, 133 S. Ct. 2223, 2227 (2013) (Breyer, J.); *Pac. Bell Tel. Co. v. Linkline Commc'ns Inc.*, 555 U.S. 438, 453 (2009) (Roberts, C.J.); *Leegin Creative Prods. v. PSKS*, 551 U.S. 877, 894 (2007) (Kennedy, J.); *F.T.C. v. Phoebe Putney Health Sys.*, 568

U.S. 216, 228 (2013) (Sotomayor, J.); *Verizon Commc'ns v. Law Offices of Curtis V. Trinko*, 540

U.S. 398, 411 (2004) (Scalia, J.); *Novell, Inc. v. Microsoft Corp.*, 731 F.3d 1064, 1070 (10th Cir. 2013) (Gorsuch, J.) (citing Phillip Areeda & Herbert Hovenkamp, *Antitrust Law: An Analysis of Antitrust Principles and their Application* ("Areeda & Hovenkamp")).[1]

*Amici*'s interest in this case runs deep for two reasons. First, this Court has encountered few opportunities to offer substantial guidance to the lower courts on how to apply the rule of reason. It is thus particularly important that the Court's opinion here make that doctrine—which already confounds many lower courts—clearer rather than murkier. Second, the ideas introduced by the Second Circuit's decision below are particularly pernicious; they are small but potentially serious fractures to important, structural bones of antitrust doctrine that will cause lasting harm if not properly set by this Court.

As the District Court's careful analysis showed, existing doctrines already provide accurate answers to questions like those this case posed. And as is often true, the introduction of special rules to deal with individual cases or isolated phenomena will tend to do much more harm than good. Special rules are obviously much more harmful if they are themselves inaccurate—as the Second Circuit's were. But whether theoretically accurate or not, they also introduce occasions for lower courts to miss the forest for a tree they have misunderstood and that was never necessary to plant.

---

1 All citations to the treatise are to the online edition that includes the 2017 supplement, and made by ¶ number.

We strongly believe this is true with respect to the Second Circuit's (inaccrate) rules regarding so-called "two-sided markets."[2] These business models are certainly important to scholars of business strategy—and increasingly so as their prevalence grows in today's technological environment. But the prevailing view among antitrust economists and scholars is that two-sidedness does not require changing the settled rules of antitrust law, which can already analyze competitive issues in such "markets" with straightforward doctrinal tools that provide accurate results.

## SUMMARY OF ARGUMENT

At bottom, this case concerns two critical, related, and mistaken ideas that the Second Circuit introduced into antitrust law and economics, and that this Court should reject. One is that a "relevant market" for antitrust purposes must (or even can) include "both sides" of a two-sided platform; the other is that competitive harms and benefits must be (or even can be) "netted" across relevant markets in rule of reason cases. These ideas are not only wrong, but in direct tension with core principles animating antitrust law.

In contrast, the District Court's opinion straightforwardly applies settled doctrine—accepting the facts as found, we believe it properly concluded that there was an antitrust violation in this case by determining that (1) American Express (AmEx) had sufficient market power to successfully impose a restraint eliminating horizontal price competition among its competitors, and (2) this led, in turn, to several anticompetitive effects, including supracompetitive prices for merchant network services. While AmEx was free to introduce evidence of offsetting procompetitive benefits, the District Court found that it did not, in part because the "benefits" it pointed to could not be deemed legitimate or procompetitive. We believe any proper rule of reason analysis should reach the same outcome on the facts as found, and it is evident that the Second Circuit only did otherwise by indulging its two mistaken ideas about "two-sided" antitrust markets.

This brief thus proceeds in two parts. Part I explains certain basic tools of antitrust analysis—both how *and why* we use them in rule of reason cases—using the District Court's legally sound analysis as a guide. Part II explains the critical errors in the Second Circuit's two-sided-market analysis: Section II.A explains briefly why multiple "sides" of a multi-sided platform or business model cannot be included in the same relevant market; Section II.B explains that the Second Circuit's "netting" exercise is unsound and ultimately antithetical to the basic purposes of the Sherman Act. Section II.B.ii also includes an explanation of how existing rule of the reason doctrine permits courts to consider relevant arguments about two-sided platforms in a case like this one, while the Second Circuit's novel approach, even if sound, substantially increases the risk of lower-court error.

---

2 Because, as explained *infra* p.28-31, the language of "two-sided markets" is confounding for antitrust purposes, we believe it clearer to refer to the general phenomenon as a two-sided "platform" or "business model." The "two-sided-market" terminology having caught on below, however, we use the terms interchangeably here.

Were we to boil all that down to a few sentences, however, we would just say this. Efficient allocation of resources in the economy depends on undistorted competitive price signals. The correct "balance" between, say, merchant prices and consumer rewards in related or even interdependent markets is thus determined *by competition itself*; that role cannot be filled by a judicial scale-balancing exercise balancing different market participants' welfare because that lies well beyond any judge's (or economist's) ken. That AmEx manipulated this balance through a restraint that virtually eliminated horizontal price competition is the antitrust *problem*—not a defense— because antitrust law endeavors to preserve competition on all sides of any business's operations, and let the free market's invisible hand take the wheel from there.

## I. The District Court Correctly Applied Rule of Reason Analysis To The Facts It Found.

### A. How the rule of reason works.

The rule of reason, which is correctly laid out in petitioners' briefs, U.S.Br.20-22; OhioBr.20-22, is a three-step heuristic courts have developed to determine the lawfulness of an alleged restraint with potentially ambiguous competitive effects. The plaintiff begins by showing that the restraint is plausibly anticompetitive; the defendant responds by proffering any legitimate, procompetitive justification it has for the restraint; and the plaintiff responds by attempting to prove that any proffered justifications are either factually false (*i.e.*, the restraint does not serve them) or at least available through "a substantially less restrictive alternative." Areeda & Hovenkamp ¶1502. Even if there are no less restrictive alternatives, courts may still find that the restraint is harmful on balance to competition in the relevant market—though even this in-market balancing exercise by courts is (appropriately) rare. *See, e.g.*, Michael Carrier, *The Rule of Reason: An Empirical Update For The 21st Century*, 16 Geo. Mason L. Rev. 827, 827-29 (2009) (finding balancing step reached in only 2.2% of cases from 1999 to 2009, and 4% of cases from 1977 to 1999). Below, we briefly elaborate these three steps and the tools antitrust law uses to conduct them.

### 1. Step one and "marketpower"

The first step—the plaintiff's showing that the restraint is "*prima facie* anticompetitive," *Cal. Dental Ass'n v. F.T.C.*, 526 U.S. 756, 771 (1999)—can be made in one of two ways. Both implicate, albeit differently, the critical concept of **market power**. The "direct method" involves direct proof of an actual anticompetitive effect, which proves *a fortiori* that the defendant has sufficient market power to bring that effect about. The "indirect method" involves independent proof of both market power and a restraint that plausibly harms competition.

This Court has said that "market power" is the power to get a purchaser "to do something that he would not do in a competitive market."[3] *Eastman Kodak Co. v. Image Technical Servs., Inc.*, 504 U.S. 451, 464 (1992). More rigorous economic definitions are available—the most accepted being the power to profitably raise price above marginal cost, *see* William Landes & Richard Posner, *Market Power in Antitrust Cases*, 94 Harv. L. Rev. 937, 939 (1981)—and that definition is frequently helpful in contexts like merger analysis. But in a case like this, the definition from *Eastman Kodak* expresses the critical conceptual point.

Market power matters in a restraint case like this one because, in its absence, merchants themselves could fight anticompetitive contract terms like AmEx's non-discrimination provisions (NDPs) by simply diverting their business to competitors. Antitrust law prefers trusting competition itself to protect the market in this way, which competition will do *in the absence of market power*. As Justice Scalia put it, certain potentially anticompetitive restraints "are completely without force when the participants lack market power." *Eastman Kodak*, 504 U.S. at 488 (dissent) (citing Areeda & Hovenkamp); *see also F.T.C. v. Indiana Fed'n of Dentists*, 476 U.S. 447, 460 (1986) ("[T]he purpose of the ... market power [inquiry] is to determine whether an arrangement has the potential for genuine adverse effects on competition[.]"). Thus, in a restraint case, the question is whether the defendant has sufficient market power to make the alleged restraint effective.

In cases involving the "direct method," like this one, the market-power showing is effectively subsumed by the plaintiff's direct proof that the alleged restraint is causing anticompetitive effects. In that case, we know the defendant has sufficient market power to generate those effects because it *is* generating them. Thus "'proof of *actual* detrimental effects'... can 'obviate the need for an inquiry into market power.'" *Indiana Fed'n*, 476 U.S. at 460-61 (citing Areeda & Hovenkamp) (emphasis added). In fact, it can establish that the requisite market power exists more directly "than calculations of elusive market share[s]" or other indirect inquiries. *Todd v. Exxon Corp.*, 275 F.3d 191, 206 (2d Cir. 2001) (Sotomayor, J.). Notably, as the United States emphasizes, U.S. Br. 23-34, this case involved very strong proof under the direct method—especially the evidence that AmEx's rules entirely suppress horizontal price competition among AmEx and its competitors. *See* Pet.App. 204a-207a & n.43 (discussing Discover testimony); *id.* 197a-198a (discussing AmEx's own acknowledgement so flack of pricing competition).

In "indirect method" cases, market power must be proven independently. Typically, after identifying the alleged restraint, the factfinder will define the **relevant market** in which that restraint operates (discussed *infra* pp.12-13, 17-20), and then attempt to infer market power from the defendant's estimated market share and other factors. Particularly in restraint cases, this inquiry is a rough proxy at its very best; sufficient market power to insist on some restraints can arise from a small share of a very

---

3 Notably, no coercion need be involved; the "power" comes solely from the presence (and elasticity) of consumer demand and the lack of substitute sources of supply.

concentrated market (like AmEx has here), and can other times be absent even when market share is very high (for example, when entry is easy). *See, e.g.*, Areeda & Hovenkamp ¶515 ("A firm could have substantial market power without accounting for all or even most of a market. By the same token, the power of a firm with a dominant market share might be very high or negligible [.]"); Louis Kaplow, *Why (Ever) Define Markets?*, 124 Harv. L. Rev. 437 (2010) (expressing skepticism that market definition truly aids in assessing market power). Some restraints can also be easier to impose with less unilateral market power because (as here)they are good for one's own competitors as well, and lead to reinforcing behavior in oligopolistic settings, *see, e.g.*, Areeda & Hovenkamp ¶¶530b,574a— as happened when Visa and Mastercard adopted their own NDPs. Pet.App. 180a. It is thus frequently preferable to look for direct proof of market power, which may include (among other things) a defendant's ability to raise prices repeatedly without losing share, very high and persistent economic profits, or ready success in thwarting counter-parties' efforts to resist the imposition of disfavored restraints. *See* Pet.App. 158a-163a (detailing considerable evidence in this regard); *accord United States v. Microsoft*, 253

F.3d 34, 58 (D.C. Cir. 2001) (pointing to Microsoft's pricing conduct and pattern of exclusionary behavior as direct evidence of monopoly power).

Before moving on, it is critical to emphasize that there is *nothing illegal about having market power*. The Sherman Act does not condemn its mere acquisition or existence; it is, in this context, only an indication that an allegedly anticompetitive restraint *might work*. Put otherwise, "[w]hile market power is a necessary condition for an anticompetitive restraint under the rule of reason, it is never a sufficient condition." Herbert Hovenkamp, *The Rule of Reason* p.17 (Fla. L. Rev. forthcoming 2018) ("*Rule of Reason*"), https://goo.gl/4CL5jx.

The Second Circuit thus erred quite seriously when it held that AmEx's "cardmember insistence" could have no bearing on its market power, particularly because it derived from "cardmember satisfaction" and so couldn't be a bad thing. Pet.App. 45a-48a. In this case, it was not relevant where AmEx's market power *came from*; the law cares only whether it exists, and so might make a putatively anticompetitive restraint possible. Accordingly, if merchants so wanted AmEx that they felt bound to accept it, that demonstrates market power without regard to why that dynamic exists.[4] The District Court was thus quite right to regard "cardholder insistence" as strong evidence of market power, and the Second Circuit quite wrong to reject it while expressly noting, several times, that "cardholder insistence is precisely what makes accepting AmEx cards worthwhile for merchants to do." *See id.* That which makes "accepting AmEx cards worthwhile" is *exactly* what gives AmEx market power.

---

4 Relatedly, note that creating "worthwhile" products often creates market power while even a patent "monopoly"on other products would not. The patent-holder on a cure for cancer would have enormous market power; the patent-holder on a new head ache remedy likely wouldn't, given competing alternatives. *See* Areeda & Hovenkamp ¶518e; *Illinois Tool Works v. Independent Ink*, 547U.S.28(2006).

## 2. Step two

Once the plaintiff makes its *prima facie* showing under either the direct or indirect method, the burden shifts to the defendant to proffer any legitimate, procompetitive justifications it may have for the restraint. This burden shift follows from basic principles of proof that are not specific to antitrust. "The defendant, being the author of the restraints, is in a better position to explain why they are profitable and in consumers' best interests." Areeda & Hovenkamp, ¶1505.

It is important to note, however, that not every justification that generates welfare somewhere in the economy—even by lowering prices—can be deemed "legitimate" or "procompetitive." Instead, this requirement must exclude (at least) one type of justification. Because promoting competition is the goal of the antitrust laws, "defendants' expectation of profit" from a restraint must come "from something other than a restriction of competition" itself. *Rule of Reason*, p.22. Put otherwise, "[a]n effective defense must be able to show that a practice has social benefits that *do not depend on the exercise of market power*." *Id.* p.23 (emphasis added). Accordingly, at an absolute minimum, a defendant's justification cannot be that it will use a restraint to generate monopoly rents or restrict output in one aspect of its business and then reinvest that revenue elsewhere—including, of course, in its own bottom line.

As an example, this Court in *NCAA v. Board Of Regents of University of Oklahoma*, 468 U.S. 85,116- 17 (1984), did not permit the NCAA to defend a restriction on televising college football games on the theory that it would "protect live attendance." That justification rested on the view that exercising market power and restricting output (*i.e.*, limiting broadcasts) would lead to benefits elsewhere in the economy, and so was "inconsistent with the basic policy of the Sherman Act." *Id.* As this Court put it, "'the Rule of Reason does not support a defense based on the assumption that competition itself is unreasonable.'"*Id.* at 117(quoting *Nat'l Soc'y of Prof'l Engr's v. United States*, 435 U.S. 679, 696 (1978)). In contrast, this Court explained that restrictions aimed at protecting "the integrity of [the product] as … distinct and attractive," or promoting the NCAA's non-competition-related ends (like preserving a "revered tradition of amateurism in college sports") could be legitimate, so long as they rested on evidence that the restriction pro-competitively increased output in the relevant market, rather than on the impermissible intuition that restricting output was somehow "pro-competitive." *See id.* at 116-17, 120.

## 3. Step three

If legitimate justifications for the restraint are offered, the burden shifts back to the plaintiff to demonstrate that a "substantially less restrictive alternative" could achieve the same benefits. Areeda & Hovenkamp ¶1502. "By this stage of the controversy, most cases will be resolved. If not—and rarely—the harms and benefits must be compared to reach a net judgment whether the challenged behavior is, on balance, reasonable." *Id.* Notably, this balancing occurs *within* the relevant market, *see infra* pp.20-27; the factfinder is not asked to balance the welfare of one set of consumers against another's somewhere else.

## B. The District Court's analysis

The District Court applied this settled framework to the facts as it found them, which are amply described in petitioners' briefs. *See* U.S. Br. 2-12, 23- 34; Ohio Br. 1-13. Without unduly revisiting those facts, the following section briefly reviews the District Court's legal analysis of them to demonstrate how the rule of reason properly operates in practice.

The court began by defining the **relevant market**. Pet.App. 111a-148a. This was the appropriate first step for two reasons. First, because the plaintiffs purported to carry their *prima facie* burden through both the direct and indirect method of proof, a market definition was needed to assess AmEx's market power using its market share and other factors. Second, and more important here, a basic mapping of the relevant market is necessary to set the scope of the ensuing inquiry, even under the direct method. It is true that, because the "purpose of the inquiries into market definition and market power is to determine whether an arrangement has the potential for genuine adverse effects on competition, proof of actual detrimental effect[s]" can be "sufficient to support a finding that the challenged restraint was unreasonable even in the absence of elaborate market analysis." *Ind. Fed'n*, 476 U.S. at 461. Even then, however, courts must ultimately establish the basic boundaries of the market in which the restraint operates.[5] To both ends, market definition must be tied to the set of *substitutes* reasonably available to the market participants at issue if it is to serve its purpose. *See infra* pp.17-20 (elaborating this point); *United States v. E.I. du Pont de Nemours & Co.*, 351

U.S. 377, 395 (1956) ("In considering what is the relevant market ... no more definite rule can be declared than that" it consists of "commodities reasonably interchangeable by consumers for the same purposes[.]").

Here, the District Court engaged in rigorous market definition, looking to both well-established economic tests and a pragmatic analysis of competitive realities supported by the testimony of market participants. It found that the relevant market encompassed "general purpose credit and charge card network services" offered to merchants. That market is highly concentrated; those services are supplied by only three major players (AmEx, Visa, and Mastercard) and one minor one (Discover). Among other things, the District Court declined to include debit-card services within

---

5 In cases that use the "direct method," it may not be necessary to *start* with market definition because "[e]vidence of competitive effects can inform market definition, just as market definition can be informative regarding competitive effects."USDOJ & FTC, *Horizontal Merger Guidelines* §4(2010). *See also id.* (further noting that "analysis need not start with market definition" because "although evaluation of competitive alternatives available to customers is always necessary at some point in the analysis,"some analytic tools"to assess competitive effects do not rely on market definition").

the relevant market by determining that debit and credit card services were not "reasonably interchangeable" and merchants would not substitute one for the other. Pet. App. 122a-143a.

Having defined the market, the District Court undertook the market-power analysis required for at least the indirect method of establishing a *prima facie* case. After analyzing AmEx's market share in combination with a set of other relevant factors including entry barriers, the high degree of industry concentration, and the "amplifying effect" of AmEx's "highly insistent or loyal cardholder base," it found that AmEx had market power. Pet.App. 150a-165a; *supra* pp.9-10. It also relied on direct indicia of market power, including AmEx's ability to repeatedly raise prices without losing share, *id.* 165a-180a, and on-point testimony establishing that even the largest national merchants cannot drop AmEx in response to its NDPs—though some have tried (and rapidly failed). *E.g.*, Pet.App.162a-164a.

After finding that AmEx had market power, the District Court concluded its step-one analysis by also finding direct proof of anticompetitive effects. It found that the challenged NDPs virtually eliminated horizontal price competition for merchant network services, impeded entry by low-cost business models, stifled innovation, and raised prices for both merchants and their customers. Pet.App. 191a-214a. It thus held (correctly, on these facts) that plaintiffs had satisfied their *prima facie* burden through both the direct and indirect method. At a minimum, it is certain as a matter of antitrust law that a firm's exercise of market power to frustrate price competition among its competitors "to the point of near irrelevance," Pet.App. 195a, at least *plausibly* causes anticompetitive harm.

The District Court then turned to AmEx's proffered legitimate justifications at step two. Pet.App. 228a-258a. It began by carefully parsing AmEx's argument that the NDPs and their restrictions on steering were necessary to sustain AmEx's "spend-centric" business model. *Id.* 230a-240a. The District Court determined that, at bottom, this was an argument that the high merchant discount rates sustained by the NDPs were necessary for AmEx to offer more lucrative rewards to cardholders, effectively "shift[ing] the bulk of interbrand competition in the credit and charge card industry to the cardholder side of the platform." *Id.* 234a-241a. The court found this argument both factually unsupported and fundamentally incompatible with the Sherman Act. Among other things, it (correctly) cautioned that AmEx seemed to be defending the viability of its own business model rather than competition as such, Pet. App. 235a, and that "the law does not permit American Express to decide on behalf of the entire market which legitimate forms of interbrand competition should be available and which should not." Pet.App. 240a; *see supra* p.10 (noting that suppression of com- petition is not a "legitimate"or "procompetitive"justification).

Because AmEx's proffered justifications were deemed both unsupported and illegitimate, the court did not proceed to step three. Instead, it properly concluded that the profound effect that the NDPs have on horizontal price competition in the relevant market for merchant network services—and the resulting supracompetitive prices imposed on merchants by AmEx *and* its competitors—constituted a violation of the Sherman Act.

In our view, this was a prototypical and straightforward application of rule of reason analysis that appears to have reached the correct result—at least on the facts as the District Court found them. In fact, any analysis leading to a contrary result is necessarily suspicious. While vertical restraints like AmEx's frequently have only limited effects on *inter*brand competition (and may promote it), *see, e.g., Leegin*, 551 U.S. at 890, the District Court found here that AmEx's NDPs had profoundly restricted *horizontal* price competition not just between AmEx and its competitors, but *among all* competing providers. With the NDPs in place and secured by AmEx's market power, none of AmEx's competitors had any incentive to lower price; merchants' inability to steer customers to lower-cost cards (or even give customers truthful information about the cards' merchant fees) had severed the connection between prices to merchants and their quantities of card usage. Pet.App. 228a. In fact, Discover had testified—credibly, from an economic perspective—that it simply could not gain share by cutting merchant prices, and so rapidly raised them instead. Pet.App. 206a. The court found that supracompetitive prices and other anticompetitive effects had in fact resulted. Pet.App. 191a-214a. This established a violation of the Sherman Act, and certainly sufficed for a *prima facie* case.

## II. The Second Circuit's "Two-Sided-Market" Innovations Are Fundamentally Unsound.

Given the District Court's sound analysis, the Second Circuit's reversal was erroneous. But the much more critical point here is that the *reasons* the Second Circuit gave for reversing—both of which sounded in the "two-sidedness"of AmEx's business— are highly problematic. Neither is logically sound and both threaten to undermine basic principles of antitrust law and economics. It is imperative the Court reject both.

### A. The relevant market cannot encompass both sides of AmEx's platform.

As noted above, a relevant market for antitrust purposes is defined by the identification of reasonable substitutes for the product at issue. This can be done with relatively rigorous economic analysis where necessary—including measurements of cross-elasticities of demand among putative substitutes—but it can often be done with a more practical analysis of "commercial realities" and participant behavior. *See, e.g., Eastman Kodak*, 504 U.S. at 482; *Brown Shoe Co. v. United States*, 370 U.S. 294, 325 (1962); *DuPont*, 351 U.S. at 394.

Either way, the products that AmEx sells on the two "sides" of its platform do not exhibit the characteristics of "reasonably interchangeable" substitutes in any respect. Merchants do not buy and have no use for the services sold to cardholders and cardholders do not buy and have no use for the services sold to merchants. There is *zero* cross-elasticity of demand: A merchant cannot switch to purchasing cardholder services in response to an increase in the price of merchant services, and vice versa. Far from being substitutes, these services act more as complements and so cannot belong in the same relevant market. *See* Areeda & Hovenkamp ¶565 (explaining that the Court of Appeals "incorrectly conclud[ed] that the relevant market in which to consider American Express's anti-steering rules was not limited to the market for network [merchant] services but also included consumers....[T]hose two groupings are not substitutes for one another but rather behave more as complements."). Separate markets do not become a single relevant market for antitrust purposes simply because one defendant sells two services as part of the same platform. *See id.* (Second Circuit "was apparently misled by the fact that AmEx obtained revenue from two sources, ... but the fact that a firm obtains its profits from two different, non-substitutable groups does not serve to place the[m] ... into the same relevant market").

As the United States correctly notes, U.S. Br. 35- 40, there is in fact no logical way to include two different "sides" of a company's platform or business model in one antitrust market. Among other things, they do not include the same participants—a point the District Court emphasized in rejecting this argument. Pet.App. 119a. On the merchant "side," AmEx competes only with Visa, Mastercard, and Discover in a highly concentrated market; on the cardholder "side," AmEx competes with Discover, Chase, Capital One, Citibank, and thousands of other banks that issue credit cards. Visa has a 45% share on the merchant "side" and essentially a 0% share in issuing cards or providing cardholder rewards—the individual banks do that. Were it an important consideration here, how would Visa's "combined" share of the merchant/cardholder market be calculated? Is it 45%, 22.5%, 0% or something else altogether? There is no logical or practicable way to provide an answer.

Relatedly, but perhaps more importantly, attempting to combine these two-sides of AmEx's business into one antitrust relevant market (however that might be done) would undermine the very reasons for performing a market definition in the first place. We define markets in antitrust analysis to determine whether market power exists in the relationship between two sets of economic counterparties; we want to know whom the market participants facing a restraint or price increase might look to in an effort to discipline the anticompetitive behavior of a seller through competition itself. One need not measure cross-elasticity of demand to see that a merchant dissatisfied with AmEx's imposition of the NDPs on anyone *accepting* AmEx cards cannot respond by *taking out* a new credit card with Chase or Capital One.

Indeed, generally, the competitive dynamics that determine the effect of a restraint or price increase that a company imposes on customers in one aspect of its business are not predictably affected one way or another by the nature of competition in that company's other market relationships. This is to say that effects occurring in other, closely interrelated markets may ameliorate an anticompetitive effect in the restrained market, they may exacerbate it, or (as likely happened here) they may have no plausible effect at all because of how the restraint itself muffles competitive price signals. Thus, even if there are cases where we have good reason to believe that out-of-market effects cause "feedback" effects in the restrained market, *see infra* p.31, the solution cannot be to lump two markets for non-substitutes into the same "market."

In sum, we care about market definition in restraint cases because it sets the appropriate scope of the rule of reason inquiry—establishing the sphere in which the coupling of market power and an anticompetitive practice can cause the kind of distortion and welfare loss that matters to antitrust law. If competition across that relationship has been harmed or destroyed, that is sufficient to cause resources to be diverted inefficiently both within that relationship and across related parts of the economy in ways that untainted price signals would avoid. Defining the market more broadly to include other aspects of the restraining party's business will lead to over-looking those distortionary, anticompetitive effects, and ensure that market definition itself fails to answer the questions for which it is asked.

## B. "Netting" or "balancing" competitive effects across both sides of a two-sided platform is fundamentally unsound.

The Second Circuit's holding that a plaintiff's *prima facie* case must also show "net" anticompetitive effects across both sides in a case involving a two-sided platform is also pernicious. Both logically and practically, this is deeply unsound. Logically, it ignores that the balance of prices across the platform's "sides" should be set *by competition*, not skewed by competitive restraints and then excused by *ad hoc* judicial balancing. And practically, it asks courts to perform complex analyses they will find confusing or impracticable, not the least of which is attempting to pin down the ill-defined phenomenon of "two-sided markets" itself.

### 1. The Second Circuit's "netting" exercise is erroneous.

Though hard to define, *see infra* pp.28-31, two-sided platforms are certainly a recognizable phenomenon, and increasingly important to students of business strategy and industrial organization. The District Court concluded that AmEx was a two-sided platform because it "sells different products or services to two separate yet inter-related groups of customers who, in turn, rely on the platform to intermediate some type of interaction between them." Pet.App. 77a-78a (citing Evans & Schmalensee, *Industrial Organization of Markets with Two–Sided Platforms*, 3 COMPETITION POL'Y INT'L 150 (2007); Rochet & Tirole, *Two–Sided Markets: A Progress Report*, 37 RAND J. Econ. 645 (2006). For now, we adopt this as a working definition.

Note, however, that it is quite broad and encompasses ubiquitous business models like newspapers (which sell to and unite readers and advertisers), brokers of all stripes (who sell to and unite buyers and sellers), cable companies (which sell to and unite content providers and viewers), and many more. From a competition policy perspective, these industries do share certain characteristics: For example, there is the "cross-platform network effect" the District Court identified, where "the number of agents or the quantity of services bought on one side … affects the value that an agent on the other side of the platform can realize." Pet.App. 79a. But these businesses also vary widely and there may be very little salience to their two-sidedness in any given case— especially relative to other traditional considerations like market concentration and barriers to entry.[6]

In any event, the ubiquity of two-sided business models means this Court has confronted them before and rejected the Second Circuit's special rule. In *Times-Picayune Publ'g Co. v. United States*, 345 U.S. 594 (1953)—which concerned the sale of advertising space by a newspaper—this Court was faced with a classic two-sided platform: The paper sells ad space to advertisers on one side and reporting to readers on the other. Recognizing that "every newspaper is a dual trader in *separate* though interdependent markets," *id.* at 610 (emphasis added), this Court held that, because the restraint at issue was applied only in one of them, the decisive question was whether the defendant had economic dominance in *that* market alone. *Id.* In other words, this Court held, in a case where the defendant operated a two-sided platform, that each side represented a "separate … market" and that injuring competition in the restrained market alone was sufficient to violate the Sherman Act. This Court's analytical approach was correct then and remains so today; it need only adhere to this precedent to correctly decide this case.

*Times-Picayune* aside, however, *amici* would still strenuously urge this Court not to approve of any "netting" or "balancing" analysis across relevant markets—even if they are "both sides" of a two-sided platform—because that exercise is fundamentally inconsistent with the antitrust laws' core purposes. *See* Areeda & Hovenkamp ¶1505 (criticizing Second Circuit's "conclusion that when a restraint is alleged in a two-sided market, a *prima facie* case requires the plaintiff to allege net harm aggregated across both sides"). This idea finds its most damaging expression in the Second Circuit's notion that AmEx should be allowed to use its NDPs to obstruct price competition and keep merchant prices high because "a reduction in revenue that AmEx earns from merchants' fees may decrease the optimal level of cardholder benefits." Pet.App. 49a-50a. Antitrust law and policy should not even indulge *arguendo* a defendant's excuse that it is robbing Peter to pay Paul; basic antitrust policy requires that "*competition* should choose the optimal mix of revenue between the two sides"— not AmEx's near-total obstruction of horizontal competition among AmEx and its competitors on one side or the other. *See* Areeda & Hovenkamp, ¶562e.

For this reason, while we believe this Court should reverse the Second Circuit and affirm the District Court's judgment, we would urge the Court *not* to rely in any respect on the District Court having already "balanced" the benefits and harms across AmEx's merchant and cardholder markets, and/or having concluded that AmEx

---

6 Indeed, the most salient aspect of two-sided platforms from an antitrust perspective may be that their network effects make entry by new platforms difficult, *increasing* the prospect of durable market power.

still harmed competition in the market as the Second Circuit defined it. Petitioners understandably advance these alternative arguments as litigants, but we believe these analyses are ultimately unintelligible and should not be encouraged even as alternative considerations for future factfinders. Ultimately, they can only confuse the correct analysis.

Notably, AmEx's putatively "procompetitive" justification that high merchant prices lead to more rewards and competition for cardholders is plainly of the illegitimate form described above, *supra* p.15—it clearly depends on the exercise of market power to work. AmEx's justification for its restraint is simply that it will extract monopoly rents from merchants in order to use (some of) them to entice new cardholders to its platform. This is an unmitigated negative from an antitrust perspective. As the United States correctly explains, U.S. Br. 45-46, antitrust law must reject the distortionary effects of dictating prices through restraints rather than competition because it disrupts the "central nervous system of the economy," *United States v. Socony-Vacuum Oil Co.*, 310 U.S. 150, 226 n.59 (1940).

To put the same point differently, it is important that lower courts not confuse mere "lower prices" somewhere in the economy with a "procompetitive effect." In important respects, the reality can be the exact opposite: By "disrupt[ing] the proper functioning of the price-setting mechanism"—that is, by using a restraint to increase prices over here and lower them over there—a practice necessarily undermines the competitive process and so can violate the rule of reason "even absent proof that it resulted in higher prices." *Indiana Fed'n*, 476 U.S. at 461-62. Accordingly, this Court has made clear that "[a] restraint that has the effect of reducing the importance of consumer preference in setting price" is inconsistent "with th[e] fundamental goal of antitrust law," *NCAA*, 468 U.S. at 107 & n.30, and that conduct that "'impedes the ordinary give and take of the marketplace,' and substantially deprives the customer of 'the ability to utilize and compare prices'" adversely affects competition. *Nat'l Soc'y*, 435 U.S. at 692-93. In the end, the goal is not to ensure that *somebody* benefits from an alleged restraint; rather, it is to ensure that the challenged restraint is not disrupting competition in *its* market, causing a misallocation of resources to or from other areas of the economy.

Indeed, indulging a "netting" or "balancing" approach across two-sided platforms would immediately vitiate the rationale for the best-known rule in all of antitrust law—the *per se* proscription against price fixing. Cartelists almost always have a story as to why their price increases or output restrictions are a net positive for the economy: They alleviate a supply glut, keep failing firms in business, increase wages, or minimize waste. Antitrust law accepts none of these excuses not because they could never be true, but because we are confident that the distortionary effects on price signals are bad, even if there are (no doubt) some parties throughout the economy who benefit from the cartelists' behavior. *See Socony Vacuum Oil*, 310 U.S. at 226 n.59. ("Whatever economic justification particular price-fixing agreements may be thought to have, the law does not permit an inquiry into their reasonableness. They are all banned because of their actual or potential threat to the central nervous system of the economy."). The law would no more accept those justifications for horizontal price fixing in the context of two-sided platforms; courts would certainly condemn the elimination of horizontal price competition the District Court found here had it been created by agreement among AmEx and its competitors. The distortionary effect of the cartel would be an antitrust policy problem without regard to whether fully 100% of the resulting rents are passed over to cardholders. And the very same principle explains why netting or balancing across the platform is inappropriate here, too.

Moreover, while the Second Circuit suggests that AmEx passes on high merchant fees to cardholders as part of its business model, this phrasing somewhat obscures reality. AmEx is a profit-maximizing firm, not a wealth-redistribution engine; to the extent it increases rewards or decreases fees to cardholders, it is only because competition for cardholders makes it so. Notably, *that* market is healthy: There are thousands of rival firms issuing cards and competing to win a share of consumers' wallets, entry is relatively easy, and there is constant innovation in offers and rewards models. In contrast, the market is quite unhealthy on the merchant "side" because it is both quite concentrated and restricted by AmEx's NDPs. Eliminating the NDPs will help to heal that market and so will undoubtedly affect both AmEx's and its competitors' bottom lines, because they will now have to compete for both cardholders *and* merchants. But given the robustness of existing competition over cardholders, there may be no substantial decreases in reward expenditures at all. And even if there are, antitrust policy prefers to have two healthy markets rather than one, because that leads to more efficient resource allocation as between them.

Importantly, none of this is to say that AmEx should be constrained in choosing the pair of prices *it* wants to charge merchants and cardholders in its own business model. The sole point is that it should not be free to use its market power to prevent merchants from fostering price competition *among* AmEx and its competing card networks and benefitting from the lower prices other competing networks might offer merchants as a result. Nor should AmEx be free to choose for consumers whether they prefer to forego AmEx's rewards in favor of other inducements merchants might offer them for using the merchants' favored cards. *See* Areeda & Hovenkamp ¶1505 ("[C]*ompetition* is what determines how revenue is assessed with respect to each side. Some card issuers pursue a strategy of obtaining high market fees while offering more generous terms to customers, while others do the opposite. [AmEx's] policy effectively made customers indifferent to merchant charges and to the extent those charges could be expected to be higher, restrained competition[.]"). Contrary to the Second Circuit's view, AmEx cannot have "a legitimate interest" in restricting free-market forces. The interaction of those forces—not AmEx's NDPs—must be allowed to determine the optimal level of both merchant prices and cardholder rewards.

## 2. A special "net" price or benefit rule for two-sided platforms is an unnecessary invitation to error in the lower courts.

It is widely accepted that antitrust law must be implemented by an imperfect system that forces difficult economic judgments on lay judges and juries, and that it must therefore account for the risk of errors that harm competition in its pursuit of consumer welfare. *See, e.g.*, Frank Easterbrook, *The Limits of Antitrust*, 63 Tex. L. Rev. 1 (1984). That insight applies with special force to the inauguration of a new set of rules for two-sided markets that would require courts to attempt to create "net prices" or to aggregate and balance competitive benefits and harms across a two-sided platform. Even if this were theoretically possible, it is certainly impracticable and likely to create repeated errors in the lower courts that will contribute to market-wide in efficiency.

For example, efforts to balance competitive effects across relevant markets or generate "net" prices face intractable "commensurability" problems. The District Court found that AmEx itself was unable to propose a workable net price measurement that accounted for prices on both sides of its platform, Pet. App. 184a, and that result is hardly surprising. AmEx extracts merchant discount fees in dollars and pays out rewards in "miles," "points," progress toward status rewards, and other nonmonetary benefits. AmEx also charges ever-changing fees and interest rates that in part reflect the consumer "price" for card usage. There is thus no ready way to even approximate the per-transaction dollar price to cardholders for using their AmEx card, let alone "balance" a cardholder's price against a merchant's price for two different services.

Creating a special rule that permits cross-market balancing of benefits and harms for "two-sided markets" will also lead to vexing questions about how even to define which markets are "two-sided." Based on various (easily confused) definitions, so-called two-sided markets might encompass anything from businesses with plain-vanilla, vertical supply chains to what AmEx calls its "two-sided transaction market." *See* Pet.App. 78a. These definitions appear to us orthogonal to underlying antitrust principles, and so should not be turned into important doctrinal boxes that come with different rules and defenses. Instead, as we explain below, the underlying antitrust principles can themselves be used, through ordinary antitrust analysis, to capture whatever is special about a business model's two-sidedness in any given case.

Begin by noting that two-sidedness is ultimately a description of *a business model*, not a "market" at all. Uber, Lyft, taxi cabs, and typical livery services all compete directly in the market for riders, but their business models are different, and there may or may not be substitution among them in the driver or labor market. A rule that permits or requires cross-platform balancing for cases involving "two-sided markets" is thus inherently confusing: Does it apply whenever the *defendant* operates a two-sided platform, when its closest *competitors* are also two-sided platforms, when *some competitors* are also platforms, or on some other basis? Why can Uber try to excuse a restraint that injures its drivers based on benefits to riders when a livery or cab company could not?

Note, also, that every business has *far* more than two "sides." Apple and Google have similar platforms for selling online music, but also compete vigorously for specialized labor, real estate in Silicon Valley, mobile operating system usage, and more. Suppose Google imposes a restraint on performers selling music in the Google Play store and defends it as generating higher profits it can use to sell its Pixel phones more cheaply in competition with iPhones, or to set its salaries for programmers higher so as to be more competitive in that market. What makes these exercises in cross-market balancing—which clearly violate the Court's focus on individual markets in *Times-Picayune* and *NCAA*—any different from AmEx's argument here?

Next, imagine an online consignment operation for consumer electronics that returns a discounted portion of every sale to the original owner, while offering buyers a reward for every transaction. So far as we can tell, this is a "two-sided transaction market" that mirrors AmEx's business model quite precisely. Pet.App. 78a. But even from a colloquial perspective, what "market"does this consignment business occupy? Is it a consumer-electronics market? A used consumer-electronics market? A consignment based, used consumer-electronics sales market? An online electronics resale platform market? Merely adverting to the company's two-sided business model tells us nothing about its *markets*, or whether it qualifies for a special cross-market balancing rule.

The natural answer in terms of antitrust market definition, of course, is that putting this business in a market depends on what the case is about. The *relevant* market depends on why we care: If our online consignment operation is merging with a brick-and-mortar retailer of new electronics, it may cause unacceptable concentration in the market for consumer electronic sales (where both parties compete), but probably not in the market for repurchasing used electronics from original owners (because only one operates there). It may also cause no problems at all, depending on the nature of substitution between new and used sales and online and local sales. The important point, however, is that the antitrust answer to the question of what market our consignment business occupies may lie on either side of a company's "platform" and may encompass business models with ordinary vertical supply chains or not, all depending on the case or restraint at issue. For similar reasons, there is no way to know *ex ante* whether the two-sidedness of a defendant's platform will affect market definition, market power, anticompetitive effects, or anything else antitrust law cares about. The two-sided-market category is the tail, not the dog.

That said, the United States is certainly correct that the two-sidedness of a company's business *can* be relevant in any given case. U.S.Br.50-54. Its relevance, however, is already captured by the ordinary tools of antitrust analysis as the District Court applied them. Clarifying how those tools work— rather than adding new, hard-to-implement rules for new, hard-to-define categories—is far more likely to help the lower courts avoid serious errors.

For example, it is already understood that when two aspects of a company's business model are closely related or "interdependent," that may mean that competitive effects or anticompetitive distortions on one side of its business will strongly affect the other over time, and vice versa, causing "feedback" effects that may ameliorate or exacerbate the original distortion. *See, e.g.*, Areeda & Hovenkamp ¶562e. These "dynamic" considerations or "feedback" effect may constrain *or* reinforce anticompetitive exercises of market power; it depends entirely on industry-specific context. In any case, however, a defendant is free to argue that its market power in one market is illusory in fact because the close interrelationship between that market and another disciplines its ability to raise prices or impose anticompetitive conditions in the relevant market.

But, importantly, if that argument *is* presented, it requires no special two-sided-market rules to analyze; all it needs are the conventional tools for deciding whether market power exists or not. And particularly where (as here) the proof of market power and anticompetitive effects is established through *direct evidence*, there is no reason to worry that we have incorrectly assessed a defendant's power in the relevant market by ignoring a price effect somewhere else in the economy. We know the requisite market power exists because the anticompetitive effect occurred.

Indeed, notice that AmEx could not possibly make such an argument here, because the very anticompetitive effect of its restraint is to *sever* the connection between the merchant and cardholder sides of its platform. Competition for cardholder transactions does not benefit merchants (or constrain the exercise of market power over them) because merchants lack the ability to steer cardholders away from cards that charge the ma higher price. The two sides of the AmEx platform may be interdependent in some ways, but—given the NDPs—they are not interdependent in the important sense that competition for cardholders will (or even can) feedback into improved pricing conditions or competitive dynamics on the merchant side. The restraint itself prevents the feedback.

Defendants can also potentially argue that the feedback effect is one that improves the competitive process operating on *both* aspects of its two-sided platform at once through a conventional step-two, rule of reason argument. We take this to be the United States' suggestion that the defendant can show "at the second step" that the restraint is "reasonably *necessary* to achieve legitimate *procompetitive* benefits in a closely related and *interdependent* market." U.S. Br. 52 (emphasis added).[7] This entails a frankly difficult showing that the "dynamic"effects of a restraint are ultimately good for the restrained party in the medium-run in a way the antitrust laws can accept. Often, this requires showing that a product could not exist without the restraint. And, importantly, that showing needs to be made for the *product*—not just the defendant's version of it—to ensure that this argument does not reduce to the view that "competition should be restrained because it would hurt *my* ability to compete with my competitors (and their potentially superior business models)." That argument, of course, is the one this Court has rightly rejected as unacceptable throughout antitrust law.

---

7 Formally, this does not entail balancing of out-of-market "benefits" with in-market "harms"—an analysis the United States itself rejects. U.S. Br. 41, 45-46. Instead, it entails looking to out-of-market effects in interdependent markets because they may improve (or reflect improved) competition in the relevant market itself.

*See supra* pp.10-11 (discussing *NCAA*); *Brown Shoe*, 370 U.S. at 320 (antitrust law is "concern[ed] with the protection of *competition*, not *competitors*") (emphasis added).[8]

Ultimately, we believe the consideration of out-of-market benefits in cases involving two-sided platforms (or other interdependent markets) is at best an oblique way of getting to the simpler question of whether competition continues to protect or ultimately benefits the restrained parties, and while such "dynamic" analyses might theoretically prove profitable, we doubt the game is worth the several boxes of candles it will take the lower courts to play it. The "out-of-market benefit" inquiry tends in the direction of weighing the welfare of one set of consumers against the welfare of another, which is what antitrust law seeks to *avoid* in favor of reliance on competition itself. Meanwhile, the hypothetical causal chain that makes an out-of-market benefit procompetitive overall is typically attenuated and will be hard for lower courts to follow, so this Court should regard the risk of lower-court error as both high and very costly. Because the ultimate concern remains on the avoidance of competitive distortions within any properly defined set of market relationships—that is, within a relevant market—the better course is for this Court to simply instruct the lower courts to look for evidence of off-setting benefits solely within the relevant market itself.[9] That is particularly so because the kind of multi-step causal tracing exercise involved in the consideration of out-of-market benefits is precisely the kind of complexity this Court's antitrust rules have endeavored to avoid. *See, e.g., Illinois Brick Co. v. Illinois*, 431 U.S. 720 (1977); *Hanover Shoe, Inc. v. United Shoe Machinery Corp.*, 392 U.S. 481 (1968).

Whatever the Court says in this regard, however, it should make clear that it cannot help AmEx for the reasons the District Court gave below. AmEx's fundamental argument is that it must prevent steering away from its cards in order to keep its rewards high and support its business model. That argument depends on using an exercise of market power to raise prices and direct the benefits elsewhere, and imposes a restraint that ensures that those benefits *cannot* redound to merchants' benefit through the competitive process. It is thus neither legitimate nor procompetitive, and so the District Court properly rejected it. Pet. App. 234a-241a. This Court should thus reverse the Second Circuit's decision and, for the sake of clarity in future cases, affirm the sound application of the rule of reason by the District Court.

---

8 In any event, the general condition on this showing is the one emphasized at the beginning, *supra* pp.10-11, and that the Court *must* make clear: A legitimate justification must not depend on the existence of market power to work. *See* Areeda & Hovenkamp ¶1505.

9 *Accord* Douglas H. Ginsburg & Joshua Wright, *Dynamic Analysis and the Limits of Antitrust Institutions*, 78 Antitrust 1 (2012) (concluding that courts should hesitate in incorporating "dynamic effects" analysis, even if theoretically useful, because of high risk of error); *cf. Horizontal Merger Guidelines* §10 n.14 (noting that agencies properly consider any anticompetitive effect in a relevant market sufficient to challenge a merger, and consider "efficiencies not strictly in the relevant market" only as a matter of prosecutorial discretion).

# CONCLUSION

This Court should reverse the Court of Appeals and affirm the judgment of the District Court.

Respectfully submitted,

December 14, 2017

Eric F. Citron

*Counsel of Record*
GOLDSTEIN & RUSSELL, P.C.
7475 Wisconsin Ave.

Suite 850

Bethesda, MD 20814

(202) 362-0636

ec@goldsteinrussell.com

# Addendum

# ADDENDUM
## Identity of *Amici Curiae*

The *amici* listed below are distinguished antitrust law professors and scholars. University affiliations are listed only for purposes of identification. Listed professors are acting only in their individual capacities and do not purport to represent the views of their universities.

**Herbert Hovenkamp**, James G. Dinan Professor at the Law School and the Wharton School of the University of Pennsylvania. He has been the Rockefeller Foundation Fellow, Harvard Law School; Fellow of the American Council of Learned Societies, Harvard Law School; Faculty Scholar, University of Iowa; Presidential Lecturer, University of Iowa; and the recipient of the University of Iowa Collegiate Teaching Award. He is the senior surviving author of *Antitrust Law* (formerly with Phillip Areeda & Donald Turner), currently 22 volumes.

**Harry First**, Charles L. Denison Professor of Law at New York University School of Law and Co-Director of the law school's Competition, Innovation, and Information Law Program. From 1999-2001 he served as Chief of the Antitrust Bureau of the Office of the Attorney General of the State of New York. Professor First is the co-author of the casebook *Free Enterprise and Economic Organization: Antitrust* (7th Ed. 2014). He was twice a Fulbright Research Fellow in Japan and taught antitrust as an adjunct professor at the University of Tokyo. Professor First is a contributing editor of the *Antitrust Law* Journal, foreign antitrust editor of the *Antitrust Bulletin*, a member of the executive committee of the Antitrust Section of the New York State Bar Association, and a member of the advisory board and a Senior Fellow of the American Antitrust Institute.

**Einer R. Elhauge**, Petrie Professor of Law at Harvard Law School, where he writes and teaches on Antitrust Law and Economics. Professor Elhauge is author of *U.S. Antitrust Law & Economics*, co-author of *Global Antitrust Law & Economic*, co-author of *Antitrust Law, Vol X* with Areeda, Elhauge & Hovenkamp, editor of the *Research Handbook on the Economics of Antitrust Law*, and the author of articles on antitrust law and economics that have won awards and appeared in peer reviewed economics journals and top law reviews. He is also President of Legal Economics, LLC, former FTC Special Employee on Antitrust Issus, member of the editorial board for the Competition Policy International, and member of the advisory boards for the Journal of Competition Law & Economics and for the Social Sciences Research Network on Antitrust Law & Policy.

**Eleanor M. Fox**, Walter J. Derenberg Professor of Trade Regulation at New York University School of Law. She was awarded an inaugural Lifetime Achievement Award in 2011 by the *Global Competition Review* for "substantial, lasting, and transformational impact on competition policy and practice." She received the inaugural award for outstanding contributions to the competition law community in 2015 by the Academic Society for Competition Law, the world network of academic law and economic competition experts.

**Stephen Calkins**, Professor of Law, Wayne State University. Professor Calkins is the author of one of the seminal Antitrust text books–*Antitrust Law: Policy and Practice* (4th ed. 2008) (with C. Paul Rogers III, Mark R. Patterson and William R. Andersen). He is also the author of *Antitrust Law and Economics in a Nutshell* (5th ed. 2004) (with Ernest Gellhorn and William Kovacic) and served as a co-editor of the *ABA Antitrust Section, Consumer Protection Law Developments* (2009). Professor Calkins is a life member of the American Law Institute, a fellow of the American Bar Foundation and a member of the advisory boards for the American Antitrust Institute, Sedona Conference and National State Attorneys General Program Advisory Project at Columbia Law School. For the American Bar Association, he has served on the Councils of the Sections of Administrative Law and Regulatory Practice and the Section of Antitrust Law (two, three-year terms). He is a former chair of the Association of American Law School's Antitrust and Economic Regulation Committee.

**Tim Wu**, Professor of Law, Columbia Law School. Professor Wu has co-authored several books, including "Network Neutrality Broadband Discrimination" (2003), Who Controls the Internet (2006), The Master Switch (2010), and The Attention Merchants (2016). Wu was a law clerk for Justice Stephen Breyer and Judge Richard Posner, and has also worked at the White House National Economic Council, at the Federal Trade Commission, for the New York Attorney General, and in the Silicon Valley telecommunications industry.

**Barak Richman**, Edgar P. and Elizabeth C. Bartlett Professor of Law and Professor of Business Administration at Duke University. He previously served as a law clerk to Judge Bruce M. Selya of the United States Court of Appeals for the First Circuit, and from 1994-1996 he handled international trade legislation as a staff member of the United States Senate Committee on Finance. He writes regularly on issues related to economics and antitrust. Professor Richman is the author of Stateless Commerce, which was published by Harvard University Press.

**Thomas Greany**, Visiting Professor, UC Hastings College of Law. Professor Greaney was the Chester A. Myers Professor of Law and Director of the Center for Health Law Studies at Saint Louis University School of Law. Prior to joining the SLU Law faculty, he served as an Assistant Chief in the Department of Justice, Antitrust Division, specializing in health care antitrust litigation, and completed a visiting professorship at Yale Law School.

**Peter Carstensen**, Fred W. & Vi Miller Chair in Law Emeritus, University of Wisconsin Law School. He previously served as an attorney in the Antitrust Division of the United States Department of Justice. Professor Carstensen is also a Senior Fellow of the American Antitrust Institute.

**Spencer Weber Waller**, Interim Associate Dean for Academic Affairs, Professor and Director for Consumer Antitrust Studies at Loyola University of Chicago, School of Law.

**Darren Bush**, Professor of Law and Law Foundation Professor, University of Houston Law Center. Professor Bush served as a co-author with Harry First and the late John J. Flynn on the antitrust casebook FREE ENTERPRISE AND ECONOMIC ORGANIZATION: ANTITRUST (7th Ed.) with Foundation Press.

**Chris Sagers**, James A. Thomas Distinguished Professor of Law. He is a member of the American Law Institute, a Senior Fellow of the American Antitrust Institute, and a leadership member of the ABA Antitrust Section.

**Robert H. Lande**, Venable Professor of Law, University of Baltimore School of Law. Professor Lande is a co-founder and a Director of the American Antitrust Institute, a past chair of the AALS Antitrust Section, and has held many positions in the ABA Antitrust Section. He is also an elected member of the American Law Institute.

**Robin Feldman**, Harry & Lillian Hastings Professor of Law & Director of the Institute for Innovation Law, U.C. Hastings College of Law. Professor Feldman previously chaired the Executive Committee of the Antitrust Section of the American Association of Law Schools and clerked for The Honorable Joseph Sneed of the U.S. Court of Appeals for the Ninth Circuit. She is also a Fellow of the American Antitrust Institute.

**Jeffrey Harrison**, Huber C. Hurst Eminent Scholar Chair in the Levin College of Law at the University of Florida. He is the co-author of Understanding Antitrust and its Economic Implications, (6th ed., Matthew Bender, 2013) with E.T. Sullivan. Professor Harrison's casebook on Law and Economics is in the third edition. His Nutshell on Law and Economics is in its sixth edition.

**John B. Kirkwood**, Professor of Law, Seattle University School of Law. He is a Senior Fellow of the American Antitrust Institute and an Adviser to the Institute of Consumer Antitrust Studies. Professor Kirkwood previously directed the Planning Office, the Evaluation Office, and the Premerger Notification Program at the FTC's Bureau of Competition in Washington, D.C. and later managed cases and investigations at the Northwest Regional Office.

**Joshua P. Davis**, Associate Dean for Academic Affairs, Director of the Center for Law and Ethics, Professor, and Dean's Circle Scholar, University of San Francisco, School of Law. Dean Davis is on the board for the American Antitrust Institute, and he previously served as a Fellow at the Center for Applied Legal Studies at Georgetown University Law Center and as the clerk to the Hon. Patrick E. Higginbotham on the Fifth Circuit Court of Appeals.

**Norman W. Hawker**, Professor of Finance and Commercial Law, Western Michigan University. He is also a Senior Fellow of the American Antitrust Institute.

**Max Huffman**, Professor of Law and Director of Corporate and Commercial Law Graduate Certificate program, University of Indiana, Robert H. McKinney School of Law.

**Warren Grimes**, Associate Dean for Research and Irving D. and Florence Rosenberg Professor of Law, Southwestern Law School. Dean Grimes is co-author of the definitive antitrust law text for lawyers and law students, *The Law of Antitrust: An Integrated Handbook* with the late Professor Lawrence Sullivan. Dean Grimes has chaired the Los Angeles County Bar Association Antitrust and Trade Regulation Section and is a member of the Executive Committee, and he serves on the Advisory Board of the American Antitrust Institute.

**Mark R. Patterson**, Professor of Law, Fordham University School of Law. Professor Patterson has also been a visiting professor at several law schools in the U.S. and at Bocconi University in Milan. He was a co-author of *Antitrust Law: Policy and Practice* (4th ed. 2008) (with C. Paul Rogers III, Stephen Calkins, and William R. Andersen) and is the author of the forthcoming book Antitrust Law in the New Economy: Google, Yelp, LIBOR, and the Control of Information (Harvard 2017).

**Marina Lao**, Professor of Law, Seton Hall Law. Professor Lao was previously awarded a Fulbright Fellowship. She currently serves as a member of the advisory board of the American Antitrust Institute, and was Chair of the Section of Antitrust and Economic Regulation of the Association of American Law Schools.

**Michael A. Carrier**, Professor of Law, Rutgers Law School. Professor Carrier is a co-author of the leading IP/antitrust treatise, *IP and Antitrust Law: An Analysis of Antitrust Principles Applied to Intellectual Property Law* (2d ed. 2009, and annual supplements, with Hovenkamp, Janis, Lemley, and Leslie). He is a member of the Board of Advisors of the American Antitrust Institute and is a past chair of the Executive Committee of the Antitrust and Economic Regulation section of the Association of American Law Schools.

**Edward Cavanagh**, Professor of Law, St. John's University. Professor Cavanagh is currently a member of the Council of the ABA Antitrust Section. He has previously served as co-chair of the ABA Antitrust Section Public Service Committee. He has also served as co-chair of the Antitrust Section's Civil Practice and Procedure Committee. Professor Cavanagh is a past chair of the New York State Bar Association Antitrust Section and currently a member of its Executive Committee. Professor Cavanagh is a member of the Association of the Bar of the City of New York and has served on its Antitrust and Trade Regulation Committee and its Federal Courts Committee.

**Barak Orbach**, Professor of Law and Director of the Business Law program, University of Arizona, James E. Rogers College of Law. Professor Orbach is the author of a leading casebook: *Regulation: Why and How the State Regulates* (Foundation Press, 2012). Professor Orbach previously served as an Advisor for Law & Economics to the Israeli Antitrust Commissioner.

**Jon Baker**, Research Professor of Law at American University Washington-College of Law. Professor Baker served as the Chief Economist of the Federal Communications Commission from 2009 to 2011,and as the Director of the Bureau of Economics at the Federal Trade Commission from 1995 to 1998. Previously, he worked as a Senior Economist at the President's Council of Economic Advisers, Special Assistant to the Deputy Assistant Attorney General for Economics in the Antitrust Division of the Department of Justice, an Attorney Advisor to the Acting Chairman of the Federal Trade Commission, and an antitrust lawyer in private practice. Professor Baker is the co-author of an antitrust casebook, a past Editorial Chair of Antitrust Law Journal, and a past member of the Council of the American Bar Association's Section of Antitrust Law. He has published widely in the fields of antitrust law, policy, and economics.

**Andrew Chin**, Professor of Law, University of North Carolina School of Law. Professor Chin is the recipient of a Rhodes Scholarship and a National Foundation Graduate Fellowship. He clerked for Judge Henry H. Kennedy Jr. of the United States District Court for the District of Columbia and assisted Judge Thomas Penfield Jackson and his law clerks in the drafting of the findings of fact in United States v. Microsoft Corporation.

**Thomas J. Horton**, Professor of Law and Heidepriem Trial Advocacy Fellow at the University of South Dakota School of Law.

# Brief for *Amici Curiae* John M. Connor, Martin Gaynor, Daniel Mcfadden, Roger Noll, Jefferey M. Perloff, Joseph A. Stiglitz, Lawrence J. White, and Ralph A. Winter in Support of Petitioners

No. 16-1454

IN THE

# SUPREME COURT OF THE UNITED STATES

STATES OF OHIO, CONNECTICUT, IDAHO, ILLINOIS, IOWA, MARYLAND, MICHIGAN, MONTANA, RHODE ISLAND, UTAH, AND VERMONT,

*Petitioners,*

v.

AMERICAN EXPRESS COMPANY, AND AMERICAN EXPRESS TRAVEL RELATED SERVICES COMPANY, INC.,

*Respondents.*

## On Petition for a Writ of Certiorari to the United States Court of Appeals for the Second Circuit

## BRIEF FOR *AMICI CURIAE* JOHN M. CONNOR, MARTIN GAYNOR, DANIEL MCFADEN, ROGER NOLL, JEFFREY M. PERLOFF, JOSEPH A. STGLITZ, LARENCE J. WHITE, AND RAPH A. WINTER IN SUPORT OF PETITIONERS

**ANTHONY J. BOLOGNESE**
*Counsel of Record*

BOLOGNESE & ASSOCIATES, LLC
1500 JFK Boulevard, Suite 320
Philadelphia, PA 19102
(215) 814-6750

ABolognese@Bolognese-Law.com

*Counsel for AmiciCuriae*

July 6, 2017

WILSON-EPES PRINTING CO., INC. – (202) 789-0096 – WASHINGTON, D. C. 20002

# Table of Contents

INTEREST OF *AMICI CURIAE*.................................................................................................188

SUMMARY OF ARGUMENT.................................................................................................188

ARGUMENT..........................................................................................................................190

    I.  "TWO-SIDENESS".......................................................................................................190

    II.  PLATFORM COMPETITION IN TWO-SIDED MARKETS.............................................191

    III. THE AmEx RESTRAINTS HARM HORIZONTAL COMPETITION AMONG CREDIT CARD PLAT-
FORMS...........................................................................................................................194

    IV. CROSS-MARKET EXTERNALITIES.........................................................................198

CONCLUSION......................................................................................................................199

APPENDIX A........................................................................................................................201

# Table of Authorities

**Cases**

*Leegin Creative Leather Prods., Inc. v. PSKS, Inc.,* 551 U.S. 877(2007)..............................................194

*Times Picayune Pub. Co. v. United States,* 345 U.S. 594(1953)..........................................................189

U.S. Airways, Inc. v. Sabre Holdings Corp., 2017 U.S. Dist. LEXIS 40932 (S.D.N.Y. Mar. 21, 2017)....190

*United States v. Microsoft Corp.,* 253 F.3d 34 (D.C. Cir.2001)............................................................189

**Other Authorities**

A. Boik & K. Corts, *The Effects of Platform Most- Favored Nation Clauses on Competition and Entry,* J. of Law & Econ. (2016)..............................................................................................................192

D. Carlton & R. Winter, *Vertical MFN's and the Credit Card No-surcharge Rule*....................191, 192

G. Stigler, *Price and Non-Price Competition,* 76 J. Pol. Econ. 149 (1968)......................................198

J. Johnson, *The Agency Model and MFN Clauses* (Jan. 25, 2017)....................................................192

Jean-Charles Rochet & Jean Tirole, *An Economic Analysis of the Determination of Interchange Fees in Payment Card Systems,* 2 Rev. Network Econ. 69 (2003)....................................................196

Jean-Charles Rochet and Jean Tirole, "Two-Sided Markets: A Progress Report," *Rand Journal of Economics* 37 (3) (2006)..........................................................................................................................190

Lear, *Can "Fair" Prices Be Unfair? A Review of Price Relationship Agreements,* UK Office of Fair Trading, Paper#1438 (2012).................................................................................................................192

Marc Rysman, "The Economics of Two-Sided Markets," *Journal of Economic Perspectives* 23 (3) (2009).............................................................................................................................................190

S. Salop & S. Morton, *Developing an Administrable MFN Policy,* Antitrust (2013).........................192

S. Schuh et al., *An Economic Analysis of the 2011 Settlement Between the Department of Justice and Credit Card Networks,* J. of Competition Law & Econ. (2012)...................................192

**Treatises**

P. Areeda & H. Hovenkamp, Antitrust Law § 562e, p. 101 (Supp.2017)..........................................194

## INTEREST OF *AMICI CURIAE*

The *amici* are eight economists – scholars and experts in competition, industrial organization, and the economic analysis of antitrust issues.[1] *Amici* support the States' Petition for a Writ of Certiorari. The Second Circuit's ruling sets new antitrust standards for analysis in two-sided markets. However, the Second Circuit's decision is based on an incorrect interpretation of the economics of two-sided markets and, as a result, will have serious and adverse impact on antitrust cases that involve or are alleged to involve two-sided platforms.

## SUMMARY OF ARGUMENTS

The court below erred by (1) assuming that that the characterization of the AmEx service as a two-sided platform should fundamentally change the antitrust principles that govern the AmEx restraints, (2) misunderstanding the nature of competition in two-sided markets,(3) placing the burden on plaintiffs to disprove that the harm from supracompetitive merchant fees are not outweighed by benefits to third parties (cardholders in this case), and most importantly (4) disregarding the critical antitrust issue – the impacts of the AmEx merchant antisteering and pricing restraints on competition among credit card platforms.

A two-sided platform refers to a seller that brings together two different sets of consumers (the two sides), *and* where increased usage on each side benefits the other side (referred to in economics as two-sided externalities). When a credit card network is new, increased merchant acceptance increases the value to cardholders of having the network's card, and increased card holding makes merchant acceptance of the card more valuable. Such networks are therefore two-sided platforms, and they compete in a two-sided market. With two-sided platforms, pricing on one side of the platform impacts demand on the other, perhaps adding complexity to the analysis of the competitive impact of supra-competitive prices on one side. However, before such complexities are considered for a mature network like AmEx, a careful analysis should be conducted to ascertain the significance and importance of any remaining two-sided externalities. The appellate court did no such analysis.

The appellate court ruling purports to be based on the economics of "two-sided markets" in the payments industry, but the ruling departs sharply from prior antitrust analyses and rulings involving two-sided markets. While formal economic

---

1  The Appendix to this Brief identifies the Amici. Counsel for *amici* provided counsel for the parties with timely notice of intent to file this brief, and the parties have consented. No counsel for a party authored this brief in whole or in part, and no counsel or party made a monetary contribution intended to fund the preparation or submission of this brief. No person other than *amici* or their counsel made a monetary contribution to its preparation or submission. The amici include Joseph Stiglitz, who is currently consulting and is a witness for a number of national supermarket and drugstore chains that have challenged AmEx's, Visa's, and Mastercard's restraints in related law suits pending in the District Court. *See* Appendix3a.

analysis of two-sided platforms is relatively new, antitrust analysis of industries involving two-sided platforms is hardly new. For over fifty years, courts have analyzed the competitive impact of restraints on one side of a two-sided platform by focusing on how competition among competing suppliers is affected.[2] In this case, the appellate court departs from this standard analysis by requiring a plaintiff to show that a competitive harm on one side of a platform (here the merchant side) is not offset by purported benefits on the other side of that same platform (the cardholder side). This is a difficult and unwarranted burden. AmEx, as the proponent of and enforcer of the merchant restraints, is clearly in the best position to understand and quantify any relevant offsetting competitive benefits. Creating a new antitrust standard that requires the victim of a restraint of trade to prove that its harm is not offset by benefits to third parties is not sound policy or economics.

Credit card platforms (AmEx, Visa, Mastercard, and Discover) compete against each other – or would, if not stymied by AmEx's anti-steering merchant restraints – through price competition. The price competition is on each side of the platform. Each credit card platform offers a price pair consisting of a price charged to merchants for the use of the platform's card acceptance services, and also a price charged to cardholders (including benefits in the form of "rewards"). One platform may choose to compete by offering a high merchant price and high rewards to cardholders. Another platform may choose to offer lower merchant fees and lower cardholder rewards, expecting that merchants will steer its customers to that platform's cards by offering discounts or other incentives at the point of sale due to the comparatively low merchant fees.

With competition in the market, each network chooses its preferred price pair. Market forces, including merchant steering and the consumer's ability to choose merchant discounts or incentives over cardholder rewards, would sort out how much of that platform's services will be demanded–that is, its success in the market. The AmEx anti-steering merchant restraints directly interfere with this competition among the credit card platforms. With AmEx's restraints in place, a rival credit card platform or a new entrant that attempts to compete against AmEx with a price pair of lower merchant fees and lower cardholder benefits will be unsuccessful because, under the AmEx restraints, merchants are unable to incentivize the cardholders in any way. Thus, a credit card platform with the different pricing model than AmEx will garner no additional sales from its competitively low merchant price; it will be driven by the AmEx restraints to mimic the AmEx pricing.

Competition requires that (1) credit card platforms are able to freely choose their prices, (2) consumers have choices for card network rewards versus the merchant-offered discounts and incentives, and (3) competitive market forces are allowed

---

2  *See, e.g., Times Picayune Pub. Co. v. United States*, 345 U.S. 594, 610 (1953) (confining competitive analysis to "advertising market, not in readership" while noting that "every newspaper is a dual trader in separate though interdependent markets."); *United States v. Microsoft Corp.*, 253 F.3d 34 (D.C. Cir. 2001) (analysis of restraints on entry of competing browsers).

to determine how much of the platform's services will be  demanded. The AmEx merchant restraints hinder such competition.

The *amici* respectfully submit that the proper analysis of restraints imposed on one side of a two-sided platform is the established rule of reason analysis previously recognized by the Second Circuit and adopted by many other Circuits. Under this standard analysis, the first step is to determine if a restraint, whether on one or both sides of a platform, *injures competition between and among platforms*. If a plaintiff satisfies this showing, the defendant can then show procompetitive benefits that may or may not offset the anticompetitive impacts.

If the ruling of the appellate court stands, the adverse competitive impact will be substantial.  Credit card platforms process trillions of dollars of transactions in the United States annually. More importantly, firms operating in two-sided markets using the internet, such as Amazon, Uber, Facebook, Google, and Airbnb, are multiplying in number and size. The appellate court decision gives firms in these rapidly developing markets latitude to act anticompetitively on one side of their platform as long as they can point to some indirect or secondary benefit on the other side of the platform populated by a different set of consumers. The appellate court ruling will make analysis of such conduct needlessly complex and, perhaps, beyond the reach of the antitrust laws.

## ARGUMENT

### I.  "TWO-SIDEDNESS"

As noted, a two-sided platform brings together two sets of consumers, and the prices to each set ("side") significantly affect the other side (indirect two-sided externalities).[3] Two-sided  industries have included newspapers, television and radio, computer operating systems, dating services, and flight reservation services.[4]

---

3  *See* Jean-Charles Rochet and Jean Tirole, "Two-SidedMarkets: A Progress Report," *Rand Journal of Economics* 37(3) (2006), pp. 645-67; Marc Rysman, "The Economics of Two-Sided Markets," *Journal of Economic Perspectives* 23(3) (2009), pp. 125-143.

4  We write "have included" because as two-sided platforms mature, the externalities from each side to the other can become unimportant and insignificant, rendering the two-sidedness of no relevance. For example, a mature flight reservation system may not attract another airline if it adds more users, and vice versa. If so, there are no remaining significant two-sided externalities. *See U.S. Airways, Inc. v. Sabre Holdings Corp.*, 2017 U.S. Dist. LEXIS 40932 at*32 (S.D.N.Y. Mar. 21, 2017).

The appellate court emphasized that AmEx must attract both cardholders and merchants to its network.[5] But this does not distinguish AmEx from any other firm that offers a service and must attract both retailers and end consumers. Nearly *any* firm dealing with merchants could offer the appellate court's improper analysis that a restraint that raises the firm's wholesale price to the merchants passes antitrust muster as long as the restraint provides the firm with revenue that it spends on enhancing the quality of the products it offers to the "other side." A new antitrust doctrine should not follow from a mere labeling of a conventional setting as a two-sided market.[6]

AmEx's credit card network is a mature business in existence since 1958. By 2012, in the United States, AmEx had over 50 million cardholders, was accepted by over 4 million merchants that account for about 95% of all retail sales, and had annual transaction volume of over $590 billion. There is no evidence that significant two-sided externalities remain – that is, that merchant acceptance would increase if AmEx increased its cardholding base, or vice versa. Nonetheless, *amici* focus on markets that are characterized by two-sided externalities in which "price changes on one side can result in demand changes on the other side." Pet.App.8a.

## II. PLATFORM COMPETITION IN TWO-SIDED MARKETS

The economic literature analyzing two-sided platforms is new, complex, and evolving. Before courts adopt a new approach to the analysis of competitive impacts in two-sided markets, the extent to which such complexities are relevant to competitive analysis should be fully understood.[7] This is especially important in the case of AmEx. Only recently has the economic literature considered the impact of restraints

---

5  *See* Pet. App. 49a-50a (stating that the District Court should have considered the effect of the AmEx restraints on both merchants and cardholders because: "[t]he revenue earned from merchant fees funds cardholder benefits, and cardholder benefits in turn attract cardholders. A reduction in revenue that AmEx earns from merchant fees may decrease the optimal level of cardholder benefits, which in turn may reduce the intensity of competition among payment card networks on the cardholder side of the market").

6  In a recent paper co-authored by one of the *amici*, the authors conclude that "[t]he two-sidedness of credit card markets does not require a new set of economic principles for assessing competition policy because the difference between the credit card setting and a conventional one-sided market is essentially a matter of labeling.... Creating different legal rules for the same economic conduct depending on whether the market can be described as one-sided or two-sided is a mistake that could lead to widespread confusion in the evaluation of vertical restriction." D. Carlton & R. Winter, *Vertical MFN's and the Credit Card No-surcharge Rule*, at 40 (working paper available at https://goo.gl/kKd2Ck).

7  For example, the appellate court cites a 2013 working paper by Filistrucchi et al. *See* Pet. App. 7a n.3 (citing Lapo Filistrucchi et al., *Market Definition in Two-Sided Markets: Theory and Practice 5*). The analysis therein emphasizes a distinction for competitive analysis between two-sided transactions markets (where, as with payment cards, the two sides directly interact with one another), and two-sided non-transactions markets (where, like newspapers, the two sides do not interact with one another). While noting this paper, the appellate court simply disregards the distinction, providing no guidance for future cases involving two-sided platforms that may differ from the credit card platforms on this account.

on competition that allow a firm like AmEx to charge higher prices to one side (here, merchants), which results in increased prices charged to all customers, and which, through competition on the other side (cardholders), may result in lower prices to that side.[8] The appellate court's analysis and ruling fails to account for this recent learning.[9]

In addition, the major impact of the AmEx restraints is direct interference in price competition among credit card platforms. The appellate court puts no importance on this paradigmatic injury to competition.

Instead, the appellate court took a novel and unprecedented approach to analyzing the competitive impact of the AmEx restraints. Rather than determining whether the restraints on merchants injured competition among platforms–that is, among competing credit card firms – the court ruled that the proper antitrust analysis must "consider the two-sided net price accounting for the effects of the [restraints] on both merchants and cardholders." Pet. App.49a. The court held that it was the plaintiffs' burden to show that AmEx's restraints had an adverse net effect on competition defined as the sum of the prices to merchants and cardholders. Only after the plaintiffs had made such a showing would AmEx be obligated to come forward with any evidence of a procompetitive justification.

If the appellate court were correct that different and new economic analysis is required in two-sided markets–a proposition with which *amici* disagree–it should be applied only after a rigorous and careful demonstration that two-sided market characteristics exist in the market, and are important to the competitive impact of a restraint. More importantly, if a market is demonstrated to consist of two-sided platforms, and if benefits to consumers using one side of a platform (here cardholders) result from restraints that harm the other side (merchants), then a simple summing of these benefits and harms is *not* informative as to the restraint's impact on competition. In addition, further examination of whether there are important cross-platform externalities from which the restraints at issue might harm other platforms needs to be conducted.

The correct approach is to determine whether a restraint on one side of a two-sided market interferes with competition among platforms in the market. The com-

---

8    Because the AmEx restraints adversely impact entry into the credit card market, there can be no presumption that the restraints result overall in lower cardholder prices.

9    The recent economic literature finds that restraints such as the AmEx restraints "typically raise platform fees and retail prices, and curtail entry or skew positioning decisions by potential entrants pursuing low-end business models." *See* A. Boik & K. Corts, *The Effects of Platform Most-Favored Nation Clauses on Competition and Entry*, J. of Law & Econ., Abstract (2016); *accord* S. Schuh et al., *An Economic Analysis of the 2011 Settlement Between the Department of Justice and Credit Card Networks*, J. of Competition Law & Econ. (2012); S. Salop & F. Scott Morton, *Developing an Administrable MFN Policy*, Antitrust (2013); Lear, *Can "Fair" Prices Be Unfair? A Review of Price Relationship Agreements*, UK Office of Fair Trading, Paper #1438 (2012); J. Johnson, *The Agency Model and MFN Clauses* (Jan. 25, 2017) (available at https://goo.gl/Vbj3tV); D. Carlton & R. Winter, *Vertical MFN's and the Credit Card No-surcharge Rule* (available at https://goo.gl/kKd2Ck).

petitive impact of restraints such as those imposed by AmEx – restraints that directly alter and impede horizontal competition among platforms – is properly demonstrated only by the impact on the competition among those platforms. The appellate court disregarded this most critical economic issue – how the AmEx restraints affect competition among AmEx, Visa, Mastercard, Discover, and potential new entrants.[10]

In order to better understand competition in two-sided markets, consider the example of platforms intermediating between hotels and travelers. These platforms can be two sided because the demand for the services by travelers can depend on the number and quality of the hotels that use the service, and vice versa. If a platform lowers its price to travelers, then it can increase the number of travelers using the platform, which may make the platform more valuable to hotels. Similarly, lowering the platform fee charged to hotels can increase the number of hotels using the platform, making the platform more valuable to travelers – the booking service providers are competing in a two-sided market.

Two-sided platforms compete, in part, via the prices offered by each platform to the two sides. For example, one hotel booking service may charge a high price to hotels and a relatively low price to travelers, while other platforms may expect more equal prices to be more profitable, resulting in a better mix of hotels and travelers. Competition is likely to result in competing platforms offering different price pairs, and those offering the price pairs that best satisfy consumer preferences will thrive.

The important economic point is that in two-sided markets, the relevant competition occurs at the *platform level* (*i.e.,* competition among the credit card companies). A competitive two-sided market, through consumers' choices, will effectively decide the preferred and competitive price relationships (the price pair) and, as an incidental matter, the overall "price level" (the sum of the prices) in the two sides. It is this platform competition that is directly interfered with by the AmEx restraints on the merchant side of the AmEx platform.

Rather than asking whether the AmEx rules prevented competitive market forces from determining the price pairs offered by the competing platforms, the appellate court considered only the impact on the AmEx prices to both sides of the platform. The court ruled that the competitive metric is whether the *sum* of the two prices increased. This is a fundamental economic error. Whether the sum of the prices goes up or not does not relate to whether restraints are or are not anticompetitive. Nor does it relate to how the restraints might distort and interfere with the competition among platforms in two-sided markets. When restraints hamper the process of platform competition, anticompetitive harm follows because the restraints alter the price

---

10  Visa and Mastercard operate as what is called four-party systems (cardholders, merchants, issuers, and acquirers, *see* Figure 2 at Pet. App. 55a-56a) in which the Visa and Mastercard platforms deal with acquiring banks that compete for merchants and issuing banks that compete for cardholders. This difference from AmEx and Discover does not impact our analysis.

pairs themselves, regardless of whether the sum of the prices increases, decreases, or remains unchanged.[11]

## III. THE AMEX RESTRAINTS HARM HORIZONTAL COMPETION AMONG CREDIT CARD PLATFORMS

The AmEx restraints bar merchants purchasing AmEx services from differentially pricing the AmEx card versus other credit cards. The restraints even bar merchants from providing their customers with accurate information about the prices charged to merchants by AmEx and alternative cards. The AmEx restraints are vertical restraints, imposed by a supplier on its customers. However, the AmEx vertical restraints have direct horizontal effects because they interfere with horizontal competitors' pricing.

The required competitive analysis of a vertical price restraint is set forth in *Leegin Creative Leather Prods., Inc. v. PSKS, Inc.*, 551 U.S. 877 (2007), and summarized in the appellate court's decision.[12] *Leegin* concerned resale price maintenance (RPM). Unlike the appellate court's ruling, this well-established analysis of RPM finds the first stage of the rule of reason satisfied by showing an increase in the retail price. The burden then shifts to the supplier imposing the restraint to show offsetting procompetitive benefits. The failure of the appellate court to follow this approach is not justified by sound economic principles.

With RPM, the suppression of competition at the retail/merchant level is a cost to the supplier imposing the restraint, as the direct effect is reduced demand for the supplier's product from the higher retail price. Therefore, to be of benefit to the supplier, the decision to impose RPM can be presumed to have some non-price, demand-enhancing effects. In contrast, with AmEx, the suppression of price competition at the retail/merchant level by AmEx provides first-order benefits to AmEx, as its competitors are effectively restrained from undercutting its price. Because of this direct reduction in horizontal price competition, AmEx's merchant restraints cannot be presumed to be motivated by non-price, overall demand-enhancing effects.

Additionally, the direct impact of RPM on competing suppliers is to increase the demand for their products. In contrast, the AmEx restraints provide no direct benefits to AmEx's platform competitors; rather, the restraints directly interfere with the other platforms' ability to compete with AmEx in pricing to merchants. Yet for analysis of RPM, simply showing an increase in the retail prices to the buyers is sufficient to satisfy the first prong of the rule of reason analysis – an anticompetitive impact. Absent the presumed demand-enhancing impact and the benefit to competitors from

---

11    *See* P. Areeda & H. Hovenkamp, Antitrust Law §562 e,p.101 (Supp. 2017) (stating that the AmEx court erred because "competition should choose the optimal mix of revenue between the two sides").

12    Pet. App. 30a-31a.

RPM, it is not sound economic policy to reject such an anticompetitive showing in the AmEx case simply because the platform may be two-sided.

The practical effect of the AmEx restraints is to drive merchants purchasing from AmEx to set equal prices for the use of all cards, regardless of their relative cost to the merchant. The result is that merchants' customers paying with credit cards perceive no difference in selecting one credit card versus another, and the customers will be motivated to choose the card considered to offer the highest cardholder benefits. Consequently, as the District Court below correctly found, if a payment card platform seeks to compete for transactions with AmEx by offering an identical net price, but with lower prices on the merchant side along with higher prices (less rewards) for card users, then its effort will be impeded, not because there is no demand for the platform's services, but because the AmEx restraints effectively suppress the demand for such a card on the merchant side. See Pet. App. 194a-203a. Therefore, platforms (such as Discover) that attempt to compete with AmEx by charging lower merchant fees and equal or possibly lower rewards will realize little benefit from the low merchant fees.[13] As a consequence, the AmEx restraints suppress horizontal competition among credit card platforms to increase transactions by charging lower merchant prices. Similarly, the AmEx restraints impede competition on the cardholder side by preventing platforms from offering lower prices to merchants in exchange for merchants offering more immediate and more valuable rewards or discounts to cardholders at the point of sale.

As a result, with the AmEx restraints in place, competing platforms will be motivated to raise their merchant price – that is, they will be driven to the AmEx business model. In so doing, the platforms have to abandon other competitive business models that they, the retail consumers, the cardholders, and the merchants might prefer.[14] The AmEx restraints directly interfere with competitors' ability to compete with alternative platform models offering different and potentially efficient price pairs. This is regardless of whether such competitive price pairs have equal, lower, or even higher total two-sided net prices.

The competitive impact of merchant pricing restraints on entry is also far reaching. The AmEx restraints result in all credit card networks competing for transactions only through cardholder benefits provided by the networks at some future point in time. Cardholder benefits and rewards are a way to reduce the net prices paid by the cardholders. But at best, the rewards are a discount on the credit card bill, and the discount accomplishes a price reduction only with a lag in time. The AmEx rules prohibit a merchant from accepting payment cards from a competing network that offered rewards in the form of a point-of-sale discount or other benefits received at

---

13 See Dist. Ct. Op., Pet. App. 203a-207a (holding that AmEx's merchant restraints effectively deny other networks the opportunity to pursue a business model that differentiates itself by offering merchants a low price for greater volume).

14 See Dist. Ct. Op., Pet. App. 216a-217a (finding that without AmEx's restraints, all four card networks' merchant prices would decrease).

the time of the sale such as a preferred checkout line. Under the AmEx rules, any such point-of-sale benefits would be considered differential pricing, which is not allowed. Thus, the AmEx restraints directly interfere with innovative and potentially efficient alternative platform pricing systems. This important anticompetitive impact was not considered by the appellate court.

With restraints in place that impede horizontal competition regarding pricing to merchants, competition on the cardholder side may or may not increase, and such competition might or might not result in a change to the net prices summed over the two sides. However, such a reduction in the cardholder price, if it occurs, is not a "pro-competitive" or an efficiency-enhancing benefit that offsets the interference with competition on the merchant side. It is, rather, a further economic distortion and inefficiency directly due to the AmEx restraints.

The appellate court recognized that in two-sided markets, a platform must "find an effective method for balancing the prices on the two sides of the market."[15] This is the essence of competition in two-sided markets – identifying and offering a price pair that attracts both sides to use the platform. Selecting and offering a preferred price pair, however, is quite different from the situation in which restraints on one side of the market allow for price increases that, through competition on the other side, may lead to price reductions to the second side. While the total two-sided price may be unaffected as the price reduction on one side may completely offset the increase on the other side, the resulting price pair has nothing to do with the competitive search for a preferred price pair.

The potential adverse consequences of the appellate court's approach—in which indirect effects on the second side of a two-sided platform must be taken into account in the first step of a rule of reason analysis – can be readily understood by viewing the court's analysis through the lens of traditional and well understood anticompetitive conduct. Consider a case in which AmEx, Visa, Mastercard, and Discover agree to fix prices by charging equal and high merchant fees. The obvious anticompetitive harm is the direct interference in platform competition regarding the merchant price. And with merchant restraints in place like those of AmEx, which do not allow other credit card platforms to offer lower merchant prices, competition through entry cannot solve the problem. However, if this hypothetical cartel of credit card platform suppliers does not control competition on the cardholder side, then the result is likely to be increased cardholder benefits with reduced cardholder prices, and in the long run, perhaps full dissipation of all the profits earned from the high merchant fees.

No reasonable antitrust scholar would consider the dissipation of profits from price fixing through competition in other markets to be an offsetting procompetitive benefit. Nothing is different about the dissipation of profits from merchant fees

---

15  Second Circuit Op., Pet. App. 8, n.4 (citing Jean-Charles Rochet & Jean Tirole, *An Economic Analysis of the Determination of Interchange Fees in Payment Card Systems*, 2 Rev. Network Econ. 69, 71 (2003)).

propped up by AmEx's merchant restraints compared to the dissipation of profits from price fixing. In addition, the hypothetical collusive price fix among credit card platforms would not be considered benign if the "net" price were unchanged because of the full dissipation of the cartel profits extracted from the merchant side through competition on the cardholder side. Of course, such a price fix would likely be judged under a *per se* standard. But that does not change the fact that the approach taken by the appellate court is economically flawed and unfounded. The outcome of "competition" with restraints such as those imposed by AmEx is little different from what would emerge from the collusion example – a non-competitive *price pair* that may or may not alter the sum of the prices.

Whether from collusion or from vertical restraints on differential merchant pricing, AmEx and its competitors may benefit during the transition to long-run equilibrium and the full dissipation of profits earned from the supra-competitive merchant prices. Those consumer cardholders that are fortunate enough to meet the credit and income requirements for high rewards cards may also benefit. However, the merchants paying higher prices to AmEx, and the merchants' customers using other payment means, are harmed. More importantly, economic efficiency is impeded as price signals are distorted regarding choice of payment means. Customers will be motivated to use their rewards cards even when cash, debit, or check would otherwise benefit them, and customers will be motivated to take inefficient actions to qualify for the high rewards cards.

The appellate court decision imposes on the plaintiffs, the victims of the high prices supported by the merchant restraints, the burden of disproving that the harm they suffer is not outweighed by any benefits to the other side of the platform. This requirement will have substantial adverse impacts on antitrust enforcement. First, as we have emphasized, the effects on cardholders should not be considered offsetting *procompetitive* effects. Any such benefits to cardholders flow from the merchant restraints that support the supracompetitive merchant fees. Foreclosure of competition effectuated on some consumers should not be justified by an increase in competition somewhere else that the foreclosure motivates.

Second, the merchant restraints are imposed by AmEx, the very party best able to understand and quantify any relevant offsetting competitive benefits for the restraints. Perverse incentives will be created if a platform can avoid antitrust liability for harm to one side of the platform, as long as the victim cannot prove that the spoils from that harm are not passed on to the other side. AmEx and cardholders control the information concerning cardholder rewards programs – how the programs work, what they cost, and what value they might provide to the cardholders. AmEx and cardholders will have no incentive to cooperate with merchants' efforts to show that restraints transferring benefits to AmEx and cardholders should not be allowed. Indeed, AmEx and cardholders will have incentives to create cardholder programs designed to obfuscate the benefits, increasing plaintiffs' burden.

Third, the appellate court's overly broad conception of two-sided markets could allow any supplier suppressing retail competition through a vertical restraint to point to the possibility of incentives for higher quality, thus shifting the burden back to the plaintiff. Because any suppression of competition in any context carries the possibility of higher quality resulting from higher prices,[16] antitrust enforcement may become needlessly complex, expensive, and uncertain.

## IV. CROSS-MARKET EXTERNALITIES

The AmEx restraints increase the price that merchants pay to AmEx and thereby raise the costs to merchants for those customers using AmEx. The AmEx restraints prevent the merchants from differentially raising retail prices to only AmEx cardholders to cover that cost increase. The AmEx restraints then motivate other credit card platforms to raise their prices to merchants, further increasing the merchants' costs. Dist. Ct. Opp., Pet. App. 207a-209a. Merchants incurring higher costs in turn raise their prices to all their customers.[17] The result is higher retail prices to all the merchants' customers, including those who use low-cost cash or debit cards. These customers, who tend to have incomes or credit scores too low to qualify for rewards credit cards, will thus end up subsidizing the rewards of more affluent cardholders. *Id.* at 210a-212a. This is further evidence of inefficient pricing and a negative externality. These harms occur even if AmEx passed on all of its high merchant fees to cardholders through higher rewards, and they are amplified when other credit card platforms increase their merchant prices and cardholder benefits in response to the AmEx restraints.

The appellate court requires that analysis in two-sided markets must go beyond the direct effects on competition on the side of the platform where a restraint is imposed. If it is economically relevant to consider the competitive impact beyond the side of the platform where the restraint is imposed, then proper analysis must also consider effects beyond the platform itself, as the restraint can have broad effects on consumers who do not participate on either side of the platform that imposes the restraint.

However, there is a sound economic basis to retain the standard rule of reason analysis in which the plaintiff focuses on the direct effects of the restraint in a two-sided market. If the plaintiff succeeds in demonstrating that the challenged merchant restraints adversely impact competition among platforms – here higher platform prices to the merchants from all platform competitors – then the plaintiff's burden should be satisfied. With this initial burden satisfied, the defendant should be required to demonstrate not simply that the other side of the platform is affected, but that there is a beneficial impact on competition among platforms.

---

16 *See* G. Stigler, *Price and Non-Price Competition*, 76 J. Pol. Econ. 149, 149-54 (1968).

17 The appellate court's ruling does not rely on market power in the retail sectors facing AmEx's restraints. Rather, the retail markets mainly impacted by the AmEx restraints are competitive to a first approximation such that the cost increase caused by higher merchant credit card fees can be presumed to be fully, or nearly fully, passed on to consumers.

Finally, the appellate court suggests that AmEx might justify its merchant restraints by a showing that AmEx's "output" – that is, the volume of AmEx transactions – increased.[18] However, if the AmEx restraints have effects beyond the AmEx platform, as is the case here, then the AmEx output alone is not a proper indicator of the welfare effect of the restraint. A relevant analogy is an exclusive dealing contract. An exclusive dealing vertical restraint may increase the "output" of the firm imposing this restraint, but at the expense of the firm's competitors. The proper measure of output would then be the size of the market served by all competitors.

Here, the fundamental product at issue is "payment." If one desired to determine indirectly through market size the procompetitive or anticompetitive nature of a credit card platform's vertical price restraints, then the proper metric is all payment transactions whether accomplished by credit card, debit card, cash, check, or other means. The effect of the restraint is to increase the subsidization of the users of credit card platforms by customers paying by other means. With increased cardholder benefits resulting from competition on the cardholder side in the face of high credit card merchant fees, customers will be motivated to switch from other payment forms to credit cards. Thus, the usage of credit cards may increase. But this is only evidence of distortion in the competitive process, not that the restraint is procompetitive. For those customers switching to credit cards only because of increased rewards, credit card use can be presumed less efficient than the prior preferred means of payment. As a consequence of the use of less efficient means of payment, the cost of transacting will increase and the total of transactions—the proper measure of output in this context— will be expected to decline.

## CONCLUSION

Based on the foregoing analyses, the Amici respectively ask the Court to grant the States' Petition for a Writ of Certiorari.

Respectfully submitted,

**ANTHONY J. BOLOGNESE**
*Counsel of Record*
BOLOGNESE & ASSOCIATES, LLC
1500 JFK Boulevard, Suite 320
Philadelphia, PA 19102
(215) 814-6750
ABolognese@Bolognese-Law.com

Dated: July 6, 2017

---

18  Pet. App.52a.

# APPENDIX A

*Amicus* **John M. Connor** is a Professor of Industrial Economics emeritus at Purdue University. Professor Connor specializes in research and teaching of empirical industrial economics and antitrust policy. His research has been cited in five court decisions and more than 75 law review articles. Professor Connor is also Senior Advisor to the American Antitrust Institute.[19]

*Amicus* **Martin Gaynor** is a Professor of Economics and the E.J. Barone Chair in Health Systems Management at Carnegie Mellon University. Professor Gaynor has consulted for the Federal Trade Commission and the U.S. Department of Justice, and also consulted for the Netherlands Competition Authority on issues involving vertical restraints and market definition.[20]

*Amicus* **Daniel McFadden** is a Nobel Laureate in economics (2000) and the E. Morris Cox Professor Emeritus of Economics and the Director of the Econometrics Laboratory at the University of California at Berkeley. Among his many honors, Professor McFadden received the John Bates Clark Medal from the American Economics Association (1975) and the Frisch Medal from the Econometrics Society (2000).[21]

*Amicus* **Roger Noll** is Professor of Economics emeritus at Stanford University and a Senior Fellow and member of the Advisory Board at the American Antitrust Institute. Before coming to Stanford, Professor Noll was a Senior Economist at the President's Council of Economic Advisers, a Senior Fellow at the Brookings Institution, and Institute Professor of Social Science and Chair of the Division of Humanities and Social Sciences at the California Institute of Technology.[22]

*Amicus* **Jeffrey M. Perloff** is a Professor in the Department of Agricultural and Resource Economics at the University of California at Berkeley. Professor Perloff has authored textbooks on economics including Modern Industrial Organization (with Dennis Carlton), Microeconomics, Microeconomics: Theory and Applications with Calculus, and Estimating Market Power and Strategies (with Larry Karp and Amos Golan).[23]

*Amicus* **Joseph A. Stiglitz** is a Nobel Laureate in economics (2001) and is University Professor at Columbia University. He is a former senior vice president and chief economist of the World Bank and a former member and chairman of the U.S. President's Council of Economic Advisors. Based on academic citations, Professor Stiglitz is the fourth most influential economist m the world today.[24]

---

19  Purdue University, John M. Connor, https://goo.gl/ZaQdzU.

20  Martin Gaynor Curriculum Vitae, http://bit.ly/2fFTvQO.

21  University of California at Berkeley, Faculty Profiles, McFadden, http://bit.ly/2eoJMk9.

22  Stanford University Public Policy Program, Roger Noll http://stanford.io/2fFUOiP.

23 University of California at Berkeley Department of Agricultural and Resource Economics, Jeffrey M. Perloff Brief Bio, http://bit.ly/2emKIWc.

24  Columbia University, Brief Biography of Joseph E. Stiglitz, https://goo.gl/s6tCkb.

Professor Stiglitz currently consulting and is a witness for a number of national supermarket and drugstore chains that have challenged AmEx's, Visa's, and Mastercard' s restraints in related lawsuits pending in the District Court.[25]

*Amicus* **Lawrence J. White** is Robert Kavesh Professor of Economics and Deputy Chair of the Economics Department at New York University's Leonard N. Stern School of Business. He has served on the Senior Staff of the President's Council of Economic Advisers, and has also served as the Director of the Economic Policy Office in the Antitrust Division of the U.S. Department of Justice. Professor White is also the General Editor of the Review of Industrial Organization, a journal that focuses on competition and monopoly in their many forms and their effects on efficiency, innovation, and social conditions.[26]

*Amicus* **Ralph Winter** holds the Canada Research Chair in Business Economics and Policy at the Sauder School of Business at the University of British Columbia.[27] He was previously a Professor of Economics at the University of Toronto, and has also served as President of the Canadian Economics

Association. Professor Winter has also consulted for the U.S. Department of Justice and the Canadian Competition Bureau.[28]

---

25  Those merchants are: Ahold U.S.A., Inc.; Albertson's, Inc.; BI-LO, LLC; CVS Health, Inc.; The Great Atlantic & Pacific Tea Company, Inc.; H.E. Butt Grocery Co.; Hy-Vee, Inc.; The Kroger Co.; Meijer, Inc.; Publix Super Markets, Inc.; Raleys Inc.; Rite Aid HDQTRS Corp.; Safeway Inc.; Supervalu, Inc.; and Walgreen Co.

26  New York University Stern School of Business, Lawrence J. White Biographical Summary, https://goo.gl/zCwff1.

27  University of British Columbia Sauder School of Business, Ralph Winter, https://goo.gl/ennG6B.

28  University of British Columbia Sauder School of Business, Ralph Winter Curriculum Vitae, http://bit.ly/2fPyrG9.

# Authors' Bios

**David S. Evans** is Chairman of Global Economics Group, based in its Boston office, and is Co-Executive Director of the Jevons Institute for Competition Law and Economics and Visiting Professor at University College London. His academic work has focused on industrial organization, including antitrust economics, with a particular expertise in multisided platforms, digital economy, information technology, and payment systems. He has authored 6 major books and more than 100 articles in these areas. His most recent book, with Richard Schmalensee, is *Matchmakers: The New Economics of Multisided Platforms*, which won the 2017 Gold Medal in Economics for the Axiom Business Book Awards. Dr. Evans has taught courses related to antitrust economics, primarily for graduate students, judges and officials, and practitioners, and has authored handbook chapters on various antitrust subjects. He has served as a testifying expert on many significant antitrust matters in the United States, European Union, and China. Several of his books and articles were cited the Supreme Court in its *State of Ohio v. American Express*. He has a Ph.D. degree in economics from the University of Chicago.

**Richard Schmalensee** served as the John C. Head III Dean of the MIT Sloan School of Management from 1998 through 2007. He was a member of the President's Council of Economic Advisers from 1989 through 1991 and served for 12 years as Director of the MIT Center for Energy and Environmental Policy Research. Richard Schmalensee is the author or co-author of 11 books and more than 120 published articles, and he is co-editor of volumes 1 and 2 of the Handbook of Industrial Organization. His research has centered on industrial organization economics and its application to managerial and public policy issues, with particular emphasis on antitrust, regulatory, energy, and environmental policies. He has served as a consultant to the U.S. Federal Trade Commission, the U.S. Department of Justice, and numerous private corporations.

Professor Schmalensee is a Fellow of the Econometric Society and the American Academy of Arts and Sciences. He was the 2012 Distinguished Fellow of the Industrial Organization Society. He has served as a member of the Executive Committee of the American Economic Association and as a Director of the International Securities Exchange and other corporations. He is currently a Director of the National Bureau of Economic Research and Chairman Emeritus of the Board of Directors of Resources for the Future.

Πs will argue that TSPM
not matter if treat OD members
as competitors.

DT is right that TSPM doesn't tell
you if it makes sense to limit OD member
comp. But TSPM is relevant in determining
if there is justif for the restraint b/c
of conseq. on s/patient side.
   We can't answer "effects"
questn just by fact of restraint on OD
comp.

What if get M.P. over 1 side comes
from pricing on other side?
   "Second" example on p.2: Huge subsidy to
senders. All want to use it. Splits returns
from power over receivers. Will not drive
out = efficient comp, but will still be rents
on receiver side that will accrue to platform.
Why is that not harm to comp like
price. pricing except stage 2 is not temporal?

   Assume a dating app that pays
we $10 to sign up. If dating apps are
me > $10 more efficient as a way to get date
   valuable, to men → can use subsidy
I to get $15 & from men. Platform pockets $2.
  Is that OK so long as no exclude other platform

Take AX. If loss of sale > AX md, then worth it to pay. AX acquired mkt power over Me by out-running V, the "bear". But why would it 3 efficient bank out-bid AX? [ Org. pricing?]

But now Factor in 3d P— CORP. It will create C/H demand by a corp. card prog that will make C/H use AX for personal purchases as well.

Is this just saying that AX = more effic & entitled to benefits of that efficiency?

Made in the USA
San Bernardino, CA
19 December 2019